W0071636

GANDHI AGAINST CASTE

GANDHI AGAINST CASTE

NISHIKANT KOLGE

OXFORD
UNIVERSITY PRESS

OXFORD
UNIVERSITY PRESS

Oxford University Press is a department of the University of Oxford.
It furthers the University's objective of excellence in research, scholarship,
and education by publishing worldwide. Oxford is a registered trademark of
Oxford University Press in the UK and in certain other countries.

Published in India by
Oxford University Press
22 Workspace, 2nd Floor, 1/22 Asaf Ali Road, New Delhi 110002, India

© Oxford University Press 2017

The moral rights of the authors have been asserted.

First Edition published in 2017
Third impression 2024

All rights reserved. No part of this publication may be reproduced, stored in
a retrieval system, or transmitted, in any form or by any means, without the
prior permission in writing of Oxford University Press, or as expressly permitted
by law, by licence, or under terms agreed with the appropriate reprographics
rights organization. Enquiries concerning reproduction outside the scope of the
above should be sent to the Rights Department, Oxford University Press, at the
address above.

You must not circulate this work in any other form
and you must impose this same condition on any acquirer.

ISBN-13: 978-0-19-947429-5
ISBN-10: 0-19-947429-X

Typeset in Bembo Std 11/15
by Tranistics Data Technologies, New Delhi 110 044
Printed in India by Manipal Technologies Limited, Manipal

To
Baba Saheb
(Dr B.R. Ambedkar)

Contents

Foreword

Many scholars have analysed Mahatma Gandhi's stand on caste, but this work by the young academic Nishikant Kolge comes across as a landmark study.

For one thing, Kolge's examination is *thorough*. He asks precise questions, and for answers, he goes to the entire range of what Gandhi said or wrote, and, quite appropriately, to what Gandhi did. Unlike 'theorists' whose doctrines may be examined without reference to their lives, those who resorted to 'action' to change the condition of their peoples—persons like Abraham Lincoln, Gandhi, B.R. Ambedkar, Mao Zedong, Nelson Mandela, and Martin Luther King, Jr, to name them in the order of their birth—cannot be understood solely from their words.

This was a point that Gandhi made himself, and frequently. Kolge informs us that Gandhi also very categorically says: 'What you do not get from my conduct, you will never get from my words.' He goes a step further and suggests that 'as a matter of fact my writings should be cremated with my body'. Another quote from him says:

'What I have done will endure, not what I have said or written.' This does not imply, however, that Gandhi's writings are not to be carefully examined; rather it means that Gandhi expects to be judged and understood by his conduct and not by his writings alone. It also implies that should some contradictions and inconsistencies appear in his writings, they should be resolved in the light of his practices. Gandhi himself says: 'To understand what I say, one needs to understand my conduct....'

Second, Kolge's analysis is *logical*. Pointing out that inconsistencies in Gandhi's writings on caste 'leave ample scope for study and analysis', Kolge argues that these inconsistences may be seen in three different ways: as evidence of contradictions in thought, as an evolution over time in his thinking, or 'as constituting part of a strategy' that Gandhi employed 'to fight the caste system'.

Which of the three is the most satisfactory explanation? Kolge's careful reasoning and the evidence found by him point to strategy. By the 'strategy' he imputes to Gandhi, Kolge has in mind not 'a clever or unfair act' but 'skilful means' that may 'persuade people towards a particular direction'.

Third, Kolge's analysis seems to be *objective*. Keeping a sharp and steady focus on the vast material before him—on what Gandhi said and did—Kolge appears to have barred all external considerations. Thoroughness, logical analysis, and objectivity have helped this study that takes us beyond earlier works on the subject.

That Gandhi implemented a strategy for national freedom is accepted by most scholars, even if they disagree with Gandhi's strategy. But what about caste? Were his verbal positions on caste or his actions on caste questions (such as the 1932 fast-unto-death against a separate Dalit electorate) ad hoc reactions to events, or part of a steadily pursued and coherent strategy?

Kolge acknowledges that 'it is not easy, simple, or straightforward to argue that Gandhi had the approach of a strategist in his fight against the caste system, as can be said with respect to his fight against the British Empire. Neither in Gandhi's own writings nor in the secondary works on him can one find evidence to give strong support for such an argument.'

However, after 'rigorously and diligently examining' all that Gandhi said *and did* about caste, Kolge concludes that there indeed was a strategy. His arguments leading to such a conclusion deserve the most serious attention.

Two years before Gandhi's death, when a coworker asked him why he 'did not make anti-untouchability work part of a wider crusade against the caste system itself,' this, Kolge points out, is how Gandhi responded:

> It is one thing for me to hold certain views and quite another to make my views acceptable in their entirety to society at large. ... I have therefore to exercise the utmost patience and be satisfied with hastening slowly ... I am wholly in agreement with you in principle. If I live up to 125 years, I do expect to convert the entire Hindu society to my view.

Kolge's research seems to confirm Gandhi's claim. He finds that though he was radical from the beginning over caste, Gandhi was careful and gradual in what he openly demanded from Indian society. However, as his own political position steadily strengthened, Gandhi felt freer to ask for tougher reforms. In Kolge's assessment, 'the inconsistencies or changes in [Gandhi's] writings were deliberate and conscious and not due to any changes in his opinion on the subjects'.

Moreover, no matter what Gandhi asked (or did not ask) Hindu society to do, Kolge finds that from 'a very young age' Gandhi attacked the notion of 'pollution' from contact with 'untouchables'. Throughout his life he remained a radical in his own domestic sphere, and in every community, ashram, school, or satyagraha team he established, whether in South Africa or in India.

In 1915, Gandhi told Kasturba that she was free to leave his newly started ashram in Ahmedabad if she could not tolerate

sharing the ashram's roof with a Dalit couple whom he had admitted. Kasturba changed her attitude and stayed, but not Maganlal
Gandhi, the talented nephew on whom Gandhi was hugely dependent, who walked out along with his wife Santok, only to return a
few months later.

In December 1920, when, as part of the Non-Cooperation
Movement, the Congress and its supporters started national schools,
Gandhi insisted, Kolge tells us, on 'actually having untouchable
children in all the sixty national schools'. This did not happen. In
early 1922, Gandhi remarked: 'I have just learnt that *Antyaj* [Dalit]
children have already been enrolled in 18 national schools. [But]
as long as there is a single national school without *Antyaj* pupils, it
cannot be said that the resolution ... has been carried out.'

Kolge cites another strong remark from Gandhi: 'He also said [in
1935] that even if the whole body of Hindu opinion were against the
removal of untouchability, he still would advise a secular legislature
like the [Central] Assembly not to tolerate that attitude.' Kolge also
shows that from the late 1930s onwards and right up to his death,
Gandhi urged circles close to him, including the Sevagram ashram
community, to foster marriages between Dalits and caste Hindus.

An important question Kolge asks is about the society Gandhi
wished to see. Kolge's answer is this: '[For Gandhi] swaraj for the
nation is not simply "a collective freedom from alien rule" but a
collective capacity of individuals to live together in harmony. The
attainment of independence for the nation also means the nurturing
and strengthening of this capacity in the individual to live with others in peace and harmony.' Adding that Gandhi saw the individual
as society's core, Kolge quotes this line: 'I want every individual to
become a full-blooded, fully developed member of society.'

Also underlined by Kolge is Gandhi's faith in 'bread labour' and
its fruit, equality. If every Indian worked physically, on land if possible and in any case on the spinning wheel, hierarchy would give
way to equality. Kolge quotes Gandhi: 'Obedience to the law of

bread labour will bring about a silent revolution in the structure of society.'

Kolge cites Gandhi's comment on the *shuddhi* campaign, started in the mid-1920s, to reconvert Dalits who had become Christians or Muslims: 'It is not the untouchables whose shuddhi I [want]— the thing would be absurd—but my own and that of the Hindu religion.' Kolge describes as 'fundamental' the differences between Gandhi's movement against untouchability and upper-caste social reform movements such as the one led in the 1920s and 1930s by prominent Arya Samaj individuals. While the latter also wanted to rid Hindu society of untouchability, their stronger dislike was of conversion to other religions.

Also, Kolge points out, while certain 'other great social reform-ers' asked 'untouchables' to 'learn Sanskrit and adopt the customs, rituals, and beliefs of the great Sanskrit tradition to empower themselves' and strive to become 'like Brahmins for their spiritual, moral, social, and economic development', Gandhi 'was very hos-tile to such methods'.

According to Kolge: 'Gandhi rejected it [Sanskritization] because it only promised a change in the hierarchical position for particular castes or subsections of castes and failed to actually bring about any definite structural changes within the caste system. On the other hand, Gandhi was asking every Hindu to be like a *Bhangi*—lowest among the low in the caste system—in thought, word, and action. It was something very radical, for by doing so, Gandhi was refus-ing to accept the superiority of Brahminical tradition, culture, and customs from which justification for caste differences was derived. By rejecting the superiority of Brahminical culture, Gandhi indeed attacked the very root of the caste system.'

Insisting that religious texts like the Hindu shastras had to pass the tests of morality and reason, Gandhi was however opposed, Kolge points out, to throwing out the shastras altogether.

Examining Dalit criticisms of Gandhi, Kolge endorses some of them. While acknowledging Gandhi's ceaseless challenge to Hindu society to face ugly realities, Kolge thinks that Gandhi neglected the unequal socio-economic structure that Dalits face and the role that the state and modernization could play in undermining the evils of caste.

He also thinks that Gandhi was paternalistic and failed to create around him Dalit leaders of the stature of Ambedkar, Nehru, or Patel.

Kolge treats Gandhi as a human and fallible everyman, not as a perfect superman. Gandhi, who said repeatedly that this was exactly how he wished to be seen, would have welcomed Kolge's scrupulous examination.

Rajmohan Gandhi
Urbana, Illinois

Acknowledgements

This book is a revised version of my PhD dissertation that was completed in 2014 at the Department of Humanities and Social Science, Indian Institute of Technology (IIT) Madras. Therefore, first and foremost, thanks must go to my supervisor, Professor Sudhir Chella Rajan, for his continuous support, encouragement, and guidance. He has always supported my writings by sharing his knowledge and insights, as well as allowing me space to think, explore, and figure out where I want to take this work. It is due to his patience and fortitude that this book is seeing the light of day. Apart from this, he has been one of the most important sources of support, academic advice, and general guidance. I also extend my sincere thanks to the examiners Dr Ramachandra Guha and Professor Tridip Suhrud, who made substantive and helpful comments on the original thesis. I would like to express my special gratitude to Dr Guha for encouraging me to convert this thesis into a book as soon as possible.

I would also like to express my deepest gratitude to my earlier supervisor Professor M.S. John whose trust, encouragement, and guidance helped me complete my thesis. Indeed I have no words to express my gratitude to him for providing the much-needed help. Also, I would like to express my special gratitude to Dr N. Sreekumar, my first supervisor and a wonderful human being, for his guidance, support, and patience. My continuous academic arguments with him trained me to approach research issues in depth and from multiple perspectives.

I would like to thank other professors in the department for their affection and encouragement, particularly Dr Veeraraghavan and Dr Jyotirmaya Tripathy. It was under Dr Veeraraghavan's supervision that I learnt to critically read a book or article. I also learnt how to make an academic argument while doing my coursework with him. I express my sincere thanks to Dr Jyotirmaya Tripathy for encouraging me to write my first research paper. My special gratitude to Dr P. Sudarsan for his guidance, affection, friendly advices, and occasional treats at Tiffany's. I also express my gratitude to Professor V.R. Muraleedharan, Professor D. Malathy, and Dr Milind Brahme for their help and encouragement on various occasions.

Particular thanks are due to Rajshri Jobanputra. I learnt many things from her when she was in IIT Madras. I attended many of her classes on philosophy and was also part of her group where we discussed a variety of topics, and all these helped me in various ways. I am deeply grateful to her for patiently reading preliminary versions of this book and for giving some valuable suggestions. The interaction with other students in the department has contributed enormously to my academic experience at IIT Madras. I wish to thank all my friends in the department for their help and encouragement.

A good number of people have also helped me in successfully completing this work. I would like to thank Ravindra Kumar, former secretary of the Gandhi Peace Foundation, New Delhi; Dr Siby K. Joseph, the dean of students, and Professor Ram Chandra Pradhan, both at the Institute of Gandhian Studies, Wardha, Maharashtra;

Dr V. Krishna Ananth, the head of the Department of History, Sikkim University; and Dr Usha Thakkar, the secretary of Mani Bhavan Gandhi Sangrahalaya, Mumbai, for giving unprecedented help whenever I approached. I would also like to thank Professor S. Poddar, Dr S. Debbarma, and other colleagues at the Department of History, Tripura University. Thanks to my friend Biplab Debnath for correcting almost all of my important documents and correspondence and for his willingness to help me in every field of life. I express my gratitude to Professor Durga Das Ghosh for reminding me that I have to finish this work as soon as possible. I would like to thank research scholars in the Department of History, Tripura University, for their encouragement and help.

I was greatly assisted in the archives and libraries I visited: the library of the Department of Humanities and Social Science and the Central Library, IIT Madras; the library of the Madras Institute of Development Studies, Chennai; Connemara Library, Chennai; National Archives of India, New Delhi; Nehru Memorial Museum and Library, New Delhi; Gandhi Smarak, New Delhi; National Gandhi Museum and Library, New Delhi; Jawaharlal Nehru University Library, New Delhi; the library of the University of Delhi; the library of the Gandhi Peace Foundation, New Delhi; and the library of the Institute of Gandhian Studies, Wardha. I thank all the staff members of the aforementioned libraries.

I could not have done this without the help of the following four persons who have always remained a source of immense help and support. First, Holger, who is the first person I think of when I am in any kind of difficulty. He taught me English and how to write research proposals, corrected preliminary versions of my all papers, and has helped me in every field of life. I express my deepest gratitude to him. The second is Pratibha, my wife, who has been helpful, encouraging, and supportive, and has shown belief in me and my work. I thank her heartily for everything she does for me. The third is Sandhya Bhagat, my sister, who has always fought for me. She has immense faith in my capabilities and always encourages me to strive for better things in life. I extend my deepest gratitude to her. The fourth is my mother, whom I love most in this world; I am highly indebted to her for her endless love, care, and prayers.

I would also like to express my gratitude to my father, Jijaji, Bhaiya, Monu, Mosa, Mosi, Aai (mother-in-law), and Baba (father-in-law). I convey thanks to all the children of my family, Kevin (my aunty's son), Honey and Anshu (my sister's children), Barbie (my brother's daughter), and Mahi and Joy (my sons) for their love. I also extend my deepest gratitude to my late Nana and Nani for their love, care, and prayers.

Finally, I would also like to express my gratitude to Professor Rajmohan Gandhi not only for writing a foreword for this book but also for always being very encouraging and supporting my entire academic endeavour. And I would take this opportunity to thank Oxford University Press for their prompt and helpful assistance with the manuscript at various stages of preparation. Any inadequacies that remain, however, are my own.

Was there a strategy in Gandhi's approach to fight against the caste system?*

[T]o understand what I say one needs to understand my conduct....
—M.K. Gandhi[1]

Can one even speak of Mahatma Gandhi (1869–1948) and 'strategy' in the same breath? Some scholars may accept that Gandhi sometimes compromised some of his basic principles to win endorsement at the highest levels of nationalist politics for his campaigns, but they might fiercely object to the use of the term 'strategy' with regard to Gandhi due to its negative connotation. For many scholars Gandhi remains basically a spiritual leader, and to them, 'the greatness of Gandhi is more in his holy living than in his heroic struggles'.[2] They hold that he involved himself in political struggles only so long as it aided his spiritual progress and that, at their core, his struggles were a search for truth; the word 'strategy' might fail to explain this spiritual essence of Gandhi's struggle. It would diminish the status of

1

Gandhi—from that of a spiritual leader to that of a strategist–social reformer or strategist–politician.

However, the term 'strategy' is alien neither to Gandhi's own writings nor to the available literature on him. Gandhi often speaks of himself as a general or soldier and uses the analogy of war to explain his stance on some matters. He says: 'I am a soldier. I am speaking therefore with a grasp of the strategy of war.'[3] He also confesses that '[t]here is room for that honest strategy in satyagraha'.[4] Sometimes Gandhi speaks as a master strategist who is making tactful choices in directing his campaigns. For instance, while reflecting on his decision to suspend the Non-Cooperation and Civil Disobedience movements, he writes: 'An able general always gives battle in his own time on the ground of his choice. He always retains the initiative in these respects and never allows it to pass into the hands of the enemy.'[5] He explains further that 'in a satyagraha campaign the mode of fight and the choice of tactics, e.g., whether to advance or retreat, offer civil resistance or organize non-violent strength through constructive work and purely selfless humanitarian service, are determined according to the exigencies of the situation'.[6] His political actions therefore appear not to be directed by moral or religious principles alone, distant from the concrete practical situations at hand. There must have been some element of strategy when he decided what issues to take up, which groups to involve, what methods to pursue, and to what lengths he should go in order to achieve the political results he was seeking.

Even ahimsa—the cardinal principle of Gandhi's philosophy— was introduced by him not as a creed, but as a method to resolve concrete political problems. In his speech at the All India Congress Committee (AICC) meeting at Wardha on 15 January 1942, Gandhi says that ahimsa, to him, is a creed, the breath of life. But he placed it before the Congress as a political weapon to be employed for solving political problems.[7] Later, in response to a question, he confesses that he remained convinced that he did well to present to the Congress non-violence as an expedient. He adds that he could not have done otherwise if he was to introduce it into politics and that if he had started with men who accepted non-violence as a creed, he might have ended with himself.[8] He also says: 'As a political method, it can always be changed, modified, altered, and even given up in preference to another.'[9] At this level, ahimsa is not a cardinal principle but a method or, to be more precise, a strategy—the strategy of non-violent struggle.

There is also a whole range of scholars who have studied Gandhi basically as a master political strategist in the use of non-violence. The best known of these are Richard Gregg, Krishnalal Shridharani, Joan Bondurant, Gene Sharp, and Bipan Chandra.[10] Robert E. Klitgaard, the author of 'Gandhi's Non-violence as a Tactic',[11] and Suchitra, who wrote 'What Moves Masses: Dandi March as Communication Strategy',[12] can also be included in the same list. For some of these scholars, 'it is essential rigorously to differentiate satyagraha as technique of action from those specific considerations of right-living with which Gandhi also concerned himself.'[13] They argue that Gandhi himself makes a distinction between non-violence as a policy, expedient, or method, and non-violence as a philosophy of life, and that he organized his political struggle with the full understanding that most of those who supported him did so as temporary and often unwilling disciples for the period of the struggle only.[14] To these scholars, a study that lays stress on Gandhi's moral character tends to force discussion away from his phenomenal achievements and their relevance today. They believe that 'Gandhi's philosophy of life had only a limited impact on the people. It was as a political leader and through his political strategy and tactics of struggle that he moved millions into political action.'[15] Therefore, they argue, it is necessary to present Gandhi's approach as strategic rather than as something directly related to values and beliefs that go beyond the immediate circumstances. To present a systematic review of all these important works is beyond the scope of this book, but the general point of importance that emerges is that Gandhi can be seen as a strategist and that his approach in several domains can perhaps be better studied in these terms.

It is evident from Gandhi's own writings and from the different works available on him that he possessed the remarkable qualities of an extraordinary strategist in conducting his struggles in the field of politics. However, the same cannot be said about his struggle against caste or varna[16] without any proper justification. Prima facie, Gandhi's own writings do not show much evidence of his being a strategist in his approach to the caste system. On many occasions, Gandhi makes confusing and often contradictory statements on caste and other related issues. There are times when Gandhi glorifies the caste system as a 'natural institution'[17] or as a 'useful institution if properly regulated'.[18] He also appreciates it because it has 'saved Hinduism from disintegration'.[19] On the other hand, there are also instances when he condemns it severely. He says that 'whilst *varna* gives life, caste kills it, and untouchability is the most hateful expression of caste'.[20] At another point he says: '[C]astes are a human manufacture, are daily weakening and have to go.'[21] Joseph Lelyveld correctly observes that 'it's never difficult to quote the Mahatma against himself'[22] while discussing his attitude towards untouchability and caste. These inconsistencies in Gandhi's writings leave ample scope for study and analysis; they can be viewed as evidence of self-contradiction in thought, or evolution in understanding, or as constituting part of a strategy deployed to fight the caste system. However, to deduce anything at this stage would be a hasty exercise.

In the available secondary literature on Gandhi and the caste system, there are several writings by scholars who hold that there is a possibility of some kind of strategy in Gandhi's approach. In his well-known book *Gandhi and His Critics*, B.R. Nanda, a biographer and Gandhian scholar, writes: 'Gandhi's reluctance to make a frontal assault on the caste system in the early years may have been a matter of tactics.'[23] Rajmohan Gandhi, another known Gandhian scholar and grandson of Gandhi himself, makes similar remarks: 'I see the Varnashrama remarks as sugar-coating for his [Gandhi's] pill for caste Hindus. He wants them to swallow his reforms.' He says: '[T]he "caste system" he [Gandhi] was "defending" was nonexistent. Attacks on his "defence" by his foes of the caste system only assured caste Hindus that Gandhi was not their enemy which he was not.'[24]

There are also many scholars who believe that Gandhi's views on caste, varna, and other related issues went through gradual change and development. Shriram Nikam writes: '[H]is [Gandhi's] views regarding Varna Vevastha, caste system and untouchability have evolved over a long period during the national movement.'[25] However, several other thinkers believe that Gandhi was the one who, more than anyone else, defended and validated the caste system in its orthodox form. For example, Parimala V. Rao writes: 'Gandhi inherited a Congress which already had a powerful pro-caste group. Added to this was the personal commitment that Gandhi himself had vis-à-vis the defence of the institution of caste.... He defended the *varnadharma* and attributed the emergence of untouchability to "a distortion of *varnadharma*". He also opposed the idea of anyone "moving" to a higher *varna*.'[26]

These above-quoted and other views held by different scholars explaining Gandhi's attitude towards the caste system can be—ignoring some variations—roughly divided into three schools of thought. The first consists of those scholars who accept that Gandhi believed in the caste system in toto as the 'natural order of society', promoting control and discipline, and sanctioned by religion. The second comprises those scholars who accept that Gandhi's attitude towards the caste system evolved over a period of time. The third is made up of a few scholars who find the possibility of some kind of tactic in Gandhi's defence of the caste system that some of his writings contain.

Clearly, it is not easy, simple, or straightforward to argue that Gandhi had the approach of a strategist in his fight against the caste system, as it can be said with respect to his fight against the British empire. Neither in Gandhi's own writings nor in the secondary works on him can one find evidence to give strong support for such an argument. Since there are only a few scholars who claim that Gandhi had a strategic approach in this matter, it is imperative to thoroughly examine the rival views. Only on rigorously and diligently examining all the three schools of thought would it be possible to justify whether or not Gandhi's approach to fighting the caste system was strategic in nature.

If these schools of thought are examined properly, it is found that the limitation common to all three is that they are largely derived from some of Gandhi's own writings or speeches and that, in the process of drawing conclusions, Gandhi's practices were not taken into consideration. Raghavan N. Iyer suggests that political thinkers are properly studied without reference to their personalities and practice, but when we turn to Gandhi, we find it peculiarly difficult to ignore his personality and his activities.[27] Gandhi also very categorically says: '[W]hat you do not get from my conduct, you will never get from my words.'[28] He goes a step further and suggests that 'as a matter of fact my writings should be cremated with my body'.[29] Another quote from him says: '[W]hat I have done will endure, not what I have said or written.'[30] This does not imply, however, that Gandhi's writings are not to be carefully examined; rather it means that Gandhi expects to be judged and understood by his conduct and not by his writings alone. It also implies that should some contradictions and inconsistencies appear in his writings, they are to be resolved in the light of his practices. Gandhi himself says: 'To understand what I say one needs to understand my conduct....'[31]

The next two sections of this chapter attempt to examine Gandhi's practices with regard to different caste restrictions and associated religious ritual obligations to obtain a better understanding of his views on caste and related issues. The first section explores

Gandhi's own personal practices related to caste restrictions and religious obligations. The second explores how community life was organized in Gandhi's ashrams. The following section examines the validity of the views held by each of the three aforementioned schools of thought on Gandhi's attitude towards the caste system, but against the background of a proper understanding of his personal practices. This is in order to find out the most appropriate view that can be carried forward into a new research inquiry. It is assumed that such an exercise will be helpful not only in clarifying some of the misunderstanding in the available literature regarding Gandhi's views on caste and other related issues, but also in seeking a possible answer to the question: was there a strategy in Gandhi's approach to the caste system?

Gandhi's Personal Practices

> I know that friends get confused when I say I am a sanatani Hindu and they fail to find in me things they associate with a man usually labelled as such.... It is a somewhat embarrassing position, I know—but to others, not to me!
>
> (M.K. Gandhi)[32]

Lavanam Gora and Mark Lindley write that in Gandhi's days, the traditional Hindu caste distinctions involved four basic rules:

1. Untouchability: to avoid touching or, in Malabar, even looking at 'untouchables' if you were not one yourself.
2. Restriction on commensality: to avoid eating with anyone of a lower caste than oneself.
3. Endogamy: to marry within your caste.
4. Hereditary occupation: to follow one's parent's vocation.[33]

Gandhi's personal attitude towards the practice of such caste rules or restrictions as well as his observance of other religious obligations will be analysed in this section.

Untouchability

The Hindu masses largely practised untouchability as part of their caste restrictions. In general, the practice lay in avoiding physical contact with particular groups of people in order to save oneself from being 'polluted'. Gandhi, in his speech at the Suppressed Classes Conference in Ahmedabad on 13 April 1921, narrated an incident from his childhood when he was hardly yet 12, in his second year at high school. The story was of Uka—a scavenger—who used to visit Gandhi's house to clean the latrines. Gandhi remembered that although he was a very dutiful and obedient child insofar as it concerned respecting one's parents, he often had tussles with them when they asked him to perform ablutions if he accidently touched Uka.[34] Referring to this story, Pyarelal Nayyar, Gandhi's personal secretary and biographer, writes that this event planted in Gandhi's soul the seed of rebellion against the institution of untouchability.[35] Another story that illuminates Gandhi's attitude towards the practice of untouchability is contained in his autobiography. He writes that when his wife refused to clear the chamber pot of his Christian clerk born of untouchable parents, he told her that he would not stand this nonsense in his house; he caught her by the hand and dragged her to the gate with the intention of pushing her out.[36] His autobiography also says that 'in South Africa untouchable friends used to come to my place and live and feed with me'.[37]

A different kind of untouchability related to menses is generally practised among many orthodox Hindu communities. Here, women are treated as untouchable during their monthly period. During this time, they are not allowed to enter places of worship or even the kitchen. Also, their physical touch is considered to be polluting. In one of his letters to Mirabehn, Gandhi described his views on these practices: 'I think I told you that so far as I am concerned, I never respected the rule even with reference to Ba herself. And when I began to see things clearer, I never felt the call to have the rule observed.'[38] Several of his letters to different persons show that he did not practice restrictions related to menstruation with other women either. He suggests in these letters that it is neither obligatory nor necessary to practise such restrictions.[39]

Besides, there are numerous other instances which reveal that, throughout his life, Gandhi never practised untouchability in any form. While writing about Gandhi's practice related to caste rule of untouchability, Tanika Sarkar writes:

> He [Gandhi] worked closely with low-caste coolies and invited Untouchable colleagues to live on his farms. He forced 'unclean' work on himself and on his family, and he accepted Untouchables in his social and domestic circles on equal terms. He made his family and associates break pollution taboos and engage in labour that was considered very profoundly polluted: shoe-making, leatherwork, cleaning of toilets.[40]

Apart from all this, it is important to know that when he returned to India from South Africa, he brought with him an 'untouchable' boy name Naiker.[41] He also adopted an 'untouchable' girl, Lakshmi, as his daughter. She used to live in his ashram and often travel with him. Therefore, it may not be difficult to argue that from a very young age, Gandhi showed a remarkable irreverence for caste restrictions of untouchability based on the notion of purity and pollution.

Inter-dining and Inter-caste Marriage

Hindus also observed several rules pertaining to endogamy and commensality. Endogamy forbade marriage among persons of different castes. One could only marry within one's own caste. The restrictions on commensality stipulated that members of one caste should not eat in the company of members of any other caste and/or should not eat food cooked by any person of a caste lower than their own. Gandhi's family belonged to the Vaishnava sect of Gujarat that followed strict restrictions on meat-eating. However, in his autobiography, Gandhi writes that in his childhood days, he had at least 'not more than half a dozen meat-feasts' in the company of a friend, a Muslim boy identified as Sheikh Mehtab by many of his biographers.[42] Also, he admitted—on being questioned by Ranchhoddas V. Patwari, the ex-dewan of Morvi (Saurashtra)—that during his stay in England, he ate at restaurants as well as at the house of an Englishman and that he had no objection to eating food prepared at European hotels, or by a Christian or a Mohammedan, if it consisted of ingredients eatable by him.[43] In his autobiography, Gandhi says that he used to invite English friends and Indian coworkers to eat at his home. He would also regularly visit a Christian family for dinner and eat his vegetarian food in their company while they ate their non-vegetarian food.[44] There is also some evidence that suggests that after coming back to India from South Africa, he attended parties where not only meat but liquor was also served.[45] When Gandhi started living in Segaon near Wardha, a person named Govind, who was an untouchable by caste, generally prepared food for him.[46] All these examples reveal that in the very early years of his life, Gandhi overcame the caste restriction of compulsorily dining within one's own caste and that throughout his life he ate with people of different faiths as well as castes, including untouchables. In his autobiography, he writes: 'I had no scruples about inter-dining.'[47]

It is a matter of fact that while in South Africa, Gandhi was instrumental in the marriage of Henry Polak, a Jew, with Millie Graham Downs, a Scottish Christian. After their marriage, this couple lived in Gandhi's Johannesburg house for almost a year. They also shifted to the Phoenix Settlement when Gandhi moved there with his family.[48] Recalling their marriage in his autobiography, Gandhi writes: 'Any expense over the wedding was out of the question, not even a special dress was thought necessary. They needed no religious rites to seal the bond. Mrs. Polak was a Christian by birth and Polak a Jew. Their common religion was the religion of ethics.'[49] According to Gandhi, their marriage was duly registered at the registrar of European marriages in the Transvaal, South Africa. Gandhi was the best man at the wedding.

It is worth taking into consideration that Gandhi not only allowed his son Ramdas[50] to marry someone who was from a different sub-caste but also allowed his son Devdas[51] to marry a girl who was from another varna altogether. He also, by design, married off his adopted daughter, Lakshmi, who was an untouchable, to a Brahmin boy[52] in 1933. On many occasions, Gandhi expressed his appreciation of inter-caste and inter-religious marriages. He also did not impose any restrictions on his own children in this respect.[53]

Hereditary Occupation

Hereditary occupation is understood to be one of the most important characteristics of the caste system. Everyone's caste is assigned a particular type of work and it is expected of every Hindu to follow his hereditary occupation as a caste restriction. It may not be a coincidence that in the first paragraph of his autobiography, Gandhi writes that over the last three generations, starting with his grandfather, his family had not been pursuing the hereditary or traditional duty assigned to them according to the caste system. He himself never earned his bread and butter by following his ancestors' calling. He also let his children choose their own professions and never pressed them to follow any pursuit prescribed for their caste. Moreover, he tried to master many activities prohibited for his caste, such as the work of a scavenger, barber, washerman, cobbler, tiller, and tailor.[54] He also taught many of these skills to his children, wife, and coworkers. It is also interesting to note that on two occasions, Gandhi mentioned his profession as 'farmer and weaver'. First, on 10 March 1922, Gandhi, along with S.G. Banker, the printer of *Young India*, was arrested for writing seditious articles. At the preliminary hearing on 11 March, Gandhi gave his age as 53 and his profession as 'farmer and weaver'.[55] Second, on 1 August 1933, Gandhi and Mahadev Desai were arrested at midnight and first taken to Sabarmati Jail and then transferred the next day to Poona's Yerwada Jail. There he was tried by Magistrate Hyam Israel. When asked his occupation, Gandhi replied, 'I am by occupation a spinner, a weaver and a farmer.'[56]

In 1908, Gandhi opened a school for the children at the Phoenix Settlement as well as for the Indian children from outside the settlement. In the school curriculum, there was no emphasis on teaching children their ancestors' calling. On the other hand, every student had to learn and respect manual labour. After returning to India from South Africa in 1917, Gandhi started a national school at his Indian ashram where every student needed to learn agriculture, hand weaving, and the use of carpenter and blacksmith tools. In this school too, there was no emphasis on preserving one's hereditary occupation. Around 1937, Gandhi introduced a plan of basic education that the Congress was expected to implement if it came to power after the general elections held under the Indian Act, 1935. Though Gandhi's basic education scheme was craft-centred, there was no insistence that one has to follow his or her hereditary craft. On the other hand, it was expected that everyone, irrespective of their caste and religion, should learn more than one craft depending on the individual's circumstances and environment. In short, Gandhi's educational scheme promoted respect for manual labour without any emphasis on furthering the idea of hereditary professions.

Sacred Books or the Question of Religious Authority

In general, the Hindu masses accept the authority of the shastras that consist of the four Vedas; the Upanishads; the Puranas; and the two great epics, the Ramayana and the Mahabharata. In Hinduism, the shastras—especially the Vedas—are considered the word

of God, and thus *sanatani* (eternal), and accepted as the highest
authority to determine truth. However, Gandhi, who proclaimed
himself a *sanatani* Hindu, said: '[N]o one can convince me, with the
help of quotations from *Shastras*.'[57] He also said: 'Early in my childhood I had felt the need of a scripture that would serve me as an
unfailing guide through the trials and temptations of life. The Vedas
could not supply that need.'[58] Though on several occasions Gandhi
said that he believed in the shastras, it is also true that he did not
accept them as the ultimate authority or the word of God. When
he was asked 'Where do you find the seat of authority?', Gandhi,
pointing to his breast, said: 'It lies here.' He also explains: 'I exercise
my judgment about every scripture, including the *Gita*. I cannot
let a scriptural text supersede my reason. Whilst I believe that the
principal books are inspired, they suffer from a process of double
distillation. Firstly, they come through a human prophet, and then
through the commentaries of interpreters. Nothing in them comes
from God directly.'[59]

It appears that although Gandhi speaks very highly of different
religious scriptures and shows strong faith in the Hindu shastras,
he never accepted them as the ultimate authority on life and never
let them override his rationality and morality. On the other hand,
'when Gandhi turned to Hindu (*Vaisnava*) texts', Ananya Vajpeyi
writes, 'what he sought from them was a moral—possibly even
a didactic—vision that could help an individual to cultivate self-
mastery and acquire self-knowledge....'[60]

Some Other Caste Restrictions and Gandhi's Practices

Gandhi, who at the age of 12 opposed the practice and doctrine of
untouchability—one of the important codes of the caste system—
also opposed other codes of the caste system at a very early age.
His autobiography tells us that during his time, it was prohibited
for his caste to voyage abroad. Although his fellow caste members

were agitated and the caste head—*sheth*—declared that if he went to England for studies he would be treated as an outcaste, he sailed for England to study law. In Hinduism, it is expected of every man of the upper three varnas or castes to wear the sacred thread— *upavita*—after going through a religious ceremony. Gandhi, as a boy belonging to one of the three upper varnas, had had such a religious ceremony in his childhood and had worn this sacred thread. But in his autobiography, he writes: 'Later, when the thread gave way, I do not remember whether I missed it very much. But I know that I did not go for a fresh one.'[61]

Gandhi's family belonged to the Vaishnava sect of Hinduism and in his childhood, as a Vaishnava, he had worn the *shikha* and the *tulasi-kanthi* (a Vaishnava necklace of *tulasi* beads) that were considered obligatory. He writes: 'On the eve of my going to England, however, I got rid of the *shikha*'; he also says, 'I got my cousin Chhaganlal Gandhi, who was religiously wearing the *shikha*, to do away with it.'[62] At another juncture, when asked when he gave up his tulasi-kanthi, he answered: 'I have never given up *tulasi-kanthi* but *tulasi-kanthi* gave me up.'[63]

Temple Visits, Idol Worship, and Public Prayer

Regular temple visits and idol or image worship constitute a part of the religious activities of a regular Hindu. In general, a Hindu visits a temple close to his or her home and worships an idol of their individual preference. Margaret Chatterjee writes that Gandhi was not a temple-goer,[64] and Joseph Lelyveld, in his recent biography of Gandhi, notes that 'Gandhi hardly ever prayed in temples'.[65] Gora and Lindley also say that 'Gandhi was not the kind of Hindu who accepts the authority of priests or even attends temple'.[66] Gandhi explains his thoughts on temple worship in his autobiography: 'Being born in the Vaishnava faith, I had often to go the *Haveli* [Temple]. But it never appealed to me. I did not like its glitter and pomp. Also I heard rumours of immorality being practised there, and lost all interest in it. Hence I could gain nothing from the *Haveli*.'[67]

Though Gandhi visited temples later in life, but his attitude towards temple worship remained the same. While on his tours, he would sometimes visit the famous temples. In his autobiography, he narrates the experience of his visit to the famous Kashi Vishwanath Temple with some disgust: 'If anyone doubts the infinite mercy of God, let him have a look at these sacred places. How much hypocrisy and irreligion does the Prince of Yogis suffer to be perpetrated in His holy name?'[68] He also very explicitly says: '... I do not visit temples. I feel no need to go to temples; hence I do not visit them.'[69] His approach to idol worship was along the same lines. He never used idols or images during his prayers. He once said: 'An idol does not excite any feeling of veneration in me.'[70]

It appears that the only caste restriction Gandhi observed consistently was vegetarianism, and the only traditional ritual he performed regularly was prayer. He was no doubt a man of prayer and was very particular and sincere about his prayers which followed a very strict timetable. However, his way of prayer was his own creation and it is difficult to find anything in the Hindu tradition that matches it. No images or idols were used in Gandhi's prayer meetings, which were held not in a temple or any special place but more often than not under the open sky. Devotional songs from different religions and readings from a variety of holy books made the core of his public prayers. Gandhi would make a 'prayer address' instead of a sermon. This would usually dwell on the political events of the day or the social challenges that needed to be met.[71] It needs to be remembered that his numerous public prayers were part of his political struggle and, for him, political struggle was part of his search for God. It appears that as far as religious practice is concerned, Gandhi was neither a temple-goer nor an idol-worshipper, and though he used to pray every day, his style of prayer was very different from the traditional manner of prayer.

Gandhi's practice of vegetarianism, too, was not a religious observation or due to caste restriction. Although a vegetarian, Gandhi comfortably ate in the company of meat eaters. In his autobiography, he confesses that he had gone to London as a convinced meat eater but had all along abstained from actually eating meat in the interest of truth and keeping in mind the vow he had made to his mother. However, he had wished at the same time that every Indian was a meat eater, and had looked forward to being one freely and openly some day and to enlisting others in the cause. He tells the reader that from the date of reading Henry S. Salt's book *Plea for Vegetarianism*, he became a vegetarian by choice.[72] At another point in his autobiography, he writes that he held his views on vegetarianism independently of religious texts.[73] Hence, though he practised very strict vegetarianism, it was basically a personal commitment for him rather than a matter of religious observation or practice arising from caste restriction.

Until this point, effort has been made to present an analysis of Gandhi's personal practices and his attitude towards several caste restrictions and other important Hindu religious observations and beliefs. It can also be seen that Gandhi's practices cannot be considered signs of orthodoxy in any way. He seems to be a reformer, if not a revolutionary, in breaking caste restrictions and other Hindu religious traditions and beliefs. To emphasize the same point further, a brief picture of the way life was organized in Gandhi's ashrams is presented in the next section.

Life in Gandhi's Ashrams

> I am going to ask the country not to judge me by either *Champaran* or *Kheda* but only by the Ashram.
>
> (M.K. Gandhi)[74]

Another way to illustrate that Gandhi was a reformer rather than an orthodox Hindu is by looking at life in Gandhi's different ashrams.

Here, life was organized along the basic principles of Gandhi's philosophy and the ashrams can be seen as an extension of Gandhi's personal practices. Once Gandhi himself said that 'the Ashram is the measuring rod by which people can judge me'.[75] In his lifetime, Gandhi founded four ashrams at different times and at different places, with a particular objective for each. The first was the Phoenix Settlement founded in 1904 near the Phoenix station in South Africa; the second, Tolstoy Farm, was established in 1910 near Johannesburg in South Africa; the third, the Satyagraha Ashram, was set up in 1915 near Ahmedabad in India; and the fourth, the Sevagram Ashram, was founded in 1936 near Wardha in India. Gandhi's own writings as well as other biographies reveal that the first ashram, Phoenix, was set up to save money in order to ensure the success of *Indian Opinion*, a weekly journal published by Gandhi. Tolstoy Farm was intended to be a home for imprisoned satyagrahis and their families. The Satyagraha Ashram would train young men, women, and children for long service to the motherland. It appears that initially there were no plans for a fourth ashram, but Wardha came up spontaneously and can be seen as an extension of the Satyagraha Ashram, its objective being similar. While each ashram had certain specific objectives, a common idea behind their establishment was to experiment with living a simple life to realize the dignity of human labour, as explained in John Ruskin's *Unto This Last*. These ashrams were clearly not established with the aim of building an ideal community along the basic principles of the Hindu caste system or *varnashrama dharma*.

Phoenix Settlement

In his autobiography, Gandhi explains that the Phoenix Settlement was the result of an instant desire to put into practice the idea of simple living as explained in Ruskin's *Unto This Last*. But it was also an effort to sustain *Indian Opinion*, which was making losses from the beginning. In his book *Satyagraha in South Africa*,

Gandhi writes: 'From the very first the paper was conducted at a loss. At last we decided to purchase a farm, to settle all the workers, who must constitute themselves into a sort of commonwealth, upon it and publish the paper from the farm.'[76]

For this purpose, Gandhi purchased 100 acres of land in the middle of the year 1904. The land lay two-and-a-half miles from the Phoenix railway station and came to be known as the Phoenix Settlement. In 1912, Gandhi gave away all that he had and made a trust of the Phoenix farm 'to put into practice the essential teaching of Tolstoy and Ruskin'.[77] The settlers of Phoenix, who initially comprised a small group of Indian and European idealists, were divided into two classes: the 'schemers' and the paid workers. The 'schemers' were those who had a personal interest in the venture. They were granted an acre of ground each with a building, and had to make a living by manual labour. Besides this, they drew USD 3 per month from *Indian Opinion*, with a right to divide the profits, if any. The others were simply paid for what they did.[78]

Not only were the settlers at Phoenix a heterogeneous group consisting of Hindus from different castes, Christians, Jews, and Muslims, but there was also no strict division of labour amongst them. Every settler, irrespective of caste, religion, or gender, had to do daily manual labour. In 1908, Gandhi opened a Phoenix school for both the children at the Phoenix Settlement and the Indian children from outside the settlement. As explained earlier, in this school's curriculum, there was no emphasis on teaching students their ancestors' calling. On the other hand, every student had to learn and respect manual labour. In *Indian Opinion*, Gandhi made it clear that in this school 'Indians of any caste or community will be admitted. No distinctions will be made in such matters as food, etc.'[79] Since there was no hostel on the premises for the students who lived outside the settlement, Gandhi made it a rule that every settler house two or three boys belonging to different castes and religions to experience inter-dining.[80] Gandhi introduced a common kitchen for the settlers around the end of 1910. Indeed, in November 1910, Gandhi wrote to Maganlal Gandhi, who was taking care of the Phoenix Settlement:

> There is only one thing uppermost in my mind and that is to introduce the common kitchen. You are not to do it forcibly. If you go on pleading with Santok and Ani gradually, they will be agreeable. ...
> Let Santok and Ani sleep together [in the same room]. It is as well if they begin to sleep together before dining together.[81]

In 1915, when some residents of the Satyagraha Ashram were hesitant about eating in the common kitchen with an untouchable family whom Gandhi had admitted in the face of great resistance from both the ashram dwellers as well as some outsiders, Gandhi wrote to one of his friends: '[I]n fact, no one should feel bad about it [eating with an untouchable family] because in Phoenix we shared food with everyone.'[82]

If there was a common kitchen at the Phoenix Settlement, there was also the practice of common prayer. All the settlers at Phoenix used to pray twice a day, and indeed the only item of prayer consisted of hymns from the different religions. Now it is evident that Gandhi's experiments with simple living and community life cannot be seen as a sign of religious orthodoxy. In no way can they be interpreted as an effort to organize human life along the basic principles of the caste system or varnashrama dharma. On the contrary, the experiments are to be seen as an effort to break all caste, community, and religious arrogance and discrimination.

Tolstoy Farm

The second ashram that Gandhi established in South Africa was Tolstoy Farm. The objective here was to house the families of jailed satyagrahis. In South Africa, Gandhi launched satyagraha against the Transvaal legislations for their racial discrimination against British Indian citizens. As a part of this struggle, some satyagrahis had to go

to jail for breaking some of the laws that were held to be discrimi-
natory and unjust. To sustain such a struggle, it was necessary that
some arrangement be made for the maintenance of the families
of the satyagrahis who were either in jail and/or in all probability
would go to jail in the near future. Due to Gandhi's own propaganda
in India about South Africa's satyagraha, he was receiving enough
money to meet these expenses. In his book *Satyagraha in South
Africa*, Gandhi says that in the beginning 'the families of jail-going
Satyagrahis were maintained by a system of monthly allowances in
cash according to their need'. However, Gandhi soon realized that
this arrangement left scope for fraud and injustice. To overcome this
and to ensure proper utilization of public money, Gandhi thought
that 'there was only one solution for this difficulty, namely that all
the families should be kept at one place and should become member of a sort of co-operative commonwealth'.[83] For this reason,
in May 1910, Hermann Kallenbach, a rich German architect and
a close friend of Gandhi, bought a farm of about 1,100 acres and
allowed the satyagrahis to use it free of any rent or charge. This
place, near Johannesburg, was used by Gandhi and other satyagrahi
families who lived there as a sort of cooperative commonwealth
community from May 1910 to January 1913 during their struggle
against racial discrimination, and came to be known as Tolstoy Farm.
The settlers of the farm hailed from Gujarat, Tamil Nadu, Andhra
Pradesh, and north India. There were Hindus from different castes,
Muslims, Parsis, and Christians. There was a single kitchen, and all
dined in a single row. The food was simple and strictly vegetarian
but Gandhi was determined that 'if the Christians and Musalmans
asked even for beef, that too must be provided for them'. However,
Gandhi was happy because 'neither the women nor the men ever
asked for meat'.[84]

D.G. Tendulkar writes: 'The settlers worked harder on the farm
than in the prisons. It was obligatory on all, young and old.' He also
notes that everyone had to perform every kind of work, including

cooking, gardening, cleaning, scavenging, shaving, and cutting hair, on a rotational basis.[85] To make the families self-supporting, small industries like sandal-making and carpentry were launched on Tolstoy Farm. Gandhi himself learnt the craft of making sandals and taught the other settlers of Tolstoy Farm. Gandhi also started a school for the young settlers. Here, an arrangement was made to impart some literary knowledge without the help of any textbooks. Gandhi also recognized the need to provide religious teaching to the young settlers. On this, he wrote that he liked the Muslims to read the Koran, the Parsis the Avesta, and the Khoja child a small *pothi* of that sect; however, it is interesting to note that he did not suggest anything for the Hindu children to read. Gandhi writes: 'I wrote out the fundamental doctrines of Hinduism according to my lights—I forget now whether it was for my own children or for the Tolstoy Farmers.'[86] In Tolstoy Farm, Gandhi experimented with co-education, which he called 'most fearless of its type'. Tendulkar called it a 'daring one'. Like the common school and common kitchen, there was also common prayer at Tolstoy Farm and it appears that the singing of devotional songs from different religions was the only item in it.

This brief sketch of life in Tolstoy Farm further strengthens the view that Gandhi seems to be a reformer and a liberal in the matter of caste and religion and the restrictions they traditionally prescribe. It is evident that though Gandhi was very interested in experimenting with living a simple community life, he did not give any thought to organizing community life along the principles of the caste system or varnashrama dharma.

Satyagraha Ashram

Gandhi came back to India in early 1915 and founded the Satyagraha Ashram on 25 May 1915 at Kochrab, a small village near Ahmedabad. Gandhi says in his autobiography that when the plague broke out in Kochrab village shortly afterwards, the ashram was shifted to the banks of the Sabarmati River, in the vicinity of the Sabarmati Central Jail. As a result, it also came to be known as the Sabarmati Ashram. But 'what he chose not to disclose was that the site was situated in close proximity to a *smashan*, a crematorium; ritually one of the most impure locations for a Hindu'.[87] Initially, there were about 25 men and women at the ashram, including one untouchable boy whom Gandhi brought with him from Africa. Soon many people from different parts of India as well as from overseas joined the ashram, which became a home of Muslims, Parsis, Christians, Jews, and Hindus from different castes, including the untouchable.

The ashram's inmates were divided into three classes: controllers, novitiates, and students. The controllers had to observe the vows of truth, ahimsa, celibacy, non-stealing, control of the palate, non-possession, swadeshi, and fearlessness of untouchability. They were also expected to 'devote some part of their time to working on the land; when that is not possible, they will perform some other bodily labour'.[88] Those who were desirous of following the afore-mentioned programme but were not immediately allowed to take the necessary vows were admitted as novitiates. It was obligatory for them to conform to all the observances that were followed by the controllers while they were in the ashram. They would acquire the status of controllers when they were able to take the necessary vows for life. Boys and girls under 12 years of age constituted the class of students.

Mark Thomson, in his book *Gandhi and His Ashrams*, writes: 'No caste distinctions were tolerated in the Kochrab and Sabarmati Ashrams and every member, child and adult alike, was required to contribute to the maintenance of the Ashram and to devote a certain amount of their time each day to the constructive work'.[89] It was desirable that all members devote some part of their time to manual work. It is a matter of fact that in the ashram, scavenging was part of day-to-day life for all the inmates, irrespective of their caste and religion.

Untouchability was not practised in any form at the ashram; even the very common practice among Hindus to treat women as untouchable during their menstruation was not practised in the ashram.[90] It also needs to be noted that common prayer and a common kitchen were part of the ashram since its founding. Gandhi writes to one of his friends about the Satyagraha Ashram kitchen: 'In the Ashram kitchen, *Luharas*, *Bhatiyas*, Brahmins, *Khatris*, Rajputs, Mussalmans, *Banias* all have been taking their meals together.'[91] All the ashram inmates were also expected to participate in the common prayer, which used to be held in the mornings from 5 a.m. to 5:30 a.m. and in the evenings, from 6:30 p.m. to 7:00 p.m. Devotional songs and readings from the holy books of different religions constituted the core of prayer at the ashram. No idols or images were used during these prayers. About idol worship at the ashram, Gandhi says:

> There is no ban against an idol at our prayers, but emphasis is given to prayer without one. It is possible that this compromise would not appeal to some. I, for one, prefer prayers without an idol. It is believed that idol worship helps by producing the effect of the place and surroundings. But this should be avoided for, after all, we have to go beyond these.[92]

Though every inmate of the ashram had to observe the vow of celibacy, many marriages were organized in the ashram. On the occasion of his son Ramdas's marriage, Gandhi said:

> The wedding just celebrated would perhaps be for the Ashram the last as between parties belonging to the same caste. It behoved people in the Ashram to take the lead in this respect, because people outside might find it difficult to initiate the reform. The rule should be on the part of the Ashram to discountenance marriages between parties of the same caste and to encourage those between parties belonging to different sub-castes.[93]

Although it was mandatory for students to learn different crafts and skills such as handloom-weaving, carpentry, and agricultural work irrespective of their caste or religion, there was no emphasis in the curriculum of the ashram's school to teach students their ancestral skills to maintain and preserve the hereditary division of labour.[94] It is evident that the Satyagraha Ashram was not organized according to the basic principles of caste or varna; neither was there any emphasis on preserving caste or varna divisions. Moreover, it is mentioned in the constitution of the Satyagraha Ashram that '[t]he Ashram does not follow the *varnashram dharma*'.[95]

Sevagram Ashram

Gandhi had declared on the Dandi March that he would not return to the Sabarmati Ashram until swaraj had been achieved and the salt tax abolished.[96] He did not return to make it his permanent home. Eventually, in 1933, Gandhi closed the ashram; the site became a trust for the assistance of untouchables and was renamed the Harijan Ashram. Late in September 1933, Gandhi moved to Wardha. Initially, he had no plans to establish an ashram there. He stayed for almost three years in a building presented to him by Jamnalal Bajaj and used it as the headquarters of the new Village Industries Association. This building was named Maganwadi in memory of the late Maganlal Gandhi who died in April 1928. In 1936, Gandhi decided to leave Wardha to settle down at Segaon, a village five miles from Maganwadi. Within a short period, Segaon became Sevagram, and another ashram was forming around Gandhi.[97] The ashram was neither organized along the basic principles of varna or caste nor observed any single caste restriction as obligatory. The cleaning of latrines, the common kitchen, and common prayer were part of the day-to-day life at the ashram.

Here, Gandhi encouraged local untouchable participation in every activity. In Sevagram, Gandhi also arranged tanning classes where the skinners were taught improved methods and a variety of ways to use the flesh and bones of animals. This was in the teeth of reactionary opposition from orthodox Hindus.[98] He also recruited local untouchables to work with him and Sushila Nayyar, to be trained in his nursing methods. He also chose a local untouchable boy to render him personal services.[99] Gandhi also allowed an untouchable to solemnize the wedding of a Brahmin, Dr A.G. Tendulkar, and an untouchable woman, Indumati, at the Sevagram Ashram on 19 August 1945.[100] It is evident that in Sevagram, as in Gandhi's other ashrams, none of the restrictions related to caste or varna was practised and there was no attempt to follow and idolize the fourfold division of Hindu society. On the other hand, it was built in such a way that it served to break down all caste arrogance and discrimination.

The brief exploration of Gandhi's personal practices and cooperative life in his ashrams helps us understand that from a very young age, Gandhi revolted against the practice of most of the important caste restrictions. He himself violated every restriction assigned to his own caste. It also helps us understand that Gandhi's personal practices served as an example to his wife, children, and other friends, and helped them overcome many caste prejudices. In no way can his actions be seen as a sign of orthodoxy or conservative attitude.

However, some of his writings, where he explicitly defends and validates some aspects of caste and some of its restrictions, reveal an entirely different picture of Gandhi's attitude towards caste. However, no proper and final conclusion about this can be drawn without providing an appropriate explanation for it.

Overview of Literature/Mystery of Gandhi's Writings

As mentioned earlier in the chapter, in the secondary sources of literature on Gandhi, there are different views seeking to explain his attitude towards the caste system. As discussed earlier, there have been different scholarly interpretations regarding Gandhi's views on the caste system that can be divided into three groups. The first group holds that Gandhi saw the caste system as a natural way of organizing human society, and that it promotes control and discipline in human life. The second group believes that the changes in Gandhi's writings on the caste system can be interpreted as a gradual evolution of his thinking about it. The third group argues that there was an inherent tactic involved in Gandhi's defence of caste in his early writings in India. Now, in the light of a clear understanding of Gandhi's personal practices regarding caste restrictions—as presented earlier—the validity of such views can be properly analysed to find out which of the three is the most appropriate for describing Gandhi's attitude towards the caste system, and to also discover the most viable line of enquiry for a new study on Gandhi and the caste system. This section of the chapter makes an effort in this direction; it examines some of the important explanations that have been advanced to explain Gandhi's attitude towards the caste system.

Gandhi's Belief in the Caste System in Toto

There are a good number of scholars who sincerely hold that Gandhi believed in the caste system in toto. These scholars can be further divided into two groups for the convenience of analysis: first are Dalit scholars; and second, Gandhian scholars. Most Dalit scholars argue that Gandhi stood against everything that demanded change in the basic social structure of Hindu society and he was one who, more than anyone else, defended and validated the caste system when its legitimacy was being seriously challenged and its existence seemed precarious.[101]

Scholar Braj Ranjan Mani writes:

Gandhi was an outstanding product of this orthodox milieu: he was a bania more brahmanised than Brahmans; his world-view and life philosophy were moulded and shaped by the age-old brahmanic values and way of life...he never gave up his basic belief in the brahmanical fundamentalism which is evident from his constant evocation of varnashrama, Ram-rajya and trustreeship....[102]

One of the important limitations of Dalit scholars' view is that the primary objective of their study is not to understand Gandhi and his views on caste and other related issues; their primary field of study is Ambedkar or Dalit movement and they place Gandhi and his movement along with or against Ambedkar to develop a better understanding about Ambedkar and his contribution to the uplift-ment of Dalits. For instance, Kancha Ilaiah writes, 'The fundamental difference between these two thinkers lies in positioning themselves from their own communities.' He further adds, 'Ambedkar was not only born in an untouchable Mahar family but all through his life stood for the suppressed, oppressed and exploited masses. Gandhi on the other hand, was born in a Baniya family and stood for the oppressor and exploiting upper castes.'[103] Therefore, in most of the Dalit scholars' studies, it is simply accepted that Gandhi believed in the caste system because of his personal commitment towards the Brahminical world view, which he inherited by virtue of being born in an upper-caste Hindu family.

However, it is difficult to accept such views about a person who openly violated most of the important restrictions of the caste system in his every personal practice, and who built ashrams that were founded on principles that rejected all the basic rules of the caste system or varnashrama dharma. Prima facie, these views clearly contradict Gandhi's personal practices and therefore seem to be problematic. It is also important to note that at this junc-ture, the present book is not engaging itself with the overall Dalit scholars' critique of Gandhi's method to deal with the issue of the caste system. This will be taken up in Chapter 4 after explaining the course of Gandhi's evolving strategy against the caste system. Since this section is reserved to identify different justifications given by different scholars to vindicate their claims regarding Gandhi's views on the caste system, it is argued here that in the light of Gandhi's actual practice, Dalit scholars' view that Gandhi believed in the caste system because he had a personal commitment towards the Brahmancial world view seems to be problematic.

In contrast to the studies of Dalit scholars, the studies of Gandhian scholars focus on Gandhi's life and his movements and provide different reasons for holding views that Gandhi believed in the caste system. The following subsections analyse some of the justifications offered by some of the Gandhian scholars to argue that Gandhi believed in the caste system in toto.

Caste Provides a Livelihood for Millions of Villagers

Prominent Gandhian scholar Margaret Chatterjee, in her book *Gandhi's Religious Thought*, makes some passing references to Gandhi's views on caste and the possible justifications for his defence of it. It is important to mention that in this work, her primary interest is to understand Gandhi's religious thoughts rather than his views on caste. She writes:

> In his early years in India, after the South-Africa experience, Gandhi spoke in favour of following one's hereditary occupation. What was behind it, I believe, was his perception of the undoubted fact that industrialisation would gradually erode the network of traditional occupations that had provided a livelihood for villagers for centuries.... Industrial civilisation would never be able to provide a livelihood for the teeming millions of India, to whom, in Gandhi's own words, God could only appear in the form of work.[104]

Although it seems to be a very unorthodox and fairly convincing argument, both of Chatterjee's claims—first that Gandhi rejected industrialization because it failed to provide a livelihood for millions of Indians and next, that he preferred and propagated traditional hereditary modes of occupation over industrialization for resolving India's economic problems—need to be examined properly before they may be accepted as appropriate explanations for Gandhi's defence of the caste system and hereditary occupation in his writings.

It is a fact that, on many occasions, Gandhi criticized industrialization because he was afraid it would lead to unemployment in India. It is also a fact that for more than two decades, Gandhi had sought to persuade the masses regarding the need of the charkha and khadi, which he propagated as an alternative to industrialization for providing a livelihood to millions in India. But in 1944, Gandhi altered this somewhat, proposing a 'New Khadi Philosophy'. This, according to him, was based on the fundamental principle that rural production must be primarily for self-consumption and not for sale. He says:

> At least this much should be clear to all that khadi is not an occupation or a craft merely for earning a livelihood. None of us should harbour this idea. For, if khadi is an industry it would have to be run purely on business lines. The difference between khadi and mill-cloth would then be that while a mill provides employment to a few thousand people in a city, khadi brings a crore of rupees to those scattered about in fifteen thousand villages. Both must then be classified as industries, and we would hardly be justified in asking anybody to put on khadi and boycott mill-cloth. Nor can such khadi claim to be the herald of swaraj. On the other hand we have claimed that the real significance of khadi is that it is a means for uplifting the villages and thereby generating in the people the spontaneous strength for swaraj. Such a claim cannot then be sustained.[105]

Indeed what Gandhi suggested now was completely different from the idea of spinning providing a livelihood to millions of Indians. Now he suggests that an attempt be made to immediately stop the spinning of yarn for sale. Instead, khadi workers should persuade and educate people to spin 'for their own use'. Moreover, when Shrikrishnadas Jaju, the secretary of the All Indian Spinners'

Association (AISA), pointed out that this would mean the khadi stores in the cities which were doing very well would have to close down and that as a result 300,000 spinners connected with the khadi organization would lose their additional income, Gandhi insists: 'Close them down.'[106]

It is obvious now that for Gandhi, the greatest danger of industrialization is not that it 'would gradually erode the network of traditional occupations that had provided a livelihood for villagers for centuries', but that it would destroy deeper values and create alienated individuals in an industrial society. He was afraid that industrialization would turn a person into a mechanical part of the production machine. He writes: '[I]t is beneath human dignity to lose one's individuality and become a mere cog in the machine. I want every individual to become a full-blooded, fully developed member of society.'[107] It seems that the 'issue of unemployment' was a 'practical' argument with which he sought to persuade to his point of view those who did not share his moral presuppositions. But basically and fundamentally, he viewed industrialization with suspicion because it destroyed the dignity and autonomy of the individual and individual labour.

Since he was also aware that hereditary occupation can crush individuality,[108] he did not at any time advocate the traditional hereditary mode of occupations (caste or varna) as an alternative to industrialization to solve the economic problems of India. Defining caste or varna as hereditary occupation and appreciating it for several reasons is one thing, and preferring and advocating it for resolving the economic problems of India is quite another. There is hardly any evidence which suggests that Gandhi, at any time, argued that it is the traditional hereditary occupations (caste or varna) that India needed to resolve her economic problems. He also did not set up any organization to persuade people to follow their hereditary occupations. There is also no reference to compulsory hereditary occupation in his proposed education scheme

(Nayee Talim) for India. Likewise, there is no reference to it in his constructive programme that he designed to create an ideal village.

As has been stated earlier, Gandhi preferred and propagated the charkha to challenge the belief of educated Indians that industrialization would solve all the economic problems of India, and the charkha, for him, was not a symbol of hereditary occupation (caste or varna) as he did not ask any particular caste alone to spin but tried to persuade everyone across caste, religion, gender, and economic status to spin every day. For him, the charkha was a symbol of self-sufficiency and dignity of labour.[109] Therefore, Chatterjee's argument that Gandhi spoke in favour of hereditary occupation (caste or varna) because it would provide a livelihood for the teeming millions of India is problematic.

Caste as an Outcome of Gandhi's Belief in Rebirth and Law of Karma

Bhikhu Parekh is another distinguished scholar who, in his book *Colonialism, Tradition and Reform*, attempts to explain Gandhi's views on caste and the possible reasons for which Gandhi might have defended caste and some of its restrictions in his writings. Since, in this book, Parekh's primary concern is to understand Gandhi's critical dialogue with the Hindu tradition and his struggle to reform it, the discussion on caste obviously acquires importance. There is a separate chapter, 'Discourse on Untouchability', where Parekh discusses in detail Gandhi's views on caste and provides a series of reasons why Gandhi defended the caste system. One of them is that 'since Gandhi believed in rebirth and the law of karma, he thought that the characteristic occupation of an individual's caste corresponded to his natural abilities and dispositions and represented a necessary moment of his spiritual evolution'.[110]

If it is true that in his writings Gandhi expresses his faith in the doctrine of karma, it is also true that it is difficult to demonstrate his faith in its orthodox interpretation where the characteristic occupation of an individual's caste *necessarily* corresponded to his natural abilities and dispositions due to their past karma. A close look at his writings where he evokes the doctrine of karma reveals that he does it often for pragmatic reasons and that, most of the time, it goes against the orthodox interpretation of the doctrine of karma. The following quote from Gandhi defending temple entry for untouchables is one of the best examples of his pragmatic interpretation of the doctrine of karma. He writes: 'If you believe that Harijans are in their present plight today as a result of their past sins, you must concede that they have the first right of worship in temples. God has been described by all the scriptures of the world as a Protector and Saviour of the sinner.'[111] One can also find other sayings of Gandhi that simply reject the orthodox understanding of the doctrine of karma—that one's destiny is the fruit of one's past karma. He writes, 'The law of karma is no respector of persons, but I would ask you to leave the orthodoxy to itself. Man is the maker of his own destiny, and I therefore ask you to become makers of your own destiny.'[112]

Not only his writings but his practices also confirm his rejection of the orthodox interpretation of the doctrine of karma, that is, one's present suffering is a result of one's past karma. For instance, his decision to end the life of an incurable calf to cut short its agony is a clear rejection of the orthodox interpretation of the doctrine of karma, which suggests that one has to suffer to atone for one's past karma. In 1928, Gandhi euthanized an incurable calf in his ashram and when some people objected to this, he vigorously defended his act and argued that he would apply the same principle to human beings in similar circumstances.[113] Now it is evident that although Gandhi for some reason did not reject the doctrine of karma, he did not believe in its orthodox interpretation. And even if Gandhi believed in rebirth, Parekh's argument that the former defended caste because he thought that due to rebirth and past karma 'the characteristic occupation of an individual's caste corresponded to his natural abilities and dispositions and represented a necessary moment of his spiritual evolution' seems to be problematic.

Greater Opportunities Afforded by Caste

Ramashray Roy, another scholar known for his two books—*Self and Society: A Study in Gandhian Thought* and *Gandhi and Ambedkar: A Study in Contrast*—attempts to understand Gandhi's views on caste and the possible reasons for which Gandhi may have advocated retention of the varnas or caste as hereditary occupation. In both of his books, Roy's conclusions are similar. He holds that 'Gandhi advocates retention of the *varna vyavastha*' because 'in his view, *varna vyavastha* is natural and affords greater opportunities than other arrangements for self-realisation and social harmony'.[114] Roy argues that 'Gandhi's rejection of modern civilization is total' and that his rejection was because primarily the goal of modern civilization, especially in its most utilitarian forms, is simply the satisfaction of one human desire after another. Self-gratification is not only accepted but also encouraged and gradually the higher purpose of life, which for Gandhi is self-realization, becomes obsolete. On the other hand, 'a social order,' Roy adds, 'of Gandhi's conception must be treated as a *yajna*. As an instance of *yajna*, society signifies an order that is based on the phenomenon of extended selves; it must reflect the values that promote harmony, non-exploitation, equality, and participation.' Roy adds: '[Gandhi] finds this possibility to exist only in a social order that is based on *varna vyavastha*.' Roy reminds the reader that 'it is in this context that we can understand why Gandhi puts so much emphasis on *varna vyavastha*, in general, and the caste system grounded in it, in particular'.[115]

There are different levels of misunderstanding in such an analysis of Gandhi's views. First, though it is true that Gandhi criticizes modern civilization because it encourages proliferation of human wants and desires, makes acquisition of goods and material comforts the core of human life, and renders obsolete the idea of self-realization, it does not mean that Gandhi completely rejected modern civilization and uncritically advocated retention of the varna vyavastha. Second, it is appropriate to say that Gandhi's conception of society signifies an order that is based on the phenomenon of extended selves; it must reflect the values that promote harmony, non-exploitation, equality, and participation. However, Roy's argument that Gandhi finds this possibility to exist *only* in a social order that is based on varna vyavastha needs to be examined properly.

Indeed Gandhi attacked all kinds of violence and domination, irrespective of whether he discovered it in the traditional way of life (varna vyavastha) or the modern (modern civilization). However, his criticism of modern civilization was more explicit than that of the traditional due to the particular historical context (Indian's struggle against colonialism) in which he found himself. For the same reason, he also chose to idealize the traditional way of life and argued that individual dignity and social harmony can be achieved within it. But this does not lead to any total rejection of modern civilization and a return to the original varna vyavastha. On the other hand, Gandhi's criticism of modern civilization shows that he believed in the possibility that individual dignity, social harmony, and the ultimate end of life, that is, self-realization, can be achieved within the boundaries of modern civilization itself. As Parel observes: '[T]he correct Gandhian metaphor for modern civilization is not "disease" but "curable disease": "civilization is not an incurable disease." Hind Swaraj, in this respect, is a short treatise on "the malaise of modernity" and Gandhi is one of its physicians.'[116]

What needs to be remembered here is that Gandhi's effort to reform modern civilization should also not be understood as his preferring modern civilization to traditional society that is organized on the basic principles of varna. Certainly, for Gandhi, it is not a matter of preference; being a practical man, he accepted that modern civilization is going to stay here, and hence needs to be improved. Indeed the dominant passion of Gandhi's life was neither the improvement of modern civilization nor the retention of varna vyavastha through the rejection of modern civilization. He firmly believed man to be a finite being and incapable of developing such social arrangements as are perfect for self-realization; therefore, there was no value in hankering after any specific arrangement. He also learnt from Indian tradition that that there were/are/will be different yugas, and therefore for Gandhi, real work consisted in defining *yugadharma* (self-realization) that must be relevant to and practicable within the context of the modern yuga. As Parekh writes: '[I]f we were to pick out the one dominant passion, the central organising principle of his [Gandhi's] life, it would have to be his search for and his struggle to establish dharma appropriate to India in the modern age.'[117] Hence, to hold that Gandhi's rejection of modern civilization was total and that he argued for the retention of a social order that is based on varna vyavastha because he found that 'it is natural and affords greater opportunities for self-realisation and social harmony' may not be appropriate.

Moreover, it is also not correct to say that 'Gandhi puts so much emphasis on *varna vyavastha*, in general, and the caste system grounded in it, in particular'. Replying to a question, Gandhi himself said: '[I]f *varnashrama* goes to the dogs in the removal of untouchability … I shall not shed a tear.'[118] Responding to another question at another point, he explains that his adherence to the idea of varnashrama should not be taken very seriously:

> I have gone no-where to defend varnadharma, though for the removal of untouchability I went to Vykom. I am the author of a Congress resolution for propagation of Khadi, establishment of Hindu–Muslim unity, and removal of untouchability, the three pillars of swaraj. But I have never placed establishment of varnashrama dharma as the fourth pillar. You cannot, therefore, accuse me of placing a wrong emphasis on varnashrama dharma.[119]

Likewise, Gandhi can be neither accused of nor appreciated for an emphasis on varnashrama dharma, as his practices speak otherwise. It is known that Gandhi was a man of action and if he really believed a society based on varna would prove to be the most conducive for self-realization, he would have lived a life in alignment with the basic principles of varna and would have also organized his ashrams along those lines. But as explained earlier, Gandhi neither lived his life nor organized any of his ashrams on the principles of varna. One can thus conclude that it is not appropriate to hold that 'Gandhi puts so much emphasis on *varna vyavastha*, in general, and the caste system grounded in it, particular'.

Gradual Changes in Gandhi's Opinions on Caste

Bipan Chandra, who is an authority on Gandhi, in his paper 'Gandhiji, Secularism and Communalism', makes some passing remarks on Gandhi's views on caste. He writes: 'Many quote his [Gandhi's] statements on the caste system, inter-caste and inter-religious dining and marriages ... and so on, from his early writings. But the fact is that, while his basic commitment to human values, truth and non-violence remained constant, his opinions on all these and other issues underwent changes—sometimes drastic—and, invariably, in more radical directions.'[120] To justify his point, Chandra quotes from two of Gandhi's writings: one from 1933 and the other from 1938. In the first, Gandhi says: 'In my search after Truth I have discarded many ideas and learnt many new things ... and, therefore, when anybody finds any inconsistency between any two writings of mine, if he has still faith in my sanity, he would do well to choose the later of the two on the same subject.'[121]

It is a fact that on more than one occasion, Gandhi says that he is not at all concerned with appearing to be consistent and suggests that his last opinion be taken as final. On the basis of this suggestion from Gandhi himself, many scholars like Chandra have argued that there was a gradual evolution and/or radical changes in Gandhi's opinion on caste and other related issues. Navajivan Publishing House, Ahmedabad, which had the copyright for Gandhi's writings, had been following the practice of printing this quote in many collections of Gandhi's different writings and speeches on varied subjects,[122] in order to make the reader aware that there were considerable changes in Gandhi's views on different subjects over time. But surprisingly enough, Gandhi never accepted that there were inconsistencies or changes in his opinions, not to speak of changes in more radical directions. Before he made the aforementioned comment, 'In my search after Truth I have discarded many ideas and learnt many new things', in the same piece of writing Gandhi also says: '[A]s I read them [own writings] with a detached mind, I find no contradiction between the two statements, especially if they are read in their full context.'[123] Indeed whenever Gandhi was charged of inconsistency in his writings—although on every occasion he said that he was not at all concerned with appearing to be consistent and suggested that his readers take his last opinion as final—he made it very clear that he personally did not find any inconsistency in his writings and this suggestion was for those friends who did find inconsistencies in his writings. He also suggested that before making their choice, these friends should also try to perceive an underlying and abiding consistency between his two seemingly inconsistent statements of different times. He wrote:

> [W]henever I have been obliged to compare my writing even of fifty years ago with the latest, I have discovered no inconsistency between the two. But friends who observe inconsistency will do well to take the meaning that my latest writing may yield unless, of course, they prefer the old. But before making the choice they should try to see if there is not an underlying and abiding consistency between the two seeming inconsistencies.[124]

Gandhi seems to be right in denying any inconsistency is his opinions on caste and its restrictions because he, from a very young age, violated most of the caste restrictions. His attitude towards the caste system remained more or less consistent throughout his life. It is obvious now that the inconsistencies or changes in his writings were deliberate and conscious and not due to any changes in his opinion on the subjects. Hence, it may not be appropriate to say that there were gradual changes or a line of development over a period of time in Gandhi's opinions on caste and other related issues.

Gandhi's Defence of Caste: A Matter of Strategy

As mentioned earlier, B.R. Nanda, in his book *Gandhi and His Critics*, has written: 'Gandhi's reluctance to make a frontal assault on the caste system in the early years may have been a matter of tactics.'[125] Apart from Nanda, there are other scholars like Rajmohan Gandhi, Ramachandra Guha, Anthony J. Parel, Judith M. Brown, David Hardiman, Dennis Dalton, and Joseph Lelyveld[126] who argue that Gandhi was a strategist in his approach to the caste system. The reason these scholars see a strategy on Gandhi's part lay in the fact that in South Africa, as early as 1909, Gandhi had publicly decried the caste system for its inequalities, but shortly after he returned to India, he understood that a conservative but powerful section of Hindus was not yet ready for radical reforms. And, for strategic reasons alone, he emphasized on the generally beneficial aspects of caste. As Judith M. Brown writes: 'Though he had rejected the whole idea far earlier and inveighed and worked against it even in South Africa, once home in India, having tested the temper of public opinion, he was aware of the strength of Hindu orthodoxy and he took care not to equate his campaign against untouchability with the question of caste as a whole.'[127]

These scholars tend to make their argument in two complementary ways. First, they refer to the following piece of writing by

Jawaharlal Nehru: 'I spoke to Gandhi repeatedly: why don't you hit out at the caste system directly? He said that he did not believe in the caste system except in some idealized form of occupations and all that; but that the present system was thoroughly bad and must go. I am undermining it completely, he said, by tackling untouchability.'[128] But Nehru's justification of some of Gandhi's writings alone may be insufficient. As Lelyveld writes: 'Nehru might be suspected of trying to gloss over the ambiguities in Gandhi's position here.'[129] More significantly, however, these scholars suggest that since in South Africa Gandhi openly criticized the caste system, his emphasis on some positive aspects of the caste system in India must be seen as part of a broader strategy to fight against the caste system. This is a more convincing justification than Nehru's. Apart from this, the argument of Gandhi being a strategist in his approach to the caste system resolves the seeming contradiction between Gandhi's personal practices where he violates most of the important caste restrictions, and his emphasis on some of the positive aspects of the caste system in some of his writings and speeches.

Based on the given discussion, it appears that the most appropriate way to interpret Gandhi's position on caste is that of the scholars who view Gandhi as a strategist; in other words, shortly after Gandhi returned to India, he understood that a conservative but powerful section of Hindus was not yet ready for radical reforms and, therefore, he wrote emphasizing the generally beneficial aspects of the caste system for strategic reasons alone. However, what is not evident in the work of these scholars is a clear narrative of the development of Gandhi's strategy over three decades in India to fulfil his personal commitment to abolish caste hierarchy.

Gandhi's writings suggest that he was not consistent in his emphasis on the beneficial aspects of the caste system and his defence of it; in fact, his writings reveal that he kept shifting his emphasis on what he meant by the caste system, varna, removal of untouchability, inter-dining, and inter-caste marriage.

If it is accepted that Gandhi wrote about the beneficial aspects of the caste system for strategic reasons alone, the inconsistencies or shifts in his writings on the issue cannot be ignored and must also be analysed as part of his long-term strategy to fight the caste system. Gandhi himself suggests, '*There is, I fancy, a method in my inconsistencies.*'[130] He also suggests to his readers that '*they should try to see if there is not an underlying and abiding consistency between the two seeming inconsistencies*'.[131] It means that the different positions assumed by Gandhi on caste, varna, untouchability, inter-dining, and inter-caste marriage at different times cannot be properly understood and historically evaluated unless they are seen as different parts of his basic strategy to fight against the caste system. But as mentioned earlier, in the available literature, there is a lack of a clear narrative of the development of Gandhi's strategy over three decades in India to fulfil his personal commitment to abolish caste hierarchy. Therefore, this study tries to explain inconsistencies in the life and writings of Gandhi on caste and other related issues as different stages of Gandhi's evolving strategy in his fight against the caste system. It also tries to see if there is continuity and a strategic relationship between one stage and another.

Organization of the Book

The book is organized into five chapters, including the present chapter. The present chapter has identified that in the available literature none of the scholars have presented a coherent analysis of the changes in Gandhi's writings on caste as part of his long-term strategy to abolish caste hierarchy. Therefore, it specified its objective to understand Gandhi's three decade-long evolving strategy to fight against the caste system and its continuous relevance for the upliftment of untouchables during our time. The following four chapters make an effort to fulfil this identified objective.

Chapter 2 tries to find out, if not the caste system or varnash-rama dharma, what was the basis of Gandhi's ideal society and ideal form of organizing human society which he aspired to achieve. This chapter carries out its investigation in the following three sections. The section on 'South Africa Experiments' describes Gandhi's various engagements in different fields of life and argues that it was in South Africa that he formulated his basic philosophical expositions on his ideals that are explained in his booklet *Hind Swaraj*. The next section, 'How to Read *Hind Swaraj*', argues that while there is little doubt that Gandhi had outlined his ideals in the booklet, there is always disagreement among scholars on how it should be interpreted for a comprehensive understanding of Gandhi's vision of ideal society, of the views he upheld, and the aims he wanted to achieve. It also explains the three major ways in which *Hind Swaraj* is generally analysed, and argues that the best way is to see it as Gandhi's effort to explain his concept of swaraj. The third section, 'What Is Swaraj', tries to explain what swaraj is for Gandhi. It takes help from Parel's essay 'Gandhian Freedoms and Self-rule'. This section, like Parel's essay, tries to understand Gandhi's concept of swaraj by analysing it under four heads: political independence of the nation, political freedom of the individual, economic freedom of the individual, and self-rule. However, if Parel focuses on explaining the meaning of different aspects of Gandhi's concept of swaraj, this section aims to comprehensively understand Gandhi's concept of swaraj in a manner that explains all the four aspects. It argues that for Gandhi, swaraj means the capacity of the individual to self-regulate or self-organize his or her life, and that achieving swaraj means nurturing such a capacity in every individual. Hence, it concludes that it is the individual and not the caste system or varnashrama dharma that is the basis of Gandhi's ideal society and that it was the autonomy of the individual which Gandhi advocated and aspired to achieve.

The third and fourth chapters chronologically analyse the inconsistencies in Gandhi's writings on the issues of untouchability, caste, varna, inter-dining, inter-caste marriage, and so on, starting from 1915 (his arrival in India from South Africa) to 1948 (his death). They analyse Gandhi's writings during five time periods on the basis of the themes that emerge during these years on issues such as untouchability, caste, varna, sanatani Hindu, inter-dining, and inter-caste marriage. The time periods are 1915–20, 1920–7, 1927–32, 1932–45, and 1945–8. These chapters also examine whether there is consistency and strategic relation among the different themes that appear in these sections of time on the same issues. However, such an exercise cannot be undertaken in isolation; Gandhi lived and worked in a specific historical context—India's struggle for political independence against colonial power. Therefore, both chapters also analyse Gandhi's writings in their particular historical context. The chapters draw attention to how the important political activities of a particular period influenced and enabled Gandhi to strategically alter his views on many key issues, and how these alterations in his writings and approaches in turn were instrumental in taking forward his movement for abolishment of the caste system to its logical end.

The fifth chapter presents a critical estimate of Gandhi's life and his strategies in order to understand the effectiveness of his evolving strategy to fight against the caste system, and thus to understand the continuing relevance of Gandhi's strategy for the upliftment of Dalits. For the same, it places Gandhi's evolving strategy against the caste system in contrast with two other contemporary movements (Ambedkar's anti-caste movement and the Arya Samaj's *shuddhi* movement) that emerged during the colonial period to tackle issues of caste. The apparent divergence between Gandhi's evolving strategy and the other two movements will highlight limitations as well as merits of Gandhi's strategy. After explaining differences between Gandhi's strategy and Ambedkar's anti-caste movement, and Gandhi's strategy and Arya Samaj's shuddhi movement, this chapter also attempts to highlight limitations, merits, and the continuing relevance of Gandhi's strategy for the upliftment of untouchables during our time. In the end, the chapter also presents a summary of all the five chapters and outlines the contribution and limitations of the present study.

A Short Note on the Word 'Strategy'

Before moving on to understand Gandhi's evolving strategy in his fight against the caste system, it is important to explain the meaning of the word 'strategy' and its usage in this context. It is not the purpose of this study to argue that Gandhi was clever or unfair in the way he dealt with the caste issue. On the other hand, this study argues that the way Buddhists understand the term 'strategy' to be 'skilful means', and not clever or unfair scheming, may be the most suitable explanation of Gandhi's approach. This Buddhist concept of 'skilful means' is described in the following words of the scholar Deane Curtin. He writes:

> The Buddhist realizes that we cannot say that truth to someone who has not yet had his or her experience in the heart of the forest. One can, however, use skilful means to direct someone to that experience. While such means cannot be entirely 'truthful'—they are not 'precise'—they are motivated by compassion and the hope of relief from suffering.[132]

It must be noted that the argument being put forward here is not to say that Gandhi learns his strategy to fight the caste system from Buddhism. Though several scholars argue that Gandhi 'consistently applied Buddhist principles to the murky work of politics',[133] the idea here is just to show a striking similarity between the Buddhist idea of 'skilful means' and Gandhi's strategy in tackling the caste system. It is argued here that like Buddha, Gandhi felt that if the masses are not yet in a state to understand the hidden evils of the caste system, it is of no use to reveal the entire truth to them; rather, gradually, step by step, their capacity to internalize the value of such radical reform should be enhanced. In one of those rare instances when Gandhi theorized his methods or strategy in dealing with the caste issue, he hinted at how his overall struggle against caste should be seen—as resembling nothing but the Buddhist idea of skilful means. In response to the question 'Why do you not make anti-untouchability work part of a wider crusade against the caste system itself?', he writes:

> It is one thing for me to hold certain views and quite another to make my views acceptable in their entirety to society at large. .... I have therefore to exercise the utmost patience and be satisfied with hastening slowly ... I am wholly in agreement with you in principle. If I live up to 125 years, I do expect to convert the entire Hindu society to my view.[134]

At another place he explains it in the following way: 'In the first place, one should never embark upon non-cooperation all of a sudden. Evil customs which have prevailed for ages cannot be eradicated in a moment. Reform is one-legged, and so proceeds haltingly. Anyone who loses patience can never become a pure saty-agrahi. The first step for a reformer is to educate public opinion.'[135]

To sum up, in this study, the 'strategy' that is being attributed to Gandhi does not mean a clever or unfair act; it means 'skilful means'—persuading people towards a particular direction. While such means, as it is understood by Buddhists, may not be truthful or precise, they are motivated by compassion and the hope to relieve others from suffering. What one wants to underline here is that when, after returning to India from South Africa, Gandhi had started talking about the positive aspects of caste system and proclaimed his faith in it, he did so because he understood that the Hindu masses were not yet ready for radical reform and that they must be first gradually educated before being asked to abandon their faith in the doctrine of the caste system and the practices based on it. And the inconsistencies in Gandhi's writings on the subject show that he was actively engaged in formulating and developing this strategy.

Notes

* This chapter has been published as 'Was Gandhi a "Champion of the Caste System"?: Reflections on His Practices' in *Economic and Political Weekly*, LII (13): 42–50.

1. M.K. Gandhi, 'Letter to Hanumanprasad Poddar', 5 November 1932, in *Collected Works of Mahatma Gandhi* (hereafter *CWMG*), Vol. 51 (New Delhi: Publications Division, Government of India, 1972), p. 353.

2. S. Radhakrishnan, 'Gandhi's Religion and Politics', in S. Radhakrishnan (ed.), *Mahatma Gandhi: Essays and Reflections* (Mumbai: Jaico Publication House, 2007), p. 1.

3. M.K. Gandhi, 'Discussion with Workers at Poona', 4 September 1924, in *CWMG*, Vol. 25 (New Delhi: Publications Division, Government of India, 1967), p. 91.

4. M.K. Gandhi, 'Discussion with Neill Statue Volunteers, Madras', 6 and 7 September 1927, in *CWMG*, Vol. 34 (New Delhi: Publications Division, Government of India, 1969), p. 467.

5. M.K. Gandhi, 'Discussion with Philipose', 15 March 1939, in *CWMG*, Vol. 69 (New Delhi: Publications Division, Government of India, 1977), p. 60.

6. Gandhi, 'Discussion with Philipose', p. 60.

7. M.K. Gandhi, 'Speech at A.I.C.C. Meeting', 15 January 1942, in *CWMG*, Vol. 75 (New Delhi: Publications Division, Government of India, 1979), pp. 219–20.

8. M.K. Gandhi, 'Question Box', 7 April 1942, in *CWMG*, Vol. 76 (New Delhi: Publications Division, Government of India, 1979), p. 11.

9. Gandhi, 'Speech at A.I.C.C. Meeting', p. 220.

10. R.B. Gregg, *The Power of Nonviolence* (London: James Clarke and Co. Ltd, 1960); K. Shridharani, *War without Violence* (Mumbai: Bharatiya Vidya Bhavan, 1962); J.V. Bondurant, *Conquest of Violence: The Gandhian Philosophy of Conflict* (California: Princeton University Press, 1958); Gene Sharp, *The Politics of Nonviolent Action* (Boston: Porter Sargent, 1973); and Bipan Chandra, 'The Long-Term Strategy of the National Movement', in B. Chandra, M. Mukherjee, A. Mukherjee, K.N. Panikkar, and S. Mahajan, *India's Struggle for Independence* (New Delhi: Penguin Books, 1989), pp. 505–17.

11. R.E. Klitgaard, 1971, 'Gandhi's Non-violence as a Tactic', *Journal of Peace Research*, 8(2): 143–53.

12. Suchitra, 1995, 'What Moves Masses: Dandi March as Communication Strategy', *Economic and Political Weekly*, 30(14): 743–6.

13. Bondurant, *Conquest of Violence*, p. 12.

14. Sharp quoted in Bob Overy, 'Gandhi as a Political Organiser', in Michael Randle (ed.), *Challenge to Nonviolence*, Issues in Peace Research (Bradford: Department of Peace Studies, University of Bradford, 2002), available at http://www.civilresistance.info/challenge (accessed on 30 May 2013).

15. Chandra, 'The Long-Term Strategy of the National Movement', p. 506.

16. In this study, caste is often used in both ways as a synonym for varna as well as a different category than varna. When caste is used as a synonym for varna, it represents the classical fourfold hierarchical and hereditary division of Hindu society into Brahmins, Kshatriyas, Vaishyas, and Shudras. When it is used as a different category than varna, it represents numerous subdivisions (endogamous groups following similar heredity occupations) within this classical fourfold division. It is used in this way because Gandhi also used it in a similar fashion.

17. M.K. Gandhi, 'The Hindu Caste System', 1916, in *CWMG*, Vol. 13 (New Delhi: Publications Division, Government of India, 1964), p. 301.

18. M.K. Gandhi, 'Letter to C.F. Andrews', 25 May 1920, in *CWMG*, Vol. 17 (New Delhi: Publications Division, Government of India, 1965), p. 534.

19. M.K. Gandhi, 'The Caste System', 8 December 1920, in *CWMG*, Vol. 19 (New Delhi: Publications Division, Government of India, 1966), p. 83.

20. M.K. Gandhi, 'Speech to Ceylon Hindus, Jaffna', 27 November 1927, in *CWMG*, Vol. 35 (New Delhi: Publications Division, Government of India, 1969), p. 336.

21. M.K. Gandhi, 'Letter to Harijan Workers', 12 January 1934, in *CWMG*, Vol. 56 (New Delhi: Publications Division, Government of India, 1973), p. 429.

22. Joseph Lelyveld, *Great Soul: Mahatma Gandhi and His Struggle with India* (New Delhi: HarperCollins, 2011), p. 22.

23. B.R. Nanda, *Gandhi and His Critics* (New Delhi: Oxford University Press, 1985), p. 26.

24. Rajmohan Gandhi, *The Good Boatman: A Portrait of Gandhi* (New Delhi: Viking, 1995), pp. 237–40.

25. Shriram Nikam, *Destiny of Untouchables in India: Divergent Approaches and Strategies* (New Delhi: Deep & Deep Publications, 1998), p. 35. Dharampal writes: '[I]n popular discussion about Gandhiji it is usually said that whatever he said or did in his later days was according to him the best.' He adds a little later that 'Gandhiji himself could have basically reverted to an earlier position after having tried out various options'. See Dharampal, *Understanding Gandhi* (Goa: Other India Press, 2003), p. 91. Suhas Palshikar writes: '[I]n the light of development of Gandhi's views on the caste issue, there is no doubt about Gandhi's ultimate preparedness to abolish caste. And yet, caste question does not become the core of Gandhi's discourse.' See Suhas Palshikar, 1996, 'Gandhi–Ambedkar Interface: …When Shall the Twain Meet?', *Economic and Political Weekly*, 31(31): 2070.

26. Parimala V. Rao, 2009, 'Gandhi, Untouchability and the Postcolonial Predicament: A Note', *Social Scientist*, 37(1 and 2): 65.

27. Raghavan N. Iyer, *The Moral and Political Thought of Mahatma Gandhi* (New Delhi: Oxford University Press, 2000), p. 4.

28. M.K. Gandhi, 'To the Readers', 2 November 1940, in *CWMG*, Vol. 73 (New Delhi: Publications Division, Government of India, 1978), p. 145.

29. Gandhi quoted in N. Dadhich. 'The Postmodern Discourse on Gandhi: Modernity and Truth', in Douglas Allen (ed.), *The Philosophy of Mahatma Gandhi for the Twenty-First Century* (New Delhi: Oxford University Press, 2009), p. 196.

30. M.K. Gandhi, *In Search of the Supreme*, Vol. 2 (Ahmedabad: Navajivan Publications, 1961), p. 286.

31. Gandhi, 'Letter to Hanumanprasad Poddar', p. 353.

32. M.K. Gandhi, 'Speech at Missionary Conference, Colombo', 16 November 1927, in *CWMG*, Vol. 35, pp. 254–5.

33. Lavanam Gora and Mark Lindley, *Gandhi as We Have Known Him* (New Delhi: National Gandhi Museum in association with Gyan Publishing House, 2007), p. 105.
34. Gandhi, 'Speech at Suppressed Classes Conference, Ahmedabad', 13 April 1921, in *CWMG*, Vol. 19, p. 570.
35. Pyarelal Nayyar, *Mahatma Gandhi, Vol. 1: The Early Phase* (Ahmedabad: Navajivan Publishing House, 1965), p. 217. For the same event, see D.G. Tendulkar, *Mahatma: Life of Mohandas Karamchand Gandhi, Vol. 1: 1869–1920* (8 vols) (New Delhi: Publications Division, Ministry of Information and Broadcasting, Government of India, 1960), p. 27; Robert Payne, *The Life and Death of Mahatma Gandhi* (New York: E.P. Dutton & Co., 1969), p. 34.
36. M.K. Gandhi, *An Autobiography or The Story of My Experiments with Truth*, Mahadev Desai (tr.), (London: Penguin, 2001), p. 255. Hereafter referred to as *An Autobiography*.
37. Gandhi, *An Autobiography*, p. 360.
38. M.K. Gandhi, 'Letter to Mirabehn', 26 August 1927, in *CWMG*, Vol. 34, p. 401.
39. M.K. Gandhi, 'Letter to N.M. Khare', 29 May 1924, in *CWMG*, Vol. 24 (New Delhi: Publications Division, Government of India, 1967), p. 135.
40. Tanika Sarkar, 'Gandhi and Social Relations', in Judith Brown and Anthony J. Parel (eds), *The Cambridge Companion to Gandhi* (New Delhi: Cambridge University Press, 2011), p. 178.
41. See Gandhi, *The Good Boatman*, p. 234; M.K. Gandhi, 'Letter to Hermann Kallenbach', 24 September 1915, in *CWMG*, Vol. 13, p. 127.
42. See Tendulkar, *Mahatma, Vol. 1*, pp. 26–7; Nayyar, *Mahatma Gandhi, Vol. 1*, pp. 209–10.
43. M.K. Gandhi, *Caste Must Go and the Sin of Untouchability* (Ahmedabad: Navajivan Publishing House, 1964), pp. 92–100.
44. Gandhi writes in his autobiography that he use to visit a Christian family for dinner every Sunday, but this practice was abruptly broken because he spoke derisively of the piece of meat on the plate of his host's son. See Gandhi, *An Autobiography*, p. 157.

45. Gandhi writes: 'At the dinner a lady was sitting on one side and a gentleman on the other side of me. After the lady had helped herself with the bottle it would come to me. It would have to pass me in order to reach the gentleman. It was my duty to pass it on to the latter. I deliberately performed my duty. I could have easily refused to pass it saying that I would not touch a bottle of liquor. This, however, I considered to be improper.' M.K. Gandhi, 'What should be Done Where Liquor is Being Served?', 22 March 1925, in *CWMG*, Vol. 26 (New Delhi: Publications Division, Government of India, 1967), p. 355.

46. Balvant Sinha, *Under the Shelter of Bapu* (Ahmedabad: Navajivan Publishing House, 1962), p. 93.

47. Gandhi, *An Autobiography*, p. 96.

48. See Thomas Weber, *Going Native: Gandhi's Relationship with Western Women* (New Delhi: Lotus/Roli Books, 2011), p. 156.

49. Gandhi, *An Autobiography*, p. 282.

50. Ramdas married Nirmala, who belonged to a different sub-caste, on 27 January 1928. See M.K. Gandhi, 'Speech at Wedding of Ramdas Gandhi', 27 January 1928, in *CWMG*, Vol. 35, p. 498.

51. Devdas married Lakshami, a Brahmin girl belonging to a different varna, in 1933. See M.K. Gandhi, 'Letter to Mirabehn', 7 June 1933, in *CWMG*, Vol. 55 (New Delhi: Publications Division, Government of India, 1973), pp. 186–8 and 'Letter to Lakshami', 7 July 1932, in *CWMG*, Vol. 50 (New Delhi: Publications Division, Government of India, 1972), p. 167.

52. Gandhi wrote a letter to Dudabhai (the biological father of his adopted daughter) in 1931: 'It is necessary to abolish the class of *Antyajas* from Hindu society, I really think that it would be good if Lakshmi could be married to a non-*Antyaja*.' See M.K. Gandhi, 'Letter to Dudabhai', 31 May 1931, in *CWMG*, Vol. 46 (New Delhi: Publications Division, Government of India, 1971), pp. 268–9. Lakshmi got married to Maruti, a Brahmin orphan boy, on 14 March 1933. See *CWMG*, Vol. 45 (New Delhi: Publications Division, Government of India, 1971), p. 15.

53. Though Gandhi did not impose any restriction on his children for marrying within their own caste, he did not allow one of his sons to marry a Muslim girl.

54. See Anu Bandyopadhyaya, *Learning from Gandhi*, available at http://www.arvindguptatoys.com/arvindgupta/bg.pdf (accessed on 8 December 2012).

55. Mahatma Gandhi, *The Gandhi Reader: A Sourcebook of His Life and Writings*, Jack A. Homer (ed.), (New York: Indiana University Press, 1956), p. 197.

56. Stanley Wolpert, *Gandhi's Passion: The Life and Legacy of Mahatma Gandhi* (New York: Oxford University Press, 2001), p. 172.

57. M.K. Gandhi, 'My Notes', 3 May 1925, in *CWMG*, Vol. 27 (New Delhi: Publications Division, Government of India, 1968), p. 21.

58. M.K. Gandhi, 'Speech at Banares Hindu University', 1 August 1934, in *CWMG*, Vol. 58 (New Delhi: Publications Division, Government of India, 1974), p. 271.

59. M.K. Gandhi, 'Discussion with Basil Mathews and Others', 24 November 1936, in *CWMG*, Vol. 64 (New Delhi: Publications Division, Government of India, 1976), p. 75.

60. Ananya Vajpeyi, *Righteous Republic: The Political Foundation of Modern India* (Cambridge: Harvard University Press, 2012), p. xix.

61. Gandhi, *An Autobiography*, p. 355.

62. Gandhi, *An Autobiography*, p. 355.

63. Gandhi, *Caste Must Go and the Sin of Untouchability*, pp. 92–100.

64. Margaret Chatterjee, *Gandhi's Religious Thought* (Notre Dame, Indiana: University of Notre Dame Press, 1983), p. 7.

65. Lelyveld, *Great Soul*, p. 194.

66. Gora and Lindley, *Gandhi as We Have Known Him*, p. 91.

67. Gandhi, *An Autobiography*, p. 45.

68. Gandhi, *An Autobiography*, p. 228.

69. M.K. Gandhi, 'What Does a Hindu Temple Mean?', 19 March 1933, in *CWMG*, Vol. 54 (New Delhi: Publications Division, Government of India, 1973), p. 129.

70. M.K. Gandhi, 'Hinduism', 6 October 1921, in *CWMG*, Vol. 21 (New Delhi: Publications Division, Government of India, 1966), p. 249.

71. Chatterjee, *Gandhi's Religious Thought*, pp. 111–13.
72. Gandhi, *An Autobiography*, p. 59.
73. Gandhi, *An Autobiography*, p. 297.
74. M.K. Gandhi, 'Ashram Inmates' 17 February 1919', in *CWMG*, Vol. 15 (New Delhi: Publications Division, Government of India, 1965), p. 92.
75. M.K. Gandhi, 'Letter to Premabehn Kantak', 13 February 1933, in *CWMG*, Vol. 53 (New Delhi: Publications Division, Government of India, 1972), p. 291.
76. M.K. Gandhi, *Satyagraha in South Africa*, Valji Govindji Desai (tr.), (Ahmedabad: Navajivan Publishing House, 2003), p. 131.
77. M.K. Gandhi, 'Mr. Polak and His Work', 7 July 1909, in *CWMG*, Vol. 9 (New Delhi: Publications Division, Government of India, 1963), p. 394; see Tendulkar, *Mahatma, Vol. 1*, p. 128.
78. See Joseph J. Doke, *M.K. Gandhi: An Indian Patriot in South Africa* (New Delhi: Publications Division, Ministry of Information and Broadcasting, Government of India, 1967), pp. 83–4; Tendulkar, *Mahatma, Vol. 1*, p. 68.
79. M.K. Gandhi, 'Phoenix School', 9 January 1909, in *CWMG*, Vol. 9, p. 135.
80. See Prabhuda Gandhi, *My Childhood with Gandhiji* (Ahmedabad: Navajivan Publishing House, 1957), p. 59.
81. M.K. Gandhi, 'Letter to Maganlal Gandhi', 7 November 1910, in *CWMG*, Vol. 10 (New Delhi: Publications Division, Government of India, 1963), p. 348.
82. M.K. Gandhi, 'Letter to Khushalchand Gandhi', 24 September 1915, in *CWMG*, Vol. 97 (New Delhi: Publications Division, Government of India, 1994), p. 14.
83. Gandhi, *Satyagraha in South Africa*, pp. 213–14.
84. Gandhi, *Satyagraha in South Africa*, p. 216.
85. Tendulkar, *Mahatma, Vol. 1*, pp. 117–20.
86. Gandhi, *Satyagraha in South Africa*, p. 220.
87. Tridip Suhrud, *Reading Gandhi in Two Tongues and Other Essays* (Shimla: Indian Institute of Advanced Study [IIAS], 2012), p. 131.
88. M.K. Gandhi, 'Draft Constitution for the Ashram', before 20 May 1915, in *CWMG*, Vol. 13, p. 95.

89. Mark Thomson, *Gandhi and His Ashrams* (Bombay: Popular Prakashan, 1993), p. 100.
90. Gandhi, 'Letter to Mirabehn', 26 August 1927, p. 400.
91. M.K. Gandhi, 'Letter to Khushalchand Gandhi', 31 August 1918, in *CWMG*, Vol. 17, p. 216.
92. Gandhi quoted in Sinha, *Under the Shelter of Bapu*, p. 22.
93. M.K. Gandhi, 'Speech at Ashram, Sabarmati', 27 January 1928, in *CWMG*, Vol. 35, p. 500.
94. M.K. Gandhi, 'Draft Constitution for the Ashram', 20 May 1915, in *CWMG*, Vol. 13, pp. 91–8.
95. M.K. Gandhi, 'Draft Constitution for the Ashram', 20 May 1915, p. 94.
96. Gene Sharp, *Gandhi Wields the Weapon of Moral Power: Three Case Histories* (Ahmedabad: Navajivan Publishing House, 1960), p. 74; Jad Adams, *Gandhi: Naked Ambition* (London: Quercus, 2010), p. 208.
97. Thomson, *Gandhi and His Ashrams*, p. 196.
98. Thomson, *Gandhi and His Ashrams*, p. 212.
99. Thomson, *Gandhi and His Ashrams*, p. 195.
100. See M.K. Gandhi, 'Letter to Nagesh V. Gunaji', 17 July 1944, in *CWMG*, Vol. 77 (New Delhi: Publications Division, Government of India, 1979), p. 396; see also M.K. Gandhi, 'Letter to Indumati Gunaji', 10 August 1945, in *CWMG*, Vol. 81 (New Delhi: Publications Division, Government of India, 1980), p. 103.
101. Braj Ranjan Mani, *Debrahmanising History: Dominance and Resistance in Indian Society* (New Delhi: Manohar, 2008), p. 348. See also Swapan K. Biswas, *Gods, False Gods and the Untouchables* (Kolkata: Orion, 1988); Gail Omvedt, *Dalit Vision: The Anti-caste Movement and the Construction of an Indian Identity*, revised edition (New Delhi: Orient Blackswan, 2006); Christophe Jaffrelot, *Analysing and Fighting Caste: Dr. Ambedkar and Untouchability* (New Delhi: Permanent Black, 2008).
102. Mani, *Debrahmanising History*, p. 348.
103. Kancha Ilaiah, 'Dalitism vs Brahmanism: The Epistemological Conflict in History', in Ghanshyam Shah (ed.), *Dalit Identity and Politics: Cultural Subordination and the Dalit Challenge*, Vol. 2 (New Delhi: SAGE, 2001), p. 126.

104. Chatterjee, *Gandhi's Religious Thought*, pp. 19–20.

105. M.K. Gandhi, 'Discussion with Shrikrishnadas Jaju', 13 October 1944, in *CWMG*, Vol. 78 (New Delhi: Publications Division, Government of India, 1979), p. 192.

106. M.K. Gandhi, 'Discussion with Shrikrishnadas Jaju', 13 October 1944, p. 191.

107. M.K. Gandhi, 'Discussion with Maurice Frydman', 1 January 1939, in *CWMG*, Vol. 68 (New Delhi: Publications Division, Government of India, 1977), p. 266.

108. Gier writes, 'Gandhi wants to protect the individual from dissolution either in a pre-modern totality or the modern bureaucratic state.' See Nicholas F. Gier, *The Virtue of Nonviolence: From Gautama to Gandhi* (Albany, NY: State University of New York Press, 2004), p. 22.

109. Ashis Nandy writes that Gandhi advocated charkha for the following three reasons. First, it did not supplant human beings; second, it symbolized the dignity and autonomy of the individual resisting the demands of modern collectives; and third, it symbolized premodern technology and non-alienated labour. See Ashis Nandy, *Traditions, Tyranny and Utopias: Essays in Politics of Awareness* (New Delhi: Oxford University Press, 1987), p. 138.

110. Bhikhu Parekh, *Colonialism, Tradition and Reform: An Analysis of Gandhi's Political Discourse* (New Delhi: SAGE, 1989), p. 226. Apart from this reason for Gandhi's defence of the caste system, Parekh had given four other reasons.

111. M.K. Gandhi, 'Speech at Public Meeting, Mandla', 6 December 1933, in *CWMG*, Vol. 56 (New Delhi: Publications Division, Government of India, 1973), p. 304.

112. M.K. Gandhi, 'Speech in Reply to "Ezhavas'" Address, Varkalail', 13 March 1925, in *CWMG*, Vol. 26, p. 294. Gandhi also writes:

Is there such a thing as the quality of mercy and pity and love, and if there is, am I to say these men and women who are dying of slow starvation and who are almost naked, are, after all, reaping the fruit of their past karma and I have no duty by them? Each for his own is the message for man. As I write these words in cold blood, I feel staggered, and if such was the implication of the

54 Gandhi against Caste

law of karma, I should become a rebel against it. Fortunately it teaches me a different lesson. On the one hand it insists on patience, and on the other it peremptorily commands me to undo the past by rearranging the present.

See M.K. Gandhi, 'Letter to Elizabeth Sharpe', 12 April 1924, in *CWMG*, Vol. 23 (New Delhi: Publications Division, Government of India, 1967), p. 422.

113. See M.K. Gandhi, 'Letter to Bhogilal', 22 September 1928, in *CWMG*, Vol. 23, pp. 297–8; 'The Feary Ordeal', 4 October 1928, in *CWMG*, Vol. 23, pp. 310–14; 'The Tangle of Ahimsa', 11 October 1928, in *CWMG*, Vol. 23, pp. 338–40.

114. Ramashray Roy, *Self and Society: A Study in Gandhian Thought* (New Delhi: SAGE, in collaboration with United Nations University, Tokyo, 1984), pp. 111–12; *Gandhi and Ambedkar: A Study in Contrast* (Delhi: Shipra, 2006), p. 140.

115. Roy, *Gandhi and Ambedkar*, p. 140.

116. A.J. Parel, 'The Doctrine of Swaraj in Gandhi's Philosophy', in U. Baxi and B. Parekh (eds), *Crisis and Change in Contemporary India* (New Delhi: SAGE, in association with the Book Review Literary Trust, 1995), p. 62.

117. Parekh, *Colonialism, Tradition and Reform*, p. 11.

118. M.K. Gandhi, 'Brahmin–Non-Brahmin Question', 24 November 1927, in *CWMG*, Vol. 35, p. 522.

119. M.K. Gandhi, 'Brahmin–Non-Brahmin Question', 24 November 1927, p. 523.

120. Bipan Chandra, 2004, 'Gandhiji, Secularism and Communalism', *Social Scientist*, 32(1 and 2): 3–4.

121. Chandra, 'Gandhiji, Secularism and Communalism', p. 4.

122. See Gandhi, *Caste Must Go and the Sin of Untouchability*, p. 2; and M.K. Gandhi, *Basic Education*, (Ahmedabad: Navajivan Publishing House, 1951), p. 2.

123. M.K. Gandhi, 'Inconsistencies?', 29 April 1933, in *CWMG*, Vol. 55, p. 60.

124. M.K. Gandhi, 'Conundrums', 25 September 1939, in *CWMG*, Vol. 70 (New Delhi: Publications Division, Government of India, 1977), p. 203.

125. Nanda, *Gandhi and His Critics*, p. 26.

126. Lelyveld, *Great Soul*, pp. 185–6; A.J. Parel, *Gandhi's Philosophy and the Quest for Harmony* (New Delhi: Cambridge University Press, 2006), pp. 90–1.

127. Judith M. Brown, *Gandhi: Prisoner of Hope* (New Delhi: Oxford University Press, 1990), p. 205. Dennis Dalton writes, 'But however much Gandhi condemned inequality of castes in South Africa, shortly after he returned to India the emphasis fell on the generally beneficial aspects of caste, and a strong defense of it for its "wonderful powers of organization."' See Dennis Dalton, *Mahatma Gandhi: Nonviolent Power in Action* (New York: Columbia University Press, 1993), p. 49. David Hardiman writes, '[I]n 1909, he condemned the caste system and "caste tyranny". On his return to India he adopted a much softer line on the question.' See D. Hardiman, *Gandhi in His Time and Ours: The Global Legacy of His Ideas* (New Delhi: Orient Blackswan, 2003), p. 126. Ramachandra Guha writes, 'The opposition that he [Gandhi] faced from his fellow Hindus meant that Gandhi had perforce to move slowly, and in stages.' See R. Guha, *An Anthropologist among the Marxists and Other Essays* (New Delhi: Permanent Black, 2001), p. 94.

128. Nehru quoted in Lelyveld, *Great Soul*, p. 187.

129. Lelyveld, *Great Soul*, p. 186.

130. M.K. Gandhi, 'My Inconsistencies', 13 February 1930, in *CWMG*, Vol. 42 (New Delhi: Publications Division, Government of India, 1970), p. 469; emphasis added.

131. Gandhi, 'Conundrums', 25 September 1939, p. 203; emphasis added.

132. Deane Curtin, 'A State of Mind Like Water: Ecosophy T and the Buddhist Traditions', in Eric Katz, Andrew Light, and David Rothenberg (eds), *Beneath the Surface: Critical Essays in the Philosophy of Deep Ecology* (London and Massachusetts: MIT Press, 2000), p. 265.

133. Pankaj Mishra, *An End of Suffering: The Buddha in the World* (Cambridge: Cambridge University Press, 2004), p. 340. Raghavan Iyer also asserts that Gandhi interpreted Hindu values 'in the light of the message of the Buddha'. See Iyer, *The Moral and Political Thought of Mahatma Gandhi*, p. 235. Douglas Allen writes, 'In many respects,

Gandhi's means–ends preventative analysis is similar to the Buddha's formulation of the Doctrine of Dependent Origination (*pratiya-samutpada or paticca-samuppada*).' See Douglas Allen, 'Mahatma Gandhi's Philosophy of Violence, Nonviolence, and Education', in *The Philosophy of Mahatma Gandhi for the Twenty-First Century*, p. 47. Nicholas F. Gier writes that he has taken 'controversial move to disengage Gandhi from his Hindu tradition and give his contextual pragmatism a Buddhist self and Buddhist ontology'. See Nicholas F. Gier, 'Nonviolence as a Civic Virtue: Gandhi and Reformed Liberalism', in *The Philosophy of Mahatma Gandhi for the Twenty-First Century*, p. 133. Joseph Prabhu argues that transformation is 'what Gandhi calls "reducing himself to zero", or again what Buddhist tradition refers to as *sunyata* (nothingness or self-emptying)'. See Joseph Prabhu, 'Gandhi's Religious Ethics', in *The Philosophy of Mahatma Gandhi for the Twenty-First Century*, p. 175.

134. M.K. Gandhi, 'Talk with Members of Harijan Sevak Sangh', 28 July 1946, in *CWMG*, Vol. 85 (New Delhi: Publications Division, Government of India, 1982), p. 24.

135. M.K. Gandhi, 'Satyagraha and Caste Reform', 13 April 1924, in *CWMG*, Vol. 23, p. 432.

What did Gandhi stand for and what did he intend to achieve?

We desire to achieve the general welfare
through the welfare of an individual.
                              —M.K. Gandhi[1]

2

In the previous chapter, it is argued that
Gandhi was a strategist in his fight against
the caste system. Other scholars have also
observed that while in South Africa, and
as early as in 1909, Gandhi had publicly
decried the caste system for its inequalities,
but that shortly after he returned to India,
he spoke with some emphasis on its generally beneficial aspects. The scholars hold
that this change on Gandhi's part was due to
strategic reasons. Gandhi probably understood that a conservative but powerful section of Hindus was not yet ready for radical
reforms and had to be brought around to
his point of view gradually. It has also been
noted that since Gandhi's own writings
contain inconsistencies in their emphasis on
and defence of the beneficial aspects of the
caste system, these inconsistencies must be

analysed to further understand the basic strategy in his fight against the caste system. This book attempts to understand Gandhi's evolving strategy to abolish the caste system by analysing the inconsistencies in the life and writings of Gandhi on issues such as untouchability, caste, varna, inter-dining, and inter-caste marriage.

However, this chapter argues that while it is true that Gandhi's approach to the caste system can be understood as a simple strategy, this strategy consisted of more than just occasional tactics. This is because the inconsistencies referred to in Gandhi's writings were not wholly determined according to the exigencies of the situation alone; they also conform to his commitment to build an ideal society and establish an ideal system of governance. In order to properly understand Gandhi's strategy for abolishing the caste system, it is important to understand the ideals he held regarding society and forms of government, for this also determined his strategy. In other words, in order to understand Gandhi's strategy better, it is important to understand what Gandhi stood for and what he intended to achieve.

Gandhi's vocal criticism of almost everything that was associated with modernity, his suspicion towards modern institutions like the state, legislature, and so on, and his glorification of caste or varna—the fourfold hereditary division of Hindu society—led many scholars to believe that it was the ancient idea of caste or varna which provided the basis for Gandhi's ideal society and his vision of ideal governance. 'In Gandhi's first-order ideal society,' Jayantanuja Bandyopadhyaya writes, 'the pure form of anarchy would be vertically organized on the basis of varna, or the four-fold division of society'.[2] Many scholars also believed that it was this ancient, original varna system that Gandhi was trying to reinforce and establish in India. However, Gandhi rejected that possibility. For him, the propagation of khadi, strengthening Hindu–Muslim unity, and removal of untouchability constituted the three pillars of swaraj. But he never propagated the establishment of varnadharma as a necessary condition to achieve swaraj.

Anthony J. Parel, a well-known Gandhian scholar, also rejects such a possibility. He writes: 'Nowhere, in his [Gandhi's] entire political career, do we find him attempting to restore the dharma of the discredited varnashrama.'[3] If it was not caste or varna, then what was Gandhi's ideal society and ideal form of governance based on? This chapter is an effort to understand the basis of Gandhi's ideal society and the kind of ideal governance he was trying to achieve for India. In the absence of this understanding, it would appear that Gandhi's position on and struggle against caste and varna are just a conglomeration of inconsistencies and not a strategy—'a plan of action designed to achieve a long-term or overall aim'.[4]

It is always important to remember that Gandhi was principally a man who believed in the importance of practice over theory. He once said of himself: 'I am not built for academic writings. Action is my domain.'[5] Definitely, this would mean that he was working to bring fundamental changes in the life and attitude of people, rather than formulating abstract theoretical speculations about an ideal society. But this should also not be read to mean that Gandhi was not concerned with epistemological enquiries or consistency in logic. Gandhi was not an armchair philosopher and his systematic philosophical expositions about an ideal society and the ideal form of governance were not expressions of his reflections that served to quench his intellectual or spiritual thirst. Rather, his writings or sayings were the outcome of his systematic thinking towards formulating strategies in response to the immediate and concrete practical situations he encountered during his struggle against racial prejudice in South Africa. However, just because his philosophical expositions on an ideal society were the result of his systematic thinking towards achieving desirable goals in the field of politics, they hardly invalidate Gandhi as a strategist.

The converse is also true: his inconsistencies, which were due to his willingness to compromise on small issues of principle in pursuit of the fruits of more important battles, do not repudiate the

perception of Gandhi as a systematic thinker or idealist.[6] Indeed
Sir Ernest Barker, a Cambridge political philosopher, is right in his
assessment of Gandhi when he writes: 'What he [Gandhi] was to
the world, and what he could do for the world, depended on his
being more things than one'; he further says that Gandhi could
mix 'the spiritual with the temporal, and could be at the same time
true to both' and 'the mixture was the essence'.[7] Gandhi also often
uses an oxymoron, 'practical idealist', to define himself. Therefore,
it is not enough to understand Gandhi's systematic philosophical
expositions on his ideal society. It is also important to understand
the inner dynamics that bring the diverse elements—that is, being
committed to certain ideals and, at the same time, formulating strategies according to the exigencies of the situation—into a fruitful
relationship with one another. Hence, this chapter not only makes
an attempt to understand the basis of Gandhi's concept of ideal
society which he developed during his 21 years of stay in South
Africa and remained committed to it until the end of his life, but
also describes those elements of Gandhi's thought that make possible the coexistence of these contradictory aspects within a single
ideological unity.

Keeping in mind the objective just described, this chapter is
divided into three sections. The first section argues that Gandhi's
basic philosophy was formulated during his life experiences in
South Africa which he penned down in *Hind Swaraj*. The second
section investigates the three major debates among scholars with
regard to the manner in which *Hind Swaraj* should be interpreted
for a holistic understanding of Gandhi's ideal society and the ways
to achieve it. After a thorough analysis of the debates, it is argued
that the best way to interpret *Hind Swaraj* is to see it as an effort to
explain Gandhi's concept of swaraj. The third section attempts to
underline a comprehensive understanding of swaraj from Gandhi's
point of view. In the process, it takes the help of Parel's essay
'Gandhian Freedoms and Self-rule' to reach the conclusion that

for Gandhi, swaraj stands for the individual's capacity to regulate their life and achieving it requires nurturing such a capacity in every individual.

South Africa Experiments

South Africa, where I had passed twenty-one years of my life sharing to the full in the sweets and bitters of human experience, and where I had realized my vocation in life.

—M.K. Gandhi[8]

In 2009, Narayan Desai could write 'Mohan became Mahatma in the course of the twenty years he spent in South Africa',[9] but in April 1893, on Gandhi's departure for South Africa, no one, not even Gandhi himself, could forecast that he would become a major political and moral force in world affairs. Before leaving for South Africa, Gandhi was drafting applications and memorials in Rajkot, after failing in both conducting his debut case at the Small Causes Court in Bombay (now Mumbai) and in getting an English teacher's job at a school in the same city. Up to this point, he had shown neither any sign of greatness nor any inclination towards political leadership. It was only in South Africa that he emerged as a great strategist of mass movement and a moral idealist. On many occasions, Gandhi himself acknowledges that 'he was born in India but was made in South Africa'.[10] On 11 April 1947, he says: 'Truly speaking it was after I went to South Africa I became what I am now.'[11]

It was definitely in South Africa where Gandhi learnt what it was to be a coloured non-European. Starting from the day of his arrival there, he had several humiliating experiences and was the target of colour prejudice.[12] A series of such unusual personal experiences forced him to seriously think about fighting colour prejudice in South Africa. This brought him into the field of politics and made it necessary for him to acquire many leadership qualities. Gandhi rapidly learnt to write political petitions, negotiate with officers/ authorities, organize political protests, and so on. He was also instrumental in the establishment of the Natal India Congress in 1894 and the Transvaal British Indian Association in 1903. Working as a secretary in both these organizations, he learnt the difficulties involved in the conduct of day-to-day affairs in a political organization. Here, he also learnt the importance of the press in educating or mobilizing public opinion for political causes. In June 1903, he started a weekly newspaper, *Indian Opinion*, which was published in four languages: Gujarati, Hindi, Tamil, and English. His articles on a variety of subjects, published in *Indian Opinion*, proved him to be an excellent journalist who used his trade very effectively as an important political tool.

It was also in South Africa in 1906, while fighting racial discrimination, that Gandhi developed and experimented with his most powerful weapon—satyagraha—which he later used in India, with great success, to challenge the British government. His fight against racial discrimination in South Africa also forced him to develop many strategies in order to run his political movements. These strategies dwelt on the issues that could be taken up, the groups with which to liaise, the methods to be pursued, and the lengths to which one could go to in order to achieve the results that were being sought. Brown observes in her influential work that 'the techniques he [Gandhi] evolved were those of the pragmatist; in particular he was limited by the people he had to organise, the audience at which he aimed, and the nature of the issues at stake'. She adds: 'As the circumstances and the grievances changed so did Gandhi's political tactics.'[13]

Gandhi's views on Hindu–Muslim unity, women's role in society, untouchability, and the caste system also got a concrete shape in South Africa. The kind of cooperation shown by both Hindus and Muslims in his struggles in South Africa helped him to develop an immense faith in Hindu–Muslim unity, and he remained committed to this until his death. The kind of courage women had shown in the South African satyagraha also helped him to recognize their capabilities and encouraged him to involve them not only in satyagraha but also in every field of life on equal terms with men. His attitude towards untouchability and caste was also shaped in South Africa. Lelyveld writes: 'He'd struggled for the equality of Indians and whites. This had led him, inevitably, to the issue of equality between Indian and Indian. He crossed the caste boundary before he crossed the class boundary.'[14]

In South Africa, Gandhi also realized that the colour prejudice he was fighting was only a small part of the exploitation, domination, and hierarchy present in human society. This led him to ponder on the deeper issues of life, such as truth, God, the nature of human beings, and the purpose of life. His fight against colour prejudice also led him to the answers to many other philosophical questions. In 1904, he gave up his family life and established the Phoenix Settlement to live a simple community life. In 1906, he took the vow of *brahmacharya*; and in 1912, he gave up his well-established practice of law and took the vow of non-possession. In this way, South Africa became the laboratory for his 'experiments with truth', also the title of his autobiography.

Lelyveld writes: 'It is not easy to pinpoint the moment in South Africa when the ambitious, transplanted barrister becomes recognizable as the Gandhi who would be called Mahatma. But it had happened by 1908, fifteen years after his arrival in the land.'[15] Lelyveld's observation appears appropriate because within the next year, that is, in 1909, in the foreword of his seminal work *Hind Swaraj*, Gandhi writes: 'I have written because I could not restrain myself. I read much, I pondered much'. He also writes: 'I consider it my duty now to place before the readers of *Indian Opinion* the conclusions, which *appear to me to be final.*'[16] Years later, when he recalled the experience of writing *Hind Swaraj*, he spoke again of the sense of urgency to share something that to him appeared final.

He writes: 'Just as one cannot help speaking out when one's heart is full, so also I had been unable to restrain myself from writing the book since my heart was full.'[17] Hence, it may not be wrong to accept that by 1908–9, Gandhi had formulated his basic philosophical expositions on ideal society, ideal governance, human nature, and so on, which, to him, seemed final and to which he remained committed until the end of his life.

Although Gandhi did not commit himself at any period of time to a fixed philosophy that might ossify into orthodoxy, and remained open all his life to acknowledging his mistakes, discarding his old beliefs, and learning new ideas, he was steadfast in his beliefs expressed in *Hind Swaraj*.[18] As late as in 1945, he wrote to Jawaharlal Nehru: 'I fully stand by the kind of governance which I have described in *Hind Swaraj*. It is not just a way of speaking. My experience has confirmed the truth of what I wrote in 1909. If I were the only one left who believed in it, I would not be sorry.'[19] This suggests that although Gandhi's opinions on various issues underwent changes over a period of time, he remained forever committed to his ideals. These ideals were the continuous source of his inspiration and determined every activity of his life, including the formulation of strategies against different forms of sociopolitical exploitation and domination.[20] At this juncture, it appears appropriate to make an attempt to understand more comprehensively Gandhi's views on ideal society and the principles by which he tries to accomplish it, as articulated in his book *Hind Swaraj*.

How to Read *Hind Swaraj*

Gandhi's political, social, and spiritual ideals, which were shaped by his South African experiences, found expression in his book *Hind Swaraj*. This book is key to understanding his philosophical expositions regarding his ideals. *Hind Swaraj* is generally held as 'the source of Gandhiji's philosophical stream'.[21] In his 'Preface' to the

1938 edition of *Hind Swaraj*, Mahadev Desai writes: 'When Lord Lothian was at Segaon, he asked me if I could give him a copy of *Hind Swaraj*, for, as he said, all that Gandhiji was teaching now lay in the germ in that little book which deserved to be read and re-read in order to understand Gandhiji properly.'[22] However, it is always a matter of great debate among scholars as to how one should read or interpret *Hind Swaraj* in order to arrive at a comprehensive picture of Gandhi's ideals.

Dietmar Rothermund, a leading historian of India and a Gandhian scholar, tells us to treat *Hind Swaraj* as a 'strategic document', a 'nationalist tract' of and for its time.[23] There is value in Rothermund's suggestion; *Hind Swaraj* was written with a very specific goal (to establish the superiority of non-violent methods over violent ones for achieving political independence for India), for a very specific group of people (Indians). It was also contextualized within a very specific historical situation (India's struggle against colonial power). This, then, indeed makes *Hind Swaraj* a 'strategic document', a 'nationalist tract' of and for its time. Such an approach to reading *Hind Swaraj* is validated by numerous studies in which Gandhi is projected as a leader of India's national struggle for political independence. Most of these studies agree that Gandhi stood for political independence of India from the British, that he was trying to achieve a constitutional state and, to use Gandhi's own terminology, a 'Parliamentary Swaraj' for India. Though there is debate over the nature of this parliamentary swaraj (for some it was *Hinduraj*—an exclusive kind of swaraj—and for others, it was more inclusive in nature, accommodating the concerns of women, Dalits, Muslims, and other minorities), there is little disagreement that it was 'parliamentary swaraj' which Gandhi advocated and tried to achieve for India. Such a reading suggests that Gandhi's struggle against the caste system, his movement for Hindu–Muslim unity, and his propaganda of the charkha were largely secondary to the struggle for political independence of India. These struggles can also be explained as constituting supplementary strategies for consolidation of the people's power between the two phases of mass struggle for political independence of India.[24]

It can be argued that if *Hind Swaraj* is to be read as a 'strategic document', a 'nationalist tract' of and for its time, then it would also reveal that Gandhi stood for replacing British rule with Indian rule without replacing their methods of governance, democratic political society, and other institutions. But in *Hind Swaraj*, Gandhi rejects this idea very explicitly. He writes: 'We want English rule without the Englishman. You want the tiger's nature, but not the tiger; that is to say, you would make India English. And when it becomes English, it will be called not Hindustan but Englistan. This is not the Swaraj that I want.'[25] He adds that 'my patriotism does not teach me that I am to allow people to be crushed under the heel of Indian princes if only the English retire'.[26]

Indeed Gandhi never held modern/Western democratic political society as an ideal, or modern/Western democratic institutions such as the state as an ideal form of governance. Gandhi regarded the state with fear and suspicion. To him, the state 'represents violence in a concentrated and organised form'. He called it 'a soulless machine' and added that 'it can never be weaned from violence to which it owns its very existence'.[27] In *Hind Swaraj*, he called parliament 'a prostitute',[28] perhaps the most derogatory word he had used to describe anything. Therefore, to reduce *Hind Swaraj* to an Indian nationalist tract only and Gandhi to a predominantly nationalist leader may not do justice to Gandhi's contribution or to the meaning contained in *Hind Swaraj*. However, this is not to reject Gandhi's valuable contribution to India's nationalist struggle against British power; it simply means that achieving political independence for India in terms of 'parliamentary swaraj' was only one of Gandhi's concerns, and perhaps not even his most important. It also means that it was not parliamentary swaraj that Gandhi stood for and tried to achieve for India; nor did he hold a democratic, political, industrialized society to be his ideal. Hence, to read *Hind Swaraj* as a 'nationalist tract' of and for its time and see Gandhi as a predominantly nationalist leader, though helpful in many ways in understanding Gandhi, yields neither a comprehensive picture of Gandhi's ideal society nor a proper understanding of the ideals he advocated and tried to achieve.

'*Hind Swaraj* was more than a book of tactics,' Bhaskar Menon writes, 'it conceptualised a clash of civilizations, held out the Indian past as a rival to European modernity.'[29] Should *Hind Swaraj* be read as conceptualizing a 'clash of civilizations' as suggested by Menon? It is a fact that in *Hind Swaraj*, Gandhi advanced a critique of modern civilization and also offered an alternative moral understanding of civilization. In Gandhi's own words, *Hind Swaraj* is 'a severe condemnation of modern civilization'. All this leads us to believe that Gandhi not only rejected the political domination of the British but also rejected modern/Western civilization itself. It is well established that Gandhi was among those who could diagnose that the British were able to hold India not because of their power, but because of the affection that Indians had developed for their (British) civilization. Gandhi argued that to make India free, it was necessary to reject modern/Western civilization; he felt every Indian should 'cling to the old Indian civilization even as a child clings to the mother's breast'.[30] This means that it was Indian civilization or India's ancient past which Gandhi stood for and tried to revive.

Although it is true that Gandhi condemned modern civilization and glorified Indian civilization in *Hind Swaraj*, he also very categorically said: 'Do not for one moment consider that I condemn all that is Western. For the time being I am dealing with the predominant character of modern civilization', that is, 'the exploitation of the weaker races of the earth'.[31] Again, it is important to remember that although Gandhi condemned modern machinery, he himself had used one of the most sophisticated printing presses of his time. Also, while he held the railways responsible for 'spreading the bubonic plague' and for 'increased frequency of famines', and hospitals for 'propagating sin', he nevertheless used the railways intensively and had undergone two minor operations at hospitals. Moreover, he acknowledged Gopal Krishna Gokhale, a Western-educated man and an admirer of that system of education, as his political guru, and chose the much westernized Nehru over the obviously more Indian Vallabhbhai Patel as his political heir. There are 20 books in the appendix of *Hind Swaraj* which Gandhi suggested for further reading; of them, only two are by Indian authors and the rest are written by 14 different European and American scholars. Therefore, it is difficult to accept that Gandhi totally rejected modern/Western civilization.

On the other hand, it is also not the case that Gandhi appreciated everything about the ancient Indian civilization. He suggested that *Hind Swaraj* 'is not an attempt to go back to the so-called ignorant, dark ages'.[32] He was well aware of the totalizing nature of traditions, especially Hindu traditions, and was not any less opposed to traditional modes of domination and hierarchy. Bhikhu Parekh says: 'For centuries Hindus had lived with the evil practice of untouchability; he declared war on it and shook its moral roots.' Parekh adds: 'Traditionally women had occupied a low position in India; he not only brought a large number of them into public life, which neither Lenin nor Mao could do, and established their equality with men.'[33] To talk of 'modern civilization' versus 'ancient civilization' or 'Western civilization' versus 'Eastern civilization/Indian civilization' in the literal sense may be useful if *Hind Swaraj* is read only as a 'strategic document', or a 'nationalist tract' of and for its time. If *Hind Swaraj* is to be read more for understanding the basis of Gandhi's ideals, it would be necessary to acknowledge that Gandhi's categorization of civilization or society was not on the basis of geography (that is, Western, Eastern, or Indian civilization) or of time (that is, modern or ancient civilization). His categories were moral and he was speaking in terms of 'true civilization' versus 'false civilization' or 'good civilization' versus 'bad civilization'. More specifically, he was speaking in terms of what a civilization ought to be.[34] Hence, Gandhi's critique of modern civilization, however severe, must be viewed as neither a complete rejection of everything that was going by the name of modern/Western civilization, nor a glorification of India's ancient past.

Although the condemnation of modern civilization and the presentation of an alternative moral understanding are important themes of *Hind Swaraj*, it has been observed by A.K. Saran that Gandhi's critique of modern Western civilization may well be peripheral to his thinking and may not constitute an essential element of it.[35] Therefore, to read *Hind Swaraj* as dwelling on the 'clash of civilizations' and to perceive Gandhi as supporting and trying to revive an ancient Indian past might be useful in many ways, but it fails to yield a comprehensive picture of Gandhi's ideal society and the matters he espoused and tried to achieve.

Richard L. Johnson writes, 'The essence of Hind Swaraj is Gandhi's interpretation of swaraj, which means both Indian home rule and self-rule (moksha), the spiritual and moral duty to develop oneself.' [36] Should *Hind Swaraj* therefore be read as Gandhi's effort to define what swaraj is? The name of the book, too, suggests that it is more closely related to the concept of swaraj than anything else. In *Hind Swaraj*, Gandhi remarked that 'all Indians are impatient to attain Swaraj, but we are certainly not decided as to what it is.'[37] In the *Harijan* of 15 July 1946, under the heading 'The Real Danger', he writes that Congressmen in general certainly do not know the kind of independence they want.[38] Moreover, the concluding part of *Hind Swaraj* very categorically says that it was written to explain the real significance of the term 'swaraj' and that it was swaraj which Gandhi stood for and tried to achieve. Here, Gandhi says: 'In my opinion, we have used the term "Swaraj" without understanding its real significance. I have endeavoured to explain it as I understand it, and my conscience testifies that my life henceforth is dedicated to its attainment.'[39]

Therefore, if *Hind Swaraj* is read as a text for an understanding of Gandhi's concept of swaraj, it will be helpful to paint a comprehensive picture of Gandhi's vision of swaraj and how he wanted to achieve it. The following section makes an effort to understand what swaraj meant for Gandhi. Although it takes *Hind Swaraj* as the primary text for this purpose, reference to other sources is also made whenever necessary.

What Is Swaraj?

Swaraj is a state of being of individuals and nations.

M.K. Gandhi[40]

Gandhi offers diverse meanings for the concept of swaraj. Sometimes he uses the term in reference to national independence and sometimes to mean spiritual freedom of the individual. He also uses it as a synonym for liberty, autonomy, political freedom of the individual, national economic freedom, freedom from poverty for the individual, self-realization, self-rule, freedom from alien rule, and so on. For the purpose of analysis, Anthony J. Parel, in his essay 'Gandhian Freedoms and Self-rule', groups these various meanings under four heads: national independence, political freedom of the individual, economic freedom of the individual, and individual spiritual freedom or self-rule. Although this section uses the same categorizations to arrive at a comprehensive understanding of swaraj, it differs from Parel in its treatment and conclusions in two ways. First, Parel focuses on explaining the meaning of the different dimensions of the concept of swaraj but not on giving a comprehensive idea of what swaraj meant to Gandhi. In this section, an attempt is made to arrive at an all-encompassing definition of swaraj which can explain all the four aspects that Parel describes. Second, Parel not only groups Gandhi's notions of swaraj into four categories but also distinguishes the first three from the fourth. This section, on the other hand, tries to argue that such a distinction may not do justice to Gandhi's philosophical position because he did not believe in any boundaries between the different aspects of human life.[41] In the following sections, as each of the four meanings of swaraj, as articulated by Parel, is further elaborated, it becomes evident that while each is distinguishable from the other, together they are inseparable.

National Independence

According to Parel, Gandhi understood swaraj for the nation as 'a collective freedom from alien rule'. He observes that there is nothing original in understanding swaraj in these terms, nor is there anything novel in the idea of fighting for its attainment. He believes that Gandhi's originality lies in his use of non-violence as a powerful method to attain swaraj. Since 1920, Gandhi's political activities in India clearly reveal that he aimed to achieve for India 'a collective freedom from alien rule', which he often called 'parliamentary swaraj'. However, this does not mean that swaraj meant nothing more than national independence to Gandhi. In an article titled 'A Word on Explanation', published on 26 January 1921, Gandhi explains his current position on *Hind Swaraj*, which itself was written in 1909. This article was used as the foreword for the next edition of *Hind Swaraj*. Gandhi writes:

> But I would warn the reader against thinking that I am today aiming at the *Swaraj* described therein. I know that India is not ripe for it. It may seem impertinent to say so. But such is my conviction. I am individually working for the self-rule pictured therein. But today my corporate activity is undoubtedly devoted to the attainment of Parliamentary Swaraj, in accordance with the wishes of the people of India.[42]

Here, Gandhi very explicitly says that although his corporate activities are devoted to the attainment of collective freedom from alien rule, which he calls 'parliamentary swaraj', this in no way exhausts his concept of swaraj for the nation as articulated in

Hind Swaraj. In *Hind Swaraj*, Gandhi very vigorously rejects the idea which equates swaraj for the nation with merely the overthrowing of the British. He conveys this on many occasions and in many ways. In fact, at one point Gandhi even affirms that by patriotism he means the welfare of all the people, and that if he could secure it at the hands of the English, he should bow down his head to them.[43]

Indeed Gandhi's analysis and understanding of swaraj for the nation is much deeper than is usually understood. From the very beginning of his active political career, he understood that it cannot be attained just by throwing the British out of India. He knew very well that the tyranny of any Indian ruler can be just as bad as that of the British. He writes that his patriotism does not teach him to allow people to be crushed under the heel of Indian princes.[44] He was also keenly aware that imperialism and colonialism not only dehumanized the colonizers but also brutalized the colonized.

The programme of satyagraha that Gandhi designed in order to attain swaraj in no way aimed at physically throwing out the British or any other opponent. It was a very unique method which sought to bring a change of heart in the opponent by means of personal suffering. Gandhi believed that human suffering has the power to melt even the stoniest heart. He placed great faith in this. He asserted that a change of heart is possible, otherwise non-cooperation (satyagraha) is of no use.[45] His satyagraha did not aim at a change of heart in the British alone, but also sought a change of heart among Indians. Non-cooperation or satyagraha, said Gandhi, 'is a plea for a change of heart, not merely in the English but equally in ourselves', and he expected the change first among Indians 'and then as a matter of course in the English'.[46] The key to understanding Gandhi's concept of swaraj for the nation lies in appreciating what he means by change of heart for the English and the Indians as well.

According to Gandhi, a change of heart for the British did not simply consist in realizing that their holding on to India is unjust and so they must leave it. As Ashis Nandy observes, all his life Gandhi sought to free the British rather than the Indians from the clutches of imperialism, and the Brahmins rather than the untouchables from the caste system.[47] He was not merely aiming at overthrowing British colonial rule by non-violent methods. Rather his aim was to overcome colonialism by changing the hearts of people. For him, a change of heart in the British meant making them realize, through personal suffering, how imperialism dehumanizes them and how it is equally important for them, too, to overcome it.

When he was talking about a change of heart among Indians, he was urging the Indian people to become capable of living together as a nation, that is, a legitimate political community, by adopting swadeshi, removing untouchability, and establishing inter- and intra-religious unity. This is how he defines his idea of swaraj or independence for the nation—as a collective capacity of individuals to live together in peace and harmony. He writes in *Hind Swaraj* that it is swaraj when we learn to rule ourselves and it is, therefore, in the palm of our hands.[48] We will see in the subsection titled 'Self-rule or Self-realization' that, for Gandhi, spiritual freedom of the individual or moksha is not something different from this. As a *karmayogi*, Gandhi believes that moksha or self-rule does not lie in an other-worldly metaphysical realm, but rather in the nurturing capacity of the individual and the nation (*praja*) to organize their own lives. Although Gandhi has many different definitions of swaraj depending on the context in which he speaks, he nevertheless keeps referring to this seminal idea of swaraj for the nation—albeit in different ways—until the end of his life.

For instance, on one occasion, he affirms that we cannot have swaraj until we have made ourselves fit for it;[49] and on another, he observes that the key to swaraj lies in self-help.[50] He has emphasized the role and importance of the individual in achieving swaraj as political independence, and he writes that this independence has to be 'experienced by each one for himself'.[51] Therefore, for Gandhi, swaraj cannot be imposed on the people from above either by alien or native rule. He believes that independence or swaraj must begin at the bottom. Fred Dallmayr argues that for Gandhi, swaraj must first be nurtured, through education at the local or village level, and then spread to larger communities and to the world through a series of oceanic circles.[52] To sum up, Gandhi means that swaraj for the nation is not simply 'a collective freedom from alien rule', but a collective capacity of individuals to live together in harmony. The attainment of independence for the nation also means the nurturing and strengthening of this capacity in the individual to live with others in peace and harmony.[53]

Political Freedom of the Individual

Political freedom of the individual is predominantly a modern, Western concept. There is no major discourse on individual political rights in the Hindu tradition.[54] Many of the modern, liberal political philosophers, from Hobbes to Rawls, assume that human beings are fundamentally brutal and mutually destructive in the natural state. They hold that human coexistence is possible on the basis of implicit, unstated contracts that define human relations and interactions. They hold that rights are the most important means by which one defends one's individual interests from illegitimate interference from others. In this way, the West defines political independence of the individual predominantly in terms of individual rights.

Arvind Sharma,[55] Beverley Birch, and Michael Nicholson,[56] along with Parel, argue that Gandhi also defines political freedom of the individual in terms of rights. Their argument can be best supported by the many quotes from Gandhi on individual rights and his arguments for the urgent need to defend them. However, it is one thing to support individual rights and fight for them, and quite another to define political freedom of the individual in terms of rights. For instance, Gandhi refused to endorse the scheme put forward by H.G. Wells, an English writer, to draw up a charter of the 'rights of man'. Instead, he suggested to Wells that the latter 'begin with a charter of duties of man, and I promise the rights will follow as spring follows winter'. Gandhi adds:

> I write from experience. As a young man I began life by seeking to assert my rights, and I soon discovered I had none—not even over my wife. So I began by discovering and performing my duty to my wife, my children, friends, companions and society, and I find today that I have greater rights, perhaps, than any living man I know.[57]

Gandhi's response to the Universal Declaration of Human Rights by the United Nations also reflects a similar attitude.[58] Therefore, it appears very difficult to accept that Gandhi understood rights to be the primary source of an individual's political freedom. Apparently, for Gandhi, the true source of political freedom of the individual lay in duty, and not in rights, and he believed that if we all discharge our duties, individual political freedom will not be far to seek.

Gandhi's understanding of individual political freedom in terms of duty is based on the assumption that man is not born to live in isolation but is essentially a social animal, independent and interdependent.[59] Unlike the social-contract theorists, he also believes that man's nature is not essentially evil, and he firmly believes in 'the essential unity of man'. Here, Gandhi largely depends on the Advaita philosophy for his understanding of man and his place in the world, in which the transcendental and metaphysical unity of human beings is assumed. In addition to his aforementioned conviction regarding human nature, Gandhi also believes that the individual is born with a set of indebtedness to the world, and that he becomes free only by recognizing his duty to others. Therefore, he sees duty as a binding factor for mankind and makes it the basis for understanding political freedom of the individual and for his concept of a good society. It is important to note that when Gandhi is speaking of duties, he is referring to moral acts (duties) and not traditional, caste-based duties. As Ronald J. Terchek reminds us: 'Gandhi's highest duty is to act morally, regardless of the consequences.' He adds that for Gandhi, non-violence is not to be pursued because there is a guarantee that each application will work but because it is the moral way to proceed.[60]

All this certainly does not mean that Gandhi has nothing to say about the concept of individual rights. He does, in fact, acknowledge the importance of the individual's rights in modern politics by introducing them using a unique method which is characterized by uncompromising non-violence in order to secure them. He, however, does not believe that they are the basic source of an individual's political freedom. In fact, for Gandhi, rights are just a licence for political freedom of the individual. Political freedom does not consist in merely being free from external obstacles in order to make choices in situations in which the individual finds himself/herself. For Gandhi, liberty is one thing and licence quite another. Gandhi acknowledges that many a time we confuse licence for liberty and lose the latter. Licence, according to him, leads one to selfishness, whereas liberty guides one to the supreme good.[61] For him, political freedom of the individual is more than just the absence of some external obstacles or barriers; it also requires the presence of something like self-determination and self-mastery. And it has to necessarily be achieved collectively. According to him, individual political freedom can be best achieved through participation in a process whereby one's community exercises collective control over its own affairs for the greatest good of all. This participation does not mean that the individual can achieve his/her political freedom by having the right to elect representatives or be elected as one. Here, participation means 'performing one's duty'; the individual can attain his/her political freedom only by performing his or her duties towards others. To sum up, for Gandhi, swaraj as 'political freedom of the individual' means the performance by the individual of his/her duty, with the situation also calling for the community exercising collective control over its own affairs for the greatest good of all.

Economic Freedom of the Individual

The third aspect of Gandhi's notion of swaraj, according to Parel, is the economic freedom of the individual, and this means freedom from poverty. To Gandhi, poverty is 'a product of an unjust social order' and is a great hindrance in the path to freedom. He says that unless poverty and unemployment are wiped out from India, he would not agree that freedom has been attained.[62] Many references in Gandhi's writings also suggest that his voluntary poverty is not to be seen as his approval of poverty. In his lecture titled 'Does Economic Progress Clash with Real Progress?', Gandhi states that 'no one has ever suggested that grinding pauperism can lead to anything else than moral degradation'.[63] On the other hand, it is also a matter of serious consideration that throughout his life, he firmly believed that if India is to attain true freedom—and through India, the world too—then, sooner or later, it must be recognized that people will have to live in villages, not in towns, and in huts, not in palaces.[64] One of the important aims of writing *Hind Swaraj*, he explains, was to see beauty in voluntary simplicity, voluntary poverty, and slowness.[65] This understanding of Gandhi about poverty is based on his belief that poverty is man's natural condition. It means that while he attacked socially constructed poverty, he did not understand economic freedom of an individual or nation to be mere freedom from poverty. Rather, he is suggesting how to overcome poverty by adopting voluntary poverty, which entails detachment and renunciation.

Even if we look at his concept of economics, which is based on decentralized agrarian practices, human skills, and trusteeship, we find that it aims neither at meeting certain economic conditions as a mark of economic development of the individual nor at abolishing the existing economic inequalities among people. Parel also observes that if certain basic needs of every individual were satisfied, Gandhi was ready to tolerate 'the existence of excessive differences between the rich and the poor'.[66] Indeed all of Gandhi's economic reforms simply aim at making every individual, and hence the community, self-sufficient and self-contained. He is very critical about the modern, Western understanding of individual economic freedom in terms of achievement of certain economic conditions; he is also critical of the belief that economic freedom can be achieved through more production and equal distribution. He strongly believes, as observed by Ronald J. Terchek, that the problems cannot be overcome with more goods or even a more equitable distribution of goods.[67] It is, therefore, one thing to say that Gandhi attacks the socially constructed concept of poverty to ensure that every individual's minimum economic needs are fulfilled (and he had certain criteria by which to judge whether a given society provides a conducive atmosphere to meet such needs) and quite another to say that he defines economic freedom of the individual or nation on the basis of certain economic conditions. He is concerned about meeting the minimum economic requirements of individuals because he believes that these essential needs are not only the primary requirements for biological survival but also essential for man's moral and spiritual development. A starving man, asserts Gandhi, cannot think of God.

As mentioned earlier, although Gandhi accepts that an individual's minimum economic needs have to be met for his/her holistic development, he is not interested in defining economic freedom of the individual in terms of certain external economic conditions. Like any other aspect of his concept of swaraj, the defining feature of Gandhi's concept of economic freedom of the individual or nation is the 'individual' and not certain economic conditions. However, for Gandhi, the fulfilment of the minimum economic needs of an individual remains the prerequisite for defining economic freedom of the individual or nation. Gandhi prefers to define it the way Ruskin did in his book *Unto This Last*:

> Therefore THERE IS NO WEALTH BUT LIFE. That country is the richest which nourishes the greatest number of noble and happy human beings; that man is richest who, having perfected the functions of his own life to the utmost, has also the widest helpful influence, both personal and by means of his possessions, over the lives of others.[68]

Gandhi similarly argues that economic freedom of the individual cannot be understood by establishing external standards that stipulate how much the individual should consume in order to be considered as having attained that economic freedom. Gandhi also says that this will, on the contrary, make an individual dependent on others. To Gandhi, therefore, economic freedom of the individual means the ability to minimize one's needs in order to be independent and to participate in the economic activities of a community to make it self-sufficient and self-contained.

Self-Rule or Self-Realization (Moksha)

In Parel's account, the fourth and the most important aspect of Gandhi's concept of swaraj is self-rule or spiritual freedom, and it consists of removal of the internal obstacles to freedom. His opinion is that Gandhi derived the idea of spiritual freedom or self-rule from the Indian tradition, especially from the Bhagavad Gita, and introduced in it a major conceptual change. Parel observes that though the notion of spiritual freedom in the Indian tradition was supposed to be apolitical and asocial, requiring withdrawal from the sociopolitical world, Gandhi reinterpreted self-rule in such a way that he gave it not only a spiritual form but also a social, political, and economic profile. Although Parel acknowledges that all the four aspects of swaraj are harmoniously interconnected, his analysis distinguishes the first three from self-rule or spiritual

freedom. He says that the first three, in some respects, are negative in character, but freedom as self-rule, in contrast, is positive
in character. Parel maintains such a distinction largely due to his
belief that, for Gandhi, the idea of self-rule lies outside the realm
of politics. Parel argues that self-rule presupposes the agency of the
spirit (individual atman) and observes that politics and political
philosophy ought to recognize moksha or spiritual emancipation
as the final end of all human striving, though politics per se is not
the pursuit of moksha.

Gandhi, quite obviously, defines the idea of self-rule/self-
realization or moksha in religious and metaphysical terms. He
writes in the introduction of his autobiography: 'What I want to
achieve—what I have been striving and pining to achieve these
thirty years—is self-realisation, to see God face to face, to attain
Moksha.'[69] There are several other instances when Gandhi explains
his idea of self-rule/self-realization in terms of realizing God or
truth. In this respect, Gandhi's idea of self-realization echoes the
traditional idea of moksha or nirvana, which is typically understood as a transcendental experience of atman/Brahman identity,
or attainment of a transcendental and superior state of consciousness beyond good and evil.[70] But it would be indulging in a risky
endeavour, and treading on slippery grounds, to try and understand
Gandhi's idea of self-realization only in this direction. As Margaret
Chatterjee observes, the 'language of self-realisation and God-
realisation which indeed even he [Gandhi] himself on occasion
uses, but which calls up an atman/Brahman identity which I do
not believe actually enters into his [Gandhi's] religious thoughts'.[71]
In fact, Gandhi remains largely agnostic about the human ability
to comprehend such notions and stresses on the limited powers
of humans in understanding such ideas. In his commentary on the
Gita, he says: 'There is violence even in the act of thinking, and so
long as that is so man cannot attain a state of perfect self-realization,
his mind cannot even comprehend such a state.'[72] This is not the

only instance of his accepting this 'terrible truth', as there are other occasions when he accepts the 'impossibility of full realisation of truth in this mortal body'.[73]

While Gandhi holds that experience of transcendence is beyond human capability, he nevertheless does not reject its possibility altogether: 'to him a culture which did not have a theory of transcendence could not be morally or cognitively acceptable'.[74] He is well aware of the practical and pragmatic utility of such ideas. He knows such ideas are required for the moral development of mankind and for sustaining faith in critical situations, because he believes, 'a mere mechanical adherence to truth and non-violence is likely to break down at the critical moment'.[75] Therefore, Gandhi's ultimate justification for the preservation of such transcendental notions of self-rule/self-realization, or truth-realization or even God-realization, is not epistemological but pragmatic. In his commentary on the Gita, Gandhi draws a parallel between his aforementioned transcendental idea of self-realization or moksha and Euclid's straight line. He says: 'Euclid has defined a straight line as having no breadth, but no one has yet succeeded in drawing such a line and no one ever will. Still we can progress in geometry only by postulating such a line.' Gandhi adds: 'What is true here is true of every ideal.'[76] To Gandhi, the ideal concept of self-rule/self-realization, which can be understood as a kind of a transcendental experience and which can be further explained with the help of the traditional idea of moksha or nirvana, is, however, unachievable in practice. He adopts it primarily for its strong pragmatic value.

It may be noted that although Gandhi values the concept of moksha/spiritual freedom (self-rule) for its pragmatic nature, his regard for it does not stop there. Being a man of action, he had a more profound understanding of moksha that could be practised. His life testifies to his being neither an escapist nor a pessimist. In his interpretation of the Gita, he explains that man cannot attain complete self-realization in the sense of being one with God in his life, but this does not mean that man should voluntarily renounce activity and sit at home quietly, or commit suicide. On the contrary, Gandhi defines his concept of moksha in very active terms. Gandhi writes in his commentary on the Gita that if we agree that man cannot attain moksha (self-realization) as it is defined earlier, we need not spend much thought or indulge in intellectual exercises over this problem. He adds that we should rather concentrate on the means, if they are right, so that the end is as good as attained.[77] In this way, by shifting attention from the end to the means, Gandhi presents a practical idea of self-rule/self-realization, that is, self-rule/self-realization through action. According to Gandhi, this is the only possible way in which humans can achieve self-rule/self-realization, and it must be ceaselessly pursued here and now.

From being an abstract transcendental state, self-rule/self-realization now becomes a process which is to be practised throughout one's life by active participation in every aspect of it. As Gandhi explains, 'If a man seeks *moksha* and still believes that he is independent, he will utterly fail in his aspiration. One who seeks *moksha* behaves as society's servant.'[78] Thus, there can be no divorce between Gandhi's first three aspects of swaraj and self-rule. In other words, for Gandhi, self-rule or moksha does not lie outside the realm of politics, but is the very ability to act well in the socio-economic–political arena. It is the ability to act with perfection in every aspect of human life, including in the socio-economic–political arena. Achievement of self-rule for the individual means nurturing such ability in him/her.

Based on the given discussion, it appears that although Gandhi uses different expressions like independence of the nation, political freedom of the individual, economic freedom of the individual, and self-rule to communicate his idea of swaraj in different contexts, they are, for him, fundamentally inseparable from each other. We may rather see these four aspects of Gandhi's idea of swaraj as different expressions of Gandhi's fundamental notion of swaraj. They may also be viewed as a process for overcoming external as well as internal slavery by nurturing the individual capacity for self-organization and self-regulation. What is important to understand here is that it is the individual that is the basis of Gandhi's definition of swaraj. As explained earlier, Gandhi defines political independence of the nation as the capacity of every individual to live in harmony and peace and not as 'freedom from alien rule'.

Gandhi also suggests that no external agency like the state can assure political freedom of the individual; rather, this is to be achieved by every individual's participation in the process, through the performance of his/her duty, whereby one's community exercises collective control over its own affairs for the greatest good of all. Similarly, for Gandhi, the ability of the individual to be self-sufficient and self-contained is more important than the meeting of certain economic conditions in determining the economic freedom of the individual or nation. Above all, to him, spiritual freedom of the individual or self-rule/self-realization is the ability of every individual to act with perfection in every aspect of human life, including in the socio-economic–political arena; it is not a mysterious transcendental experience of atman/Brahman identity. From all his definitions of swaraj, it is evident that for Gandhi, 'the individual is the one supreme consideration'.[79] And his ideal society can be perceived as 'a group of self-ruled/autonomous individuals where any kind of system to regulate people's socio-economic–political life becomes meaningless'. Explaining his ideal society, Gandhi writes:

> Representatives will become unnecessary if the national life becomes so perfect as to be self-controlled. It will then be a state of enlightened anarchy in which each person will become his own ruler. He will conduct himself in such a way that his behaviour

will not hamper the well-being of his neighbours. In an ideal State there will be no political institution and therefore no political power.[80]

* * *

Based on the given exposition, it can be claimed that it was not parliamentary swaraj, or revival of the ancient Hindu past/civilization, but autonomy of the individual that Gandhi advocated and aspired to achieve. Also, it is the individual and not the caste system or varnashrama dharma that is the ultimate basis of Gandhi's ideal society. In a society based on the principles of the caste system or varnashrama dharma, the individual works as a unit in coordination with other individuals of society acting in their respective positions as Brahmins, Kshatriyas, Vaishyas, or Shudras according to their qualities or birth. In such a system, the individual has no autonomy, and he/she is but a unit of the whole society. As explained earlier, it is the autonomy of the individual for which Gandhi stood; he very categorically says that 'if the individual ceases to count, what is left of society?'[81] It is interesting to note that Gandhi uses the analogy of the drop in the ocean rather than the human body (very often used to describe an ideal society based on the caste system, with different castes corresponding to different parts of the body) to explain the relation between the individual and society, emphasizing the autonomy of the individual. On one occasion, he says: 'What is the strength of an ocean? After all, it is made up of individual drops. Similarly, a country too is constituted of its citizens.'[82] At another point, he writes: 'Individuality is and is not even as each drop in the ocean is an individual and is not. It is not because apart from the ocean it has no existence. It is because the ocean has no existence if the drop has not, i.e., has no individuality. They are beautifully interdependent.'[83] In conclusion, it can be re-emphasized that it is the individual and not the caste system or varnashrama dharma that is the basis of Gandhi's ideal society and that it was the autonomy of the individual which Gandhi advocated and aspired to achieve.

If this is true about Gandhi, then most of his personal practices and struggles must make better sense to us if interpreted either as different methods to safeguard the autonomy of the individual, or as effective devices to minimize exploitation and domination in any form that would undermine this autonomy. For instance, his emphasis on the *vrath* of brahmacharya, non-possession (*aparigraha*), fasting as penance, simple living, and manual work can be better understood as his effort to achieve autonomy of the individual. Against such a background, his criticism of the state, the doctor, the lawyer, the railway, and the machine makes better sense to us. For Gandhi, to lose one's individuality or become a mere part of the machine constituted an affront to human dignity. He wished every individual to participate in the affairs of society as a fully independent member. About the state, he writes: '[A]lthough while apparently doing good by minimising exploitation, it [State] does the greatest harm to mankind by destroying individuality.'[84] His other doctrines, like *Sarvodaya*, trusteeship, swadeshi, and so on, can also be better understood in the same light. For example, he very explicitly says that his faith in trusteeship is based on his belief in the immense potential of the individual. In response to the question why state ownership should then not be preferable to private property to minimize violence, he says:

> It is my firm conviction that if the State suppressed capitalism by violence, it will be caught in the evils of violence itself and fail to develop non-violence at any time. The state represents violence, in a concentrated and organized form. The individual has a soul, but the State is a soulless machine, it can never be weaned from violence to which it owns its very existence. Hence I prefer the doctrine of trusteeship.[85]

Ronald J. Terchek, in his book *Gandhi: Struggling for Autonomy*, also argues that Gandhi must be considered as one who celebrated autonomy in life and fought against every internal and external assault that suppressed individuality. He writes:

> He [Gandhi] means to challenge both traditional and modern forms of determinism. As he sees it, the pre-modern world constructed its own brand of fatalism which taught that what happened to people lies beyond their comprehension and control. For all of its rationalism and science, Gandhi finds that the modern world has created its own brand of fatalism, one that assumes that reigning institutional arrangements cannot be otherwise and it is our task to adjust to them. For his part, Gandhi rejects all forms of fatalism. He continually tells his readers that they cannot make the state, culture or history responsible for what happens to them; they, and not others, must be in charge of their lives. In what follows, I read Gandhi as someone who celebrates an autonomous life and warns about the threats posed by hierarchy, indignity, and violence....[86]

Perhaps the best way to study Gandhi's life is to see how his various struggles—for political independence of India, for removal of untouchability, for Hindu–Muslim unity, for charkha and swadeshi, and so on—and his personal practices, like simple living, daily manual work, common food, and common prayer were of collective support to his flagship struggle to safeguard the autonomy of the individual. It is impossible to undertake such a gigantic task within the scope of this study, which will instead, primarily and specifically, examine Gandhi's struggle against the caste system. This line of enquiry is not aimed at arguing that, for Gandhi, the struggle against the caste system was more important than the struggle for the political independence of India or any other struggle. However, many scholars who see Gandhi as a political strategist have often relegated his struggle against untouchability or the caste system to a subset of his political struggle. They analyse his fight against the caste system along with other social reform movements undertaken by him as part of his struggle for the political independence of India. To them, it was an effective method used by Gandhi to serve two purposes, namely to discipline and prepare the masses for non-violent struggle and to consolidate the power of the people between the two phases of mass struggle for India's political independence. But, for Gandhi, the order of priority of his struggles and the web of interrelations between the struggles may not necessarily be similar.

In a letter to C.F. Andrews about the problem of untouchability and the caste system, Gandhi writes that it is a bigger one than that of gaining independence for India. Gandhi also adds, '[B]ut I can tackle it better if I gain the latter on the way.'[87] At another point, Gandhi says: 'My work of social reform was in no way less or subordinate to political work. The fact is that when I saw that to a certain extent my social work would be impossible without the help of political work, I took to the latter and only to the extent that it helped the former.'[88] Whatever may be the case—whether his struggle for political independence was more important than his struggle against the caste system or vice versa—both of his struggles were the two sides of the same coin, that is, his struggle to defend the autonomy of the individual. In this book, Gandhi's struggle against the caste system is taken as the central line of enquiry because it is usually subordinated to that of the struggle for Indian political independence and rarely studied as an independent or central campaign. As such, this book is an effort to amplify rather than replace the dominant narrative of Gandhi's life, in which he is usually understood as a political tactician and champion of non-violent resistance.

The next two chapters trace Gandhi's evolving strategy against the caste system. Both chapters show that Gandhi realized that in order to save the autonomy of the individual, he had to fight not only the colonial power but also the fatalism and determinism of the caste system. Nicholas F. Gier writes: 'Gandhi wants to protect the individual from dissolution either in a premodern totality or the modern bureaucratic State.'[89] Gandhi realized that in the present scenario, the caste system had created its own differences and hierarchy in Hindu society and also undermined the autonomy of the individual. Therefore, he felt a struggle which aimed to safeguard the autonomy of the individual must also focus on abolishing caste differences and hierarchies. The following two chapters explain how Gandhi, in different stages, attacked the moral basis of the caste system in order to abolish caste differences and hierarchies in Hindu society. The chapters also reveal how some of Gandhi's personal practices and other struggles, including those for political independence for India, abetted his efforts to safeguard the autonomy of the individual against the fatalism of the caste system.

Inconsistencies in Gandhi's Writings

It is argued in the beginning of this chapter that it is not enough to understand the ideals Gandhi upheld and what he aimed to achieve. To understand his strategies really well, it is also important to know the inner dynamism that brings the diverse elements/inconsistencies that appear not only in his writings but also in his life and thoughts into a fruitful relationship with one another. Prima facie, Gandhi's life appears to be a mixture of diverse elements and inconsistencies. For instance, Gandhi who stood up to safeguard the autonomy of the individual and saw the state and such other agencies with fear actually led political movements that were designed to create the historic state of modern India. And if he fought the fatalism of the caste system that he believed subordinated the autonomy of the individual, he also glorified the system of hereditary occupation (based on the caste system or varnashrama dharma) which undermined the autonomy of the individual. Since these are the important facts about Gandhi's life, one cannot just wave them away by accepting one fact and ignoring the others. Rather, one has to explain how Gandhi reconciles such contradictions for himself.

'A mere intellectual might read inconsistency in Gandhiji's toler-
ance of caste earlier and his denunciation of it later,' Gora writes,
referring to Gandhi's writings and speeches on the caste system.
He adds: 'But to a practical man of non-violent creed these are
stages of progress and not principles of contradiction.'[90] Indeed for
Gandhi, these are not inconsistencies or contradictions. Being a man
of action, he was aware that it is one thing to hold certain views and
quite another to make them acceptable in their entirety to society
at large. He was also aware that a change in people's attitude cannot
be wrought overnight and that anyone who aims to bring about
such a reform has to work patiently and with the principle of compromise. Since Gandhi remained primarily interested in bringing
actual changes in the attitude of the people and not in explaining
his views with accuracy, he chose rather to be charged with inconsistency and readily made strategic compromises according to the
exigencies of the situation in pursuit of the fruits of more important
battles. He called himself 'a man of compromise', and argued that
'for the simple reason that I ever compromise my own ideals even
in individual conduct is not because I wish to but because the compromise was inevitable'.[91] Hence, the best way to understand or
analyse the apparent inconsistencies or contradictions in Gandhi's
life and thought is to see them either as strategic compromises
or as 'stages of progress', as suggested by Gora. The following two
chapters examine Gandhi's strategy from 1915 (his arrival in India
from South Africa) to 1948 (his death) and try to explain the inconsistencies in Gandhi's writings on caste, varna, untouchability, and so
on as part of his evolving strategy to fight the caste system.

Notes

1. M.K. Gandhi, 'Talk with Ashram Inmates', 22 March 1934, in
   CWMG, Vol. 57 (New Delhi: Publications Division, Government
   of India, 1974), p. 302.

2. Jayantanuja Bandyopadhyaya, *Social and Political Thought of Gandhi* (Howrah: Manuscript India, 1969), p. 158.

3. Parel, *Gandhi's Philosophy and the Quest for Harmony*, p. 94.

4. See http://oxforddictionaries.com/definition/english/strategy?q= strategy (accessed on 5 January 2017).

5. Gandhi quoted in Iyer, *The Moral and Political Thought of Mahatma Gandhi*, p. 10.

6. A.L. Basham observes that 'Gandhi's willingness to compromise on matters which he considered inessential and his admitted inconsistencies hardly invalidate his sincerity'. See A.L. Basham, 'Traditional Influence on the Thought of Mahatma Gandhi', in Ravinder Kumar (ed.), *Essays on Gandhian Politics of Rowlatt Satyagraha* (Oxford: Clarendon Press, 1971), p. 27.

7. Ernest Barker, 'Gandhi as Bridge and Reconciler', in S. Radhakrishnan (ed.), *Mahatma Gandhi: Essays and Reflections on His Life and Work* (Mumbai: Jaico Publishing House, 2007), pp. 50–1.

8. M.K. Gandhi, 'Satyagraha in South Africa', 22 November 1925, in *CWMG*, Vol. 29 (New Delhi: Publications Division, Government of India, 1968), p. 268.

9. Narayan Desai, *My Life is My Message: Sadhana (1869–1915)*, Tridip Suhrud (tr.), (New Delhi: Orient Blackswan, 2009), p. 139.

10. M.K. Gandhi, 'Speech at Prayer Meeting', 28 June 1946, in *CWMG*, Vol. 84 (New Delhi: Publications Division, Government of India, 1981), p. 380.

11. M.K. Gandhi, 'Talk with Y.M. Dadoo and G. M. Naicker', 11 April 1947, in *CWMG*, Vol. 87 (New Delhi: Publications Division, Government of India, 1983), p. 257.

12. In the magistrate's court of Durban, on 23 May 1893, the day after his arrival, Gandhi was ordered to remove his turban by the magistrate. This he 'refused to do and left the court'. Two weeks later, he had another jarring experience of racial insult on a train which he took to go to Johannesburg. At the Pietermaritzburg railway station, in spite of having a first-class compartment ticket, he was thrown out of the train because a white passenger objected to having to share the space with a coloured non-European. Again, on his way

to Johannesburg by stagecoach, he fell into a clash that was overtly racial in nature.

13. Judith M. Brown, *Gandhi's Rise to Power: Indian Politics, 1915–1920* (New Delhi: Oxford University Press, 1990), pp. 3–6.

14. Lelyveld, *Great Soul*, pp. 24–5.

15. Lelyveld, *Great Soul*, p. 19.

16. M.K. Gandhi, *Hind Swaraj and Other Writings*, A.J. Parel (ed.), (New Delhi: Foundation Books, 2004), pp. 9–10; emphasis added. Hereafter referred to as *Hind Swaraj*.

17. M.K. Gandhi, 'Talks to Ashram Women', 1926, in *CWMG*, Vol. 32 (New Delhi: Publications Division, Government of India, 1969), p. 489.

18. Norman Finkelstein, in his recent book, writes: '[R]eflecting on this book [*Hind Swaraj*] at various junctures much later in his life, Gandhi expressed full satisfaction with it.' See Norman G. Finkelstein, *What Gandhi Says: About Nonviolence, Resistance and Courage* (New York: OR Books, 2012), p. 16.

19. M.K. Gandhi, 'Letter to Jawaharlal Nehru', 5 October 1945, in *CWMG*, Vol. 81, p. 319. In the original quote, Gandhi errone- ously wrote 1908 as the year of *Hind Swaraj*'s publication instead of 1909.

20. Raghavan Iyer writes, 'It is, however, necessary to accept his [Gandhi's] profound integrity as a thinker and as a seeker of truth. If we do not, we shall be constantly tempted to explain away his political statements and concepts entirely in terms of his psychological make-up or the historical conditions which shaped his thought.' See Iyer, *The Moral and Political Thought of Mahatma Gandhi*, p. 8. Akeel Bilgrami also suggests, 'Gandhi's thought and his ideas about specific political strategies in specific contexts flowed from ideas that were very remote from politics; instead they flowed from and were integrated to the most abstract epistemological and methodological commitments.' See Akeel Bilgrami, 2003, 'Gandhi, the Philosopher', *Economic and Political Weekly*, 38(39): 4159.

21. Desai, *My Life is My Message: Sadhana 1869–1915*, p. 808.

22. Mahadev Desai, 'Preface', in M.K. Gandhi, *Hind Swaraj or Indian Home Rule* (Ahmedabad: Navajivan Publishing House, 1938), p. 13. In the editor's introduction to *Hind Swaraj and Other Writings*, Parel writes:

> *Hind Swaraj* is the seed from which the tree of Gandhian thought has grown to its full stature. For those interested in Gandhi's thought in a general way, it is the right place to start, for it is here that he presents his basic ideas in their proper relationship to one another. And for those who wish to study his thought more methodically, it remains the norm by which to assess the theoretical significance of his other writings, including the *Autobiography*. It can also save them from the danger of otherwise getting drowned in the vast sea of Gandhian anthologies. No wonder that it has been called "a basic document for the study of Gandhi's thought".

See *Hind Swaraj and Other Writings*, p. xiii.

23. Rothermund quoted in Lloyd I. Rudolph and Susanne H. Rudolph, *Postmodern Gandhi and Other Essays: Gandhi in the World and at Home* (New Delhi: Oxford University Press, 2006), p. 16. See also Dietmar Rothermund, *Mahatma Gandhi: An Essay in Political Biography* (New Delhi: Manohar, 2009).

24. Bipan Chandra writes: 'Constructive work was basic to a war of position. It played a crucial role during the "passive" or non-mass movement phase in filling the political space left vacant by the withdrawal of civil disobedience. It solved a basic problem that a mass movement faces—the sustenance of a sense of activism in the non-mass movement phases of the struggle.' See Chandra, 'The Long-term Strategy of the National Movement', p. 512.

25. Gandhi, *Hind Swaraj*, p. 28.

26. Gandhi, *Hind Swaraj*, pp. 76–7.

27. M.K. Gandhi, 'Interview to Nirmal Kumar Bose', 9/10 November 1934, in *CWMG*, Vol. 59 (New Delhi: Publications Division, Government of India, 1974), p. 318.

28. Gandhi, *Hind Swaraj*, p. 30.

29. Bhaskar Menon, *Hind Swaraj II*, available at http://undiplomatic-times.com/Hind_Swaraj_II.html (accessed on 30 May 2013).

30. Gandhi, *Hind Swaraj*, p. 71.

31. M.K. Gandhi, 'Speech at Meccano Club, Calcutta', 28 August 1925, in *CWMG*, Vol. 28 (New Delhi: Publications Division, Government of India, 1968), p. 127.

32. M.K. Gandhi, 'The Unbridgeable Gulf', 10 October 1939, in *CWMG*, Vol. 70, p. 242.

33. Parekh, *Colonialism, Tradition and Reform*, p. 11.

34. A.K. Saran writes, 'The confrontation, as he [Gandhi] quite explicitly thought, was not between the colonised world and the imperial world—it was between one civilisation against another. Whether both were civilisations were also something which can be disputed. We could not, for instance, say that there were two alternative concepts of civilisation and that this struggle was of one kind of civilisation for gaining supremacy over another. It was not a conflict of that kind. It was a conflict between a human civilisation, the idea and the reality of a human civilisation and the idea and the reality of a satanic civilisation. "Satanic civilisation" is a phrase used in Hind Swaraj.' See A.K. Saran, 'Gandhi's Hind Swaraj', in Ramashray Roy (ed.), *Gandhi and the Present Global Crisis* (Shimla: IIAS, 1996), pp. 149–50.

35. Saran quoted in Roy, *Self and Society*, p. 37.

36. Richard L. Johnson, 'Three 9/11s: *Satyagrah* or Terrorism' in Douglas Allen (ed.), *The Philosophy of Mahatma Gandhi for the Twenty-First Century* (New Delhi: OUP, 2009), p. 103.

37. Gandhi, *Hind Swaraj*, p. 26.

38. M.K. Gandhi, 'The Real Danger', 15 July 1946, in *CWMG*, Vol. 84, p. 427.

39. Gandhi, *Hind Swaraj*, p. 119.

40. M.K. Gandhi, 'My Notes', 15 May 1921, in *CWMG*, Vol. 20 (New Delhi: Publications Division, Government of India, 1966), p. 99.

41. Parel himself observes that, in Gujarati, Gandhi used the same word, swaraj, in order to express all the four aspects of freedom. See A.J. Parel, 'Gandhian Freedoms and Self-rule', in *Gandhi, Freedom, and Self-rule*, p. 3; see also Parel, 'The Doctrine of Swaraj in Gandhi's Philosophy', p. 58.

42. M.K. Gandhi, 'A Word on Explanation', 26 January 1921, p. 277.

43. Gandhi, *Hind Swaraj*, p. 77.

44. Gandhi, *Hind Swaraj*, pp. 76–7.

45. M.K. Gandhi, 'Interview to Hardayal Nag', 12 May 1925, in *CWMG*, Vol. 27, p. 81.

46. M.K. Gandhi, 'Notes', 29 September 1921, in *CWMG*, Vol. 21, p. 213.

47. Ashis Nandy, 1978, 'Oppression and Human Liberation: Towards a Third World Utopia', *Alternatives*, 4(2): 172.

48. Gandhi, *Hind Swaraj*, p. 73.

49. M.K. Gandhi, 'Letter to Maganlal Gandhi', May 1918, in *CWMG*, Vol. 14 (New Delhi: Publications Division, Government of India, 1965), p. 410.

50. M.K. Gandhi, 'Message to First Railway Conference', 16 November 1918, in *CWMG*, Vol. 15, p. 62.

51. Gandhi, *Hind Swaraj*, p. 73.

52. Dallmayr, 'What Is Swaraj? Lessons from Gandhi', p. 112.

53. Gandhi's understanding of swaraj for the nation is based on the assumption that he rejects to understand national independence in terms of who is holding the government. For him, since people constitute the nation, its independence must also be defined in terms of people's condition. In *Hind Swaraj*, he writes, 'I believe that you want the millions of India to be happy, not that you want the reins of Government in your hands. If that be so, we have to consider only one thing: how can the millions obtain self-rule?' See Gandhi, *Hind Swaraj*, p. 76.

54. Jayantanuja Bandyopadhyaya writes, 'Indian literature there is practically no reference to the secular Freedom of the individual ... nowhere is there any recorded thought on the political rights of the individual.' See Bandyopadhyaya, *Social and Political Thought of Gandhi*, p. 82. Judith M. Brown writes, 'The tradition of Hindu political thinking was highly developed and sophisticated. But it has no rights discourse and did not place major emphasis on the value of the individual and his or her protection and development.' See Judith M. Brown, 'Gandhi and Human Right: In Search of True Humanity', in *Gandhi, Freedom, and Self-Rule*, p. 88.

55. Arvind Sharma, *Hinduism and Human Rights: A Conceptual Approach* (New Delhi: Oxford University Press, 2004).

56. Beverley Birch and Michael Nicholson, *Mahatma Gandhi: Champion of Human Rights* (Milwaukee: Gareth Stevens Children's Books, 1990).

57. M.K. Gandhi, 'Cable to H.G. Wells', 8 October 1940, in *CWMG*, Vol. 73, p. 90.

58. Gandhi writes, 'I learnt from my illiterate but wise mother that all rights to be deserved and preserved came from duty well done. Thus the very right to live accrues to us only when we do the duty of citizenship of the world. From this one fundamental statement, perhaps it is easy enough to define the duties of man and woman and correlate every right to some corresponding duty to be first performed. Every other right can be shown to be usurpation hardly worth fighting for. I wonder if it is too late to revise the idea of defining the rights of man apart from his duty.' See M.K. Gandhi, 'Letter to Julian Huxley', 17 October 1947, in *CWMG*, Vol. 89 (New Delhi: Publications Division, Government of India, 1983), p. 346.

59. M.K. Gandhi, 'Presidential Address at Kathiawar Political Conference, Bhavanagar', 8 January 1925, in *CWMG*, Vol. 25, pp. 550–63.

60. Ronald J. Terchek, *Gandhi: Struggling for Autonomy* (New Delhi: Vistaar, 2000), p. 29.

61. M.K. Gandhi, 'Jawaharlal Nehru', 9 January 1930, in *CWMG*, Vol. 42, p. 380.

62. M.K. Gandhi, 'Advice to Constructive Workers', 13 May 1947, in *CWMG*, Vol. 87, p. 463.

63. M.K. Gandhi, 'Speech at Muir College Economic Society, Allahabad', 22 December 1916, in *CWMG*, Vol. 13, p. 312.

64. Gandhi, 'Letter to Jawaharlal Nehru', 5 October 1945, p. 319.

65. Gandhi, 'The Unbridgeable Gulf', 10 October 1939, p. 241.

66. Parel, 'Gandhian Freedoms and Self-rule', p. 15.

67. Terchek, *Gandhi: Struggling for Autonomy*, p. 111.

68. M.K. Gandhi, *Unto This Last: A Paraphrase* (Ahmedabad: Navajivan Publishing House, 1951), pp. 21–2.

69. M.K. Gandhi, '*An Autobiography or The Story of My Experiments with Truth*, Introduction', 29 November 1925, in *CWMG*, Vol. 44 (New Delhi: Publications Division, Government of India, 1971), p. 90.

70. There may be disagreement on what kind of transcendental experience Gandhi was talking about because, at times, he speaks of it like atman/Brahman identity language of Advaita Vedanta, but on many other occasions, he also speaks like 'reduce yourself to zero' in the language of Buddhism.

71. Chatterjee, *Gandhi's Religious Thought*, p. 108.

72. M.K. Gandhi, 'Discourses on the "Gita"', 3 April 1926, in *CWMG*, Vol. 32, pp. 137.

73. Gandhi quoted in Iyer, *The Moral and Political Thought of Mahatma Gandhi*, p. 231.

74. Nandy, *Traditions, Tyranny and Utopias*, pp. 129–30.

75. Gandhi quoted in Iyer, *The Moral and Political Thought of Mahatma Gandhi*, p. 156.

76. Gandhi quoted in Rudolph and Rudolph, *Postmodern Gandhi and Other Essays*, p. 6.

77. Gandhi, 'Discourses on the "Gita"', 3 April 1926, p. 138.

78. M.K. Gandhi, 'Conclusion', 13 November 1926', in *CWMG*, Vol. 32, p. 368.

79. M.K. Gandhi, 'Discussion with G. Ramachandran', 21 and 22 October 1924, in *CWMG*, Vol. 25, p. 252.

80. M.K. Gandhi, 'Enlightened Anarchy—A Political Ideal', January 1939, in *CWMG*, Vol. 68, p. 265.

81. M.K. Gandhi, 'Plain Living and High Thinking', 9 October 1940, in *CWMG*, Vol. 73, p. 93.

82. M.K. Gandhi, 'Speech at Prayer Meeting', 9 April 1947, in *CWMG*, Vol. 87, p. 243.

83. M.K. Gandhi, 'Letter to P.G. Mathew', 8 September 1930, in *CWMG*, Vol. 44, p. 131.

84. Gandhi, 'Interview to Nirmal Kumar Bose', 9/10 November 1934, p. 319.

85. Gandhi, 'Interview to Nirmal Kumar Bose', 9/10 November 1934, p. 318.

86. Terchek, *Gandhi: Struggling for Autonomy*, p. 5.

87. M.K. Gandhi, 'Letter to C.F. Andrews', 29 January 1921, in *CWMG*, Vol. 19, p. 289.

88. M.K. Gandhi, 'Speech at Ahmedabad', 2 August 1931, in *CWMG*, Vol. 47 (New Delhi: Publications Division, Government of India, 1971), p. 246.

89. Gier, *The Virtue of Nonviolence*, p. 22.

90. Gora quoted in Anil Nauriya, 2006, 'Gandhi's Little-known Critique of Varna', *Economic and Political Weekly*, 41(19): 1837. See Gora (G. Ramachandra Rao), *An Atheist with Gandhi* (Ahmedabad: Navajivan Publishing House, 1951), p. 57.

91. M.K. Gandhi, 'Letter to B.W. Tucker', 12 March 1928, in *CWMG*, Vol. 36 (New Delhi: Publications Division, Government of India, 1970), p. 102.

Gandhi's evolving strategy to abolish the caste system: Part I

3

You see that I am in no hurry to air my views on the questions [caste system] though thereby I am exposing myself [to] being misunderstood.

—M.K. Gandhi[1]

Where I have deliberately altered an opinion, the change should be obvious, only a careful eye would notice a gradual and imperceptible evolution.

—M.K. Gandhi[2]

In the previous chapter, it was established that Gandhi developed most of his philosophical expositions on an ideal society during his 21 years of stay in South Africa; to these, he remained true until the end of his life. It was also explained that it is the individual rather than the caste system or varnashrama dharma which is the basis of Gandhi's ideal society; the autonomy of the individual was his primary concern and he fought against everything that undermined it. As such, his struggle against the Indian caste system was not a standalone struggle; rather, his struggle for political independence for India, his movement for Hindu–Muslim unity, his promotion of the charkha, his daily public prayers and common meals, and many other activities complemented each other and were together aimed at safeguarding the autonomy of the individual. Gandhi's personal practices and his individual struggles can be best interpreted as a combined effort to safeguard the autonomy of the individual. However, this study singles out his fight against the caste system as the central line of enquiry to understand his efforts towards safeguarding the autonomy of the individual against the determinism of the caste system. It also tries to explain the respective roles of his personal practice and his political strategy to achieve independence in his drive to overcome caste hierarchy.

Since Gandhi's movement against the caste system aimed to safeguard the autonomy of the individual more than anything else, it can be seen as being different from the Dalit anti-caste movements which aimed to achieve equality for everyone by assuring a higher status for the Dalits in Hindu society, either in symbolic terms (like the right to wear the sacred thread) or in real terms (like an appropriate share for them in education and political or economic power). Like the Dalit leaders of his time, Gandhi acknowledged that in the present circumstances, it was necessary to make sure that untouchables achieved equal access to education and an appropriate share in political power and economic development. However, he did not believe that this would assure eradication of the caste hierarchies and differences present in Hindu society that undermine the autonomy of the individual. Gandhi believed that achieving symbolic or higher status for untouchables, though important, would not be enough to break the prevailing caste hierarchies and differences. To break these rigidities, he held it was equally important to abolish the basic notion of purity and pollution which formed the cardinal principle and the ultimate justification for them. In this chapter and the next, an attempt is made to explain how Gandhi gradually attacked this notion of purity and pollution and thereby, strategically and step by step, worked towards undermining the legitimacy of the caste system.

In the available literature on Gandhi, it is generally held that his attitude, though consistent on the practice of untouchability based on the notion of purity and pollution, was not so consistent on caste, inter-dining, and inter-caste marriage.[3] However, it will be argued here that while Gandhi remained consistent in his militant and uncompromising attack on the practice of untouchability, his characterization of what constituted its removal, and the degree of emphasis he laid on it, changed over time. Understanding and analysing what Gandhi meant by the removal of untouchability, at different junctures and at various stages in his political struggle, would seem to be a plausible way to establish continuity in Gandhi's writings and, therefore, an evolving strategy on his part.

Gandhi's strategy is different from that of the Dalit anti-caste movements of his time in another aspect: he placed a great emphasis on restoring the dignity of manual labour as a means of removing caste hierarchies and differences. Since all of Hindu society was based on the caste system, manual labour was regarded as the duty of the people belonging to the lower strata of society. By insisting on manual labour or bread labour for everyone, Gandhi tried to restore the concept of dignity of labour. In this way his was an effort that sought to undermine the moral basis of the caste system and create a great social leveller, in the sense that it removed the stigma attached to manual labour in the minds of the upper-caste Hindus. Gandhi writes: 'Obedience to the law of bread labour will bring about a silent revolution in the structure of society.'[4] Therefore, this and the following chapter will also attempt to elucidate Gandhi's systematic emphasis on manual labour and explain why it was more than just a moral teaching. It will be shown that by stressing on manual labour in the context of the caste system, Gandhi was proposing something that was quite revolutionary.

In order to achieve the aforementioned objectives, the current and the subsequent chapters will chronologically analyse the inconsistencies in Gandhi's writings on the issues of untouchability, caste, varna, inter-dining, inter-caste marriage, and so on, starting from 1915 (his arrival in India from South Africa) to 1948 (his death). For the purpose of analysis both the chapters divide the mentioned timeframe (1915–48) into the following five time periods—1915 to 1920, 1920 to 1927, 1927 to 1932, 1932 to 1945, and 1945 to 1948—on the basis of the themes that emerge in his writings during those years on issues such as untouchability, caste, varna, sanatani Hindu, inter-dining, and inter-caste marriage. These two chapters also attempt to unearth possible consistency and a strategic relation among the different themes that appear in these time periods on the same issues. However, such an exercise cannot be undertaken by ignoring the specific historical context—India's struggle for political independence from colonial power—in which Gandhi lived and worked. This historical context was perhaps the most important among the many forces that shaped, in more than one way, Gandhi's strategy against the caste system. Therefore, it is imperative to understand the relation between changes arising in Gandhi's writings on issues such as caste, varna, untouchability, inter-dining, and inter-caste marriage, and the significant political activities of the particular period in which they were written. As a result, this and the following chapters take a careful look at the prevailing historical context while analysing Gandhi's writings. In particular, the chapters highlight the important political activities of a particular period that provide an opportunity for Gandhi to strategically alter his views on many key issues, which may take his movement of abolishing caste system in India to its logical end.

It must be noted that in talking about Gandhi's evolving strategy for abolishment of the caste system, we are not talking about any occasional tactic that he might have deployed at the highest levels of nationalist politics (such as his decision to fast unto death against the MacDonald Communal Award [1932] for the depressed classes, which assured representation of the Dalit community in elected bodies by giving them separate electorates). Here, 'evolving strategy' is seen as a continuous pattern of behaviour or a way of life that may contain the occasional tactic. The chapters will also explain how Gandhi, by personal example and by propagating simple practices like taking up the spinning wheel, sanitation works, and other manual works, tried to abolish the caste differences and hierarchies present in Hindu society.

Beginning of Strategy: From 1915 to 1920

Historical Background

Gandhi returned to India from South Africa through England on 9 January 1915. Although he had a significant reputation as the champion of Indians in South Africa, he was yet to be crowned as 'Mahatma' and as an unquestioned leader of India's struggle for political independence. Following his political guru Gopal Krishna Gokhale's advice, he refrained from commenting on any political issue, and also from involvement in debate, or controversy, or political activities during the first years of this period. Gandhi was in no hurry either to involve himself in any controversy or to enter into active politics. He wanted sufficient time to observe the prevailing social and political situation in India. Until 1918, Gandhi played a minor role in national politics and in the Indian National Congress (INC). As a matter of fact, in 1915, since he could not be elected to the Subjects Committee of the Congress, he was nominated to the committee by the Congress president.[5] Again, 'in the subject committee elections held in 1917, Gandhi suffered a heavy defeat, managing just three votes'.[6] He neither joined the home rule movement launched by Bal Gangadhar Tilak and Annie Besant in 1916 nor took active part in the negotiations which led to the Lucknow Pact (1916) between the INC and the Muslim League. He also did not attend the Congress special session held in Bombay at the end of August 1918 to discuss the Montagu–Chelmsford report for constitutional reforms in India.

Gandhi's attitude towards the British government during these initial years was cordial and loyal. After arriving in Bombay in 1915 and before leaving the city, he met the governor of Bombay, Lord Willingdon, to show his regard for the British Empire. Lord Willingdon also thanked Gandhi for his visit and reassured him saying: 'You may come to me whenever you like.'[7] Later in 1917, Gandhi also met the viceroy Lord Chelmsford again as a mark of respect towards the British Empire. In 1915, Gandhi received the Kaiser-i-Hind medal from the British government for his services in South Africa. In April 1918, with some hesitation, he accepted an invitation of Lord Chelmsford to attend a war conference. During the conference, the viceroy requested Gandhi to support the resolution on recruiting Indians to help the British Empire in the First World War. At the conference, Gandhi said: 'With a full sense of my responsibility I beg to support the resolution.'[8] After the conference was over, Gandhi issued leaflets asking the people to enlist as recruits for the First World War. During this period, he went to different parts of the country on foot, accompanied by Vallabhbhai Patel, covering about 20 miles a day, to request people to join the army to help the British Empire during those critical circumstances.

Although Gandhi was not very active in national-level politics or within the Congress, he was nevertheless busy experimenting with many other ideas with the intent of introducing them at the national level should he get the opportunity. A few days after his arrival at Bombay port from South Africa through England, Gandhi first went to Shantiniketan (the school founded by Rabindranath Tagore) in Bengal. This was because at an earlier time he had sent his Phoenix inmates to India and they were stationed at Shantiniketan. In the absence of Tagore, Gandhi removed the high-caste Brahmin cooks there and introduced self-cooking by the teachers and students. Kaka Kalelkar, who was a teacher at Shantiniketan at that time, writes about this experiment: 'I felt that he [Gandhi] was less concerned with the principle of self-help than with the dismissal of those high-caste Brahmin cooks. The institution believed in the principle of one world family, whereas its Brahmin cooks stuck to their rigid orthodoxy and allowed no one to set foot in their sacrosanct kitchens.'[9] Though Gandhi's action was appreciated initially, the old practice was reintroduced eventually. From Shantiniketan, Gandhi visited the Gurukul ashram of Mahatma Munshiram (Swami Shraddhanand) at Haridwar. Here, too, he suggested to Mahatma Munshiram to introduce manual labour and industrial training in his ashram's school curriculum. However, not much was done in this direction at the ashram.

With Gandhi there, the Phoenix party, too, visited Haridwar to help Pandit Kunzru, a member of the Servants of India Society, at the 'Kumbh Mela'.[10] The Phoenix party decided to do sanitation work at the mela. Sanitation and charkha, the two important topics for Gandhi, would be emphasized everywhere in the future by him—in personal practice, ashram discipline, public messages, Congress conferences, and so on—all to teach people the dignity of manual labour. In the Indian context, learning sanitation practice was of more value than just receiving the moral teaching of self-help. As V.S. Naipaul writes: 'Sanitation was linked to caste, caste to callousness, inefficiency and a hopelessly divided country....This is what Gandhi saw, and no one purely of India could have seen it.'[11] Gandhi's early experiments to teach sanitation to the masses taught him that it was not an easy proposition. Gandhi, writing on his experience of teaching sanitation to the villagers of Champaran where he had experimented with satyagraha for the first time in India in 1917, says: 'Sanitation was a difficult affair. The people were not ready to do anything themselves. Even the field labourers were not ready to do their own scavenging.'[12]

There was one other activity—weaving and spinning—that Gandhi was experimenting with; this activity would teach the Hindu masses dignity of manual labour and serve to destabilize caste ideology. At the end of 1916, there were three country looms and three fly-shuttle looms working in Gandhi's Satyagraha Ashram. In a few months' time, four fly-shuttle looms were added. By 1917, 10 looms in all were working in the ashram and Gandhi, with other members of the ashram, was spending nearly eight hours a day at them. But Gandhi was not satisfied with weaving. He wanted to experiment with hand spinning, which was relatively easy and a convenient means to convey the message of dignity of manual labour. In 1917, Gandhi met Gangabehn Majumdar, a widow who became instrumental in introducing the spinning wheel and its different functions to Gandhi and other ashram members. In a few months' time, the ashram itself began to manufacture wheels and other spinning accessories. Maganlal Gandhi, with the help of some other members of the ashram, made a few improvements to the traditional wheel to make it easier for individual use. By the end of 1918, Gandhi was ready to introduce the wheel as well as khadi at the national level at every opportunity. He would admit that it was only the beginning, but he was very optimistic about his campaign and professed full faith in it.[13]

As this and the next chapter unfold, it will be much clearer how Gandhi, after successfully experimenting with spinning at the ashram, systematically begins to introduce it for every individual irrespective of their caste, religion, gender, or economic status. In his view, this would help abolish caste differences and hierarchies. In 1930, he is recorded to have said: 'Invidious distinctions of rank would be abolished if everyone without exception acknowledged the obligation of bread labour.... This labour can truly be related to agriculture alone. But at present at any rate everybody is not in a position to take to it. A person can, therefore, spin or weave.'[14]

These initial and simple experiments also helped Gandhi to understand some of the difficulties he would eventually face in his long fight against the caste system. He, however, comprehended their true gravity only when he allowed an untouchable family to join the Satyagraha Ashram. In September 1915, Gandhi admitted an untouchable family (Dudabhai Malji Dafda, his wife Danibehn, and their daughter Lakshmi) into his Satyagraha Ashram, which he had founded few months before on 25 May 1915 at Kochrab near Ahmedabad. The ashram's inmates were basically members of Gandhi's Phoenix Farm who had eaten, worked, and lived together with untouchables in South Africa. However, once back in India, they were not ready for this intermingling and opposed it vigorously. Lelyveld writes that scarcely four months after starting the ashram, Gandhi faced a virtual walkout by his disciples over the presence of the so-called untouchable family in the ashram.[15] But what was most difficult and astonishing for Gandhi was the strong opposition it fetched from his own wife Kasturba Gandhi, and from his most trusted disciple Maganlal Gandhi and his wife Santok. Somehow Gandhi could manage to bring his wife around, but he had to send Maganlal and his family to Madras for six months to learn weaving in order to resolve the problem.

Besides creating some monetary problems, all this not only stirred up unrest among the ashram's inmates but also created a storm among Gandhi's orthodox Hindu friends outside the ashram. While reflecting on the event, Gandhi wrote in his autobiography: 'Their [the untouchable family's] admission created a flutter amongst the friends who had been helping the ashram.... All monetary help, however, was stopped.... With the stopping of monetary help came rumours of proposed social boycott.'[16] But none of this bothered Gandhi; he was determined to make it very clear that a vow of opposition to untouchability in his ashram was not just a pious sentiment but a fact of life, and that he would neither abandon it nor relax it at any cost. He told the ashram inmates to prepare themselves to 'go and stay in the untouchables' quarter and live on whatever we could get by manual labour'.[17] However, things did not go that far as a *sheth* (rich businessman) stepped in at that critical time to donate Rs 13,000 to the ashram.

This incident, along with other similar experiences, may have led Gandhi to realize that like his wife Kasturba and Maganlal Gandhi and his wife, many other millions of caste Hindus very honestly and sincerely believed that the existing caste system and its restrictions were an integral part of their religion. It was clearly an emotional matter to them. From this, Gandhi must have learnt that any movement which directly attacks the caste system and criticizes its traditional restrictions would not be supported by the so-called upper-caste Hindus and would fail to bring the desired changes in their attitude. He might also have been afraid that in a backlash to such a movement, the so-called upper-caste Hindus would, far from abandoning the caste system, cling to it more vigorously than ever before. He must have understood that to break down the basic precepts of caste ideology, he needed to take the so-called upper-caste Hindus into confidence and make them believe that this movement was not to destroy their religion and tradition but to purify it. The changes that started to appear in his attitude and in his writings (like his frequent claim of being a sanatani Hindu and his repeated appreciation of some aspects of the caste system) on caste and other related issues must be understood against such a background. These changes encapsulate Gandhi's efforts to communicate his struggle against the caste system in such a subtle manner that it appears to be in continuity with tradition rather than pushing for the adoption of new beliefs and values by rejecting the old ones.[18]

In the light of the given discussion, it is not surprising to find Gandhi, during this period—at the age of 47—asserting for the first time that he is a sanatani Hindu. In 1916, he said: 'I am frankly a *Sanatanist*.'[19] During this period Gandhi made his first statement endorsing the caste system when he said that he believed in its foundation.[20] These changes were taking place not only in his writings but also in his actions and approach. For instance, in the beginning of 1917 when Gandhi started the national school at his ashram, he did not publicly announce that it was open to all castes and religions as he had done earlier in South Africa when he opened a school at his Phoenix Settlement for Indian children. Even in his early involvement in a few local struggles—the Champaran and Kheda struggle for farmers and the Ahmedabad struggle for mill workers—he focused on specific local grievances and avoided attacking caste or untouchability directly. Instead, he tried to tackle these matters obliquely by taking up issues of hygiene, cleanliness, health, and sanitation.

In early 1919, we also find that Gandhi—who initially showed loyalty towards the British Raj and barely any interest in national-level politics and the workings of the Congress—started to display antagonism towards the British government. He started the satyagraha movement against them and at the same time, took active interest in both national-level politics and the Congress. During this time, we see that Gandhi attended the proceedings of the government's legislative chamber for the first and the only time in his life to hear the debate on the Rowlatt Bills. A few months later, we find him leading his first all-India satyagraha—the Rowlatt Satyagraha—against the British Raj. In October of 1919, he visited several villages in Punjab to prepare a report on the Jallianwala Bagh massacre as a member of the Congress subcommittee set up for the purpose. The next month he is reported to have presided at the All India Khilafat Conference of Hindus and Muslims in Delhi on the request of his friend Swami Shraddhanand and Hakim Ajmal Khan. In this conference, he suggested 'non-cooperation' with the government, an expression that he used for the first time and which later became central in India's struggle for political independence. Above all this, in December 1919, at the Amritsar Congress session, he was appointed a member along with two other leaders of a subcommittee formed by the Congress to rewrite the party's entire constitution. By December 1920, Gandhi had not only changed the constitution, organizational structure, and creed of the Congress, but had also become an unquestioned leader inside and outside of the Congress.

Sumit Sarkar, a well-known historian, observes that the recent writings of many scholars have described, in great detail, the process of Gandhi's rise to power or 'capture' of national leadership in 1919–20, with the accent always being that it was entirely a very skilful top-level political game on Gandhi's part.[21] These scholars are right in that Gandhi—not only during this period but also in the subsequent couple of decades—exhibited great leadership skill in top-level political games. However, at this juncture, it is vital to ask an important question: why did Gandhi assume this new role in national-level politics? Did he do so because he realized that the political independence of India was more important than anything else, or did he understand that his struggles at the social level—such as his fight against the caste system, his campaign for Hindu–Muslim unity, and empowerment of women—could not be carried forward effectively without his entering into national politics?

Gandhi's emerging role in and preoccupation with top-level politics was a matter of discussion for many during this time, and some of his close friends saw it with fear. A very close friend of his, the Anglican priest Charles F. Andrews, who alone would address him as 'Mohan', expressed such a fear to Gandhi. He wrote to Gandhi saying that in the current scenario, the latter's participation in top-level politics made him feel that more important issues like untouchability were slipping out of Gandhi's agenda. Gandhi wrote in his reply: 'You are doing an injustice to me in even allowing yourself to think that for a single moment I may be subordinating the question [untouchability] to any other.' After rejecting such a possibility, Gandhi explained that his preoccupation with top-level politics should be seen as an effort to equip himself to tackle the problem of untouchability in a better way. He told Andrews that the removal of untouchability is a much difficult task than that of achieving political independence for India, but if India attains political independence it would be easier for him to tackle the former.[22] Gandhi also explained his position on many other occasions. In 1931, at a public meeting in Ahmedabad, he said: 'I must say that the service of the so-called untouchables does not rank with me as in any way subordinate to any kind of political work.' He assured that he considered his social reform work to be as important as his political work. However, he also believed that he could not carry out his social work successfully without the help of political work; hence he took interest in the latter only to the extent that it helped the former.[23]

In what follows we examine how, in the following years, Gandhi's activities, along with his writings, reveal his strategic and systematic use of his political position to undermine the basic precepts of caste ideology on a larger scale. To this effect, the following subsection analyses the major themes that appeared in Gandhi's writings between the years 1915 and 1920.

Themes in Gandhi's Writings

Gandhi's collected writings and speeches of the period (1915–20) make for four volumes. This is still much less than his collected writings of other time periods. This could be because it was only towards the end of 1919 that Gandhi assumed editorship of two weekly journals: *Young India* and *Navajivan*. The collection of 1915–20 contains the speeches he made at various fora, personal letters to friends, and official letters. Although Gandhi wrote and spoke a lot during this period on many issues, there are not many instances of his addressing issues of caste, untouchability, and other related matters. Analysing those instances when he did, it appears that during this initial period, Gandhi was very particular and selective not only about what he said about caste and related matters but also about when he would or would not make his remarks on the subjects. The few occasions when he spoke about or wrote on such matters were political or social conferences and conferences of untouchables. He also dwelt on these matters at some of his public meetings and in his personal talks. From his writings, it appears that during this period, he was more eager to explain his position on the subject rather than starting any movement. If all of Gandhi's writings on untouchability, caste, and related issues from 1915 to 1920 are to be analysed, some of the themes they reveal are discussed ahead.

Themes in Gandhi's Writings on Untouchability

Gandhi's writings of this period show that he did not compromise at all on the issue of untouchability; he always condemned its practice and indicated his desire to remove it both as a practice and as an institution. His writings during this period also reveal that during this period—his initial years in India—he very strategically defined removal of untouchability as mere destruction of the notion that one becomes polluted merely by someone's physical touch. He said: 'I cannot believe that there is any religion in regarding it a sin to touch any particular community. To me even to *think* that it is pollution to touch any creation of God is sinful.'[24] At another time, he said: 'Why should we hesitate to touch the *Antyajas*? It is not mentioned in any religious book that this community should not be touched, or treated as we are doing now.'[25]

His writings of this period also make three other things very clear. The first is that removal of untouchability did not mean removal of the restrictions on inter-dining and inter-caste marriage. In 1918, he wrote: 'I do not want to put the prejudice of untouchability on a level with food and marriage regulations based on caste distinctions. The latter is a matter admitting of differences of opinion. For it is a question of choice. We are not bound to subscribe to promiscuous inter-dining and intermarriage.'[26] At another time, he wrote:

> There is no question here of freedom of eating with or marrying any of them. The only question is whether physical contact with them should be avoided. When a member of this community becomes a Muslim, I do not avoid such contact with him; when he becomes a Christian, I salute him; I consider it no sin to allow myself to be touched by a Muslim or a Christian after he has touched such a person, but I object to physical contact with the man himself! The very idea seems to me unjust, devoid of reason and contrary to dharma. That is why I consider myself sanctified when I touch any person of this class and have been continually beseeching the Hindus in all manner of ways, though remaining within limits of propriety, to free themselves from this stigma.[27]

The second point is that his movement for removal of untouchability was not an attack on Hinduism and its age-old traditional practices and beliefs, but a movement for saving Hinduism and traditional ideas of varna or caste by removing the excrescence of untouchability. Replying to a letter, he wrote: '... I have started a movement against *varnashrama* is a delusion of the writer's.... However, I have steadfastly endeavoured to rid *varnashrama* of the taint of untouchability by pointing out that it is a sin to refuse to touch *Bhangis* and others, and this is my purest service to Hinduism.'[28] Repeatedly, he was pointing out that untouchability was a great danger to Hinduism. He wrote: 'Untouchability is a sin, a great crime, and if Hinduism does not destroy this serpent while there is yet time, it will be devoured by it.'[29]

The third point that Gandhi's writings of this period show is that while arguing for the removal of untouchability, Gandhi did not emphasize the need for socio-economic upliftment of the untouchables, or the need for equality and justice for them. His emphasis on removal of untouchability was rather a necessary condition to not only save Hinduism but also to obtain swaraj. On one occasion, he said: 'He who demands swaraj must give swaraj to others.' So long as the practice of untouchability exists, 'the big question will remain whether we have become fit for swaraj'.[30]

Themes in Gandhi's Writings on Caste, Varna, and Sanatani Hindu

Gandhi's writings of this period show that he avoided direct criticism of the caste system and instead emphasized some of its positive aspects. For instance, he said caste is a 'useful institution if properly regulated',[31] a 'natural institution'.[32] He also appreciated it because it has 'saved Hinduism from disintegration'.[33] He not only appreciated some aspects of the caste system but also projected himself as an orthodox person 'who does not consider caste to be a harmful institution'.[34] What needs to be noted here is that while Gandhi's writings of this period show that he emphasized positively some aspects of the caste system and appreciated it for a variety of reasons, the problematic idea of hereditary occupation in relation with caste or varna is completely absent. It was only after 1920 that he started defining caste or varna essentially in relation to hereditary occupation.

Themes in Gandhi's Writings on Inter-Dining and Inter-Caste Marriage

Gandhi's writings of this period show that he adopted a similar approach to the issues of inter-dining and inter-caste marriage; he avoided criticizing restrictions on inter-dining and inter-caste marriage. On the other hand, he appreciated them as an observation of self-control. He wrote: 'Prohibition of marriage with anyone not belonging to one's community promotes self-control, and self-control is conducive to happiness in all circumstances.'[35] His writings of this period show that he also wanted to make it clear that he was not amongst those who believed inter-dining and inter-caste marriage are necessary for uniting communities. He said, 'Why did the Germans and English who belonged to the same race and same religion and who entered into marriage bonds, fight with each other, if that was necessary for unity?'[36]

It appears irrefutable that during this period, Gandhi appreci- ated caste restrictions on dining and marriage for different reasons and argued that their reform was not part of his movement for removal of untouchability. However, it is also true that Gandhi did so for strategic reasons alone, understanding that a large section of Hindu society was not ready for such radical reform and needed to be educated on such issues. What he said about Vallabhbhai Patel's Marriage Bill during this period very clearly explains how he was planning to move forward not only on the issue of inter-caste mar- riage but also on the larger issue of caste itself. When asked for his views on Vallabhbhai Patel's inter-caste Marriage Bill, he suggested that initially, inter-marriage be allowed among different sub-castes only. He said: 'This might satisfy the most ardent reformer at least as a first step, and would enable men like the Hon. Pandit Malaviya [an Orthodox Hindu] to support it.'[37] This illustrates the core of Gandhi's strategy in dealing with the caste system—to escalate activism, moving from less contentious issues to highly contentious ones, gradually educating the masses through propaganda and by personal example.

These themes on caste, varna, untouchability, inter-dining, and inter-caste marriage in Gandhi's writings and speeches continue until the end of 1920 when they start to show changes. It must be noted here that these changes were not occurring in isolation but were inevitably and intimately linked to the changes that were taking place in the Indian political scenario. In the next section, an attempt is made to first analyse how the changes in the Indian political situation influenced and enabled Gandhi to take a different stand on the issues of caste and untouchability, and then analyse the different themes on caste, varna, untouchability, inter-dining, and inter-caste marriage that occur in Gandhi's writings late 1920 onwards. It tries to show the strategic relation between Gandhi's new position on these issues during this period and his earlier position during 1915–20.

From 1920 to 1927

It has been mentioned that towards the end of 1920, there were changes in Gandhi's outlook on caste and other related issues and therefore, changes in his approach to these issues as well. These issues featured much more frequently in his writings and speeches. In almost every public speech and political debate, he spoke about caste, untouchability, and other related issues. The changes in his writings were not only in degree but also in kind. But before ana-lysing the different themes reflected in his writings of this period, it is important to understand the political changes that were happen-ing in India during this period.

Historical Background

In fact, 1920–1 is known as the beginning of the Gandhian era in Indian history. Gandhi, who could manage just three votes in the Subject Committee member elections of the INC's annual session of 1917, had, within three years, become the most powerful leader of the Congress.[38] In 1920–1, unlike in 1915–16, Gandhi was Mahatma as well as an established political leader of the Congress. In a few years' time, he had managed to capture the imagination of the people with his voluntary poverty, simplicity, humility, and saintliness. Now he was loved and respected as Mahatma—the great soul—and, for many, he seemed to be an avatar who had come down to bring about the liberation of the country. He had, over the last few years, also proved himself a champion of mass movements by organizing some local struggles successfully. By 1920, he had also refashioned the INC and, by introducing a new constitution for it, had turned it into a militant organization of mass movement in place of a forum for just annual pageants and feasts of oratory. Under the old constitution, the fundamental political aim of the Congress was to achieve Indian autonomy within the empire by 'legal and constitutional means'; Gandhi changed this to 'peaceful and legitimate means', because the methods he was going to use were bound to transgress the limits of legal and constitutional means. Under the new constitution, he prescribed a fee of 4 annas for membership of the Congress. His objective was to open the Congress to the poorest and lowliest in India. Gandhi not only changed the fundamental political aim of the Congress and opened it to the poorest, he also changed its very organizational structure. The organization was given a broad-based pyramidal structure by formation of village, taluka, district, and provincial committees, with the AICC and the working committee of 15 members at the apex. He stood above all these committees and readied himself to start a mass movement of non-cooperation to challenge the mightiest government of his time. H.N. Brailsford describes these changes in the following words:

> Visibly, all India was turning Gandhian. Once-fashionable Indians discarded their European suits and dressed in homespun. Well-to-do women also were taking to *khaddar*. Soon the villages followed the towns in adopting the white 'Gandhi' cap. Underneath it, in the mind of the average man, there reigned a fixed belief that a new era was about to dawn.... The atmosphere resembled that which has sometimes prevailed in European sects which awaited the Second Coming of Christ on a date 'revealed' by prophecy. Fortified by this conviction, it was easy for Gandhi's followers to face the sacrifices he demanded of them.[39]

It will be a mistake to think even for a moment that these changes in Indian politics were the work of a single man and that Gandhi alone could have brought about major changes in Indian politics single-handedly. There were many factors responsible for such changes, and definitely more than Gandhi's own desire and mastery in high-level politics, it was the changing political circumstances that paved the path for Gandhi's rise to power. The situation at end of 1917 and beginning of 1918 was very different: the extremists and the moderates had merged the year before, and the Muslim League and the Congress had agreed on a common platform. The need now was for mass support and politicization of the masses. If the Congress was looking for a strategy to widen its mass support, during the same time, the secretary of state for India, Edwin Montagu, and the viceroy, Lord Chelmsford, had begun their tour to gather responses to the proposed idea of political reforms. Many groups that can be identified as untouchables/Dalit met Montagu and Chelmsford, all seeking representation in the forthcoming legislative bodies. It meant that one-seventh of the Indian population that was untouchable had to be recognized as politically important. The Congress that had until now avoided the issue of untouchables/Dalits by marking it as a social issue could not afford to ignore it any more; in fact, it now had to respond to this situation. Gandhi's rise to power within the Congress can also be understood against such a background. In order to give a proper response to the new political condition, the Congress needed a leader who could keep the untouchables within the party's fold. Under such circumstances, Gandhi, who had established himself as one of the champions of the removal of untouchability, naturally rose through the ranks within the Congress, and could also manage the project of untouchability at the national level without much resistance from the party.

It is against such a backdrop that the new themes in Gandhi's writings and the changes in his attitude towards some issues need to be understood. Gandhi, as a mass leader, understood that he was now in a position to demand certain sacrifices from the upper-caste Hindu masses and that the masses also seemed to be ready for extreme sacrifices. And the new themes in his writings of this period show that as a champion of mass movement, he was ready to wrest maximum advantage from his political position, the enthusiasm of the Indian masses, and favourable political circumstances.

It was in these circumstances that in 1920, Gandhi began his all-India movement of non-cooperation against the British government by surrendering his title 'Kaiser-e-Hind' and the two medals that he got in South Africa. As a part of his non-cooperation movement, Gandhi gave a call for surrendering titles and boycotting government educational institutions, offices, and law courts. A call was also given for boycotting foreign cloth. Sources say that around 24 titles were surrendered, while around 180 lawyers gave up their legal practice by March 1921. Sumit Sarkar notes that polling was low in many places in the November 1920 elections. He adds that the educational boycott was more effective, particularly in Bengal, which saw about 20 headmasters or teachers resigning every month up to April 1921, and an exodus of students from government schools and colleges. He also tells us that the economic boycott was the most intense and successful with the value of imports of foreign cloth falling from Rs 1.02 billion in 1920–1 to Rs 0.57 billion in 1921–2.[40]

However, 'Non-cooperation', as B.R. Nanda writes, 'was in some ways a misleading description of Gandhi's programme....'[41] He feels the non-cooperation programme was designed to infuse into the people a spirit of cooperation and self-sacrifice. Nanda's observation seems to be correct, as Gandhi used this opportunity to introduce some of his experiments at the national level in order to teach people lessons in self-discipline and cooperation. For example, he now proposed that removal of untouchability become a national agenda to develop cooperation among Hindus. Sarkar writes that Gandhi deserves all credit for bringing the issue of removal of untouchability to the forefront of national politics for the very first time.[42] Gandhi, however, not only did this but also redefined its meaning to suit the immediate context. As such, removal of untouchability no longer meant merely banishing the notion that one can become polluted by the mere physical touch of someone belonging to a lower caste; rather, it would mean, among other things, entry for the untouchable children into all national schools. The changes in Gandhi's writings on such matters will be discussed in detail in the next subsection.

The charkha was another feature that Gandhi made prominent at the national level during this period. In fact, it was one of his most important concerns. He made it a symbol of swadeshi and projected it as a vital source for achieving true swaraj. During the Non-Cooperation Movement, he asked students and urban people in general to take up spinning on a voluntary basis, as a symbol of identification with the rural masses and as a quick road to swaraj. He asked educated urban women to take up the charkha to save the honour of their rural sisters. In April 1921, at the Vijayawada Congress session, the organization decided to distribute 2 million charkhas in rural India. Gandhi then turned his attention to the rural people, asking them to take up spinning to overcome their poverty. When the Congress adopted its own flag, Gandhi ensured that the image of the charkha appeared on both sides of the flag. Until the end of the Non-Cooperation Movement, Gandhi upheld the charkha as the symbol of swaraj and khadi as the uniform of the national movement. By the end of 1922, the act of spinning the charkha became a sign of struggle against the British empire. In this way, Gandhi moulded the Non-Cooperation Movement against the British empire into an attack on the notion of purity and pollution too; simultaneously, the Indian masses were taught a lesson on the dignity of manual labour. Together these various facets of the movement were also aimed at abolishment of caste differences and hierarchies.

In February 1922, in Chauri Chaura in Gorakhpur district of Uttar Pradesh, a section of the protesters, irritated by the behaviour of some policemen, set fire to a police station killing 22 policemen. On hearing this, Gandhi decided to withdraw the Non-Cooperation

Movement. He also persuaded the Congress Working Committee (CWC) to ratify his decision and so, on 12 February 1922, the Non-Cooperation Movement came to a sudden standstill. Within 20 days, the British government, which had not dared to touch Gandhi all this while, gathered courage and arrested him on 10 March 1922, sentencing him to six years of imprisonment. However, by now, Gandhi had made removal of untouchability, spinning of the charkha, and forging of Hindu–Muslim unity an integral part of India's struggle for political independence and a method for achieving true swaraj. Many individuals had so staunchly accepted this as a way of life that these constructive works continued even when the political Non-Cooperation Movement came to a halt.

After his sentencing, Gandhi was sent to Yerwada Jail in Poona. He took his spinning wheel and some religious books with him to the jail, but unfortunately, his spinning wheel was taken away by the jailers. He threatened to fast if he was not allowed to spin, and the jailers relented. While in prison, he even persuaded criminals to join him at the spinning wheel. Brown writes: 'Perhaps even more significant for the imprisoned Gandhi than his overtly religious reading or devotion was the practice of spinning.' Gandhi was so convinced about the efficacy of the spinning wheel that after his release on 5 February 1924 on health grounds, he said:

> I see a great purpose in God saving me from a serious illness in Yera-vada Prison and releasing me for your service. The purpose is that I should ... put before you the fruit of profound meditation in prison, namely, the key to swaraj lies in fulfilling three conditions alone—in the spinning-wheel, in Hindu–Muslim unity and in the removal of untouchability. The reason that I have mentioned the spinning-wheel first is that amongst these three, we are sceptical about it alone and, secondly because *it is the spinning-wheel alone which demands from us honest daily work.*[43]

By the time Gandhi was released from prison, there was a division in the Congress on the issue of council entry, the two disagreeing groups being known as the 'no-changers' and the 'pro-changers' or 'swarajists'. The 'no-changers' were advocating that the Congress should concentrate on constructive, Gandhian rural works and boycott the councils; the 'pro-changers' were of the opinion that the Congress should enter the councils. Gandhi was against the Congress's entry into the councils and insisted on non-cooperation with the British government in everything. At the Congress session at Ahmedabad in June 1924, Gandhi pressed for two resolutions: first, a minimum spinning qualification for Congress membership; and second, removal of those who had entered the councils from the ranks of Congress office-bearers. But both were defeated in the face of the pro-changers' opposition. Sarkar informs us that in November 1924, it was only by permitting swarajists to work within councils 'as an integral part of the Congress organisation' and by ending all boycott measures that Gandhi could introduce the spinning qualification for Congress membership that was so dear to him.[44]

Under the spinning qualification, or 'yarn franchise' as it was generally known, it was made obligatory for every member of the Congress to spin for half-an-hour a day, and to send 2,000 yards of hand-spun yarn every month to the All India Khaddar Board at Sabarmati. Though Gandhi could manage to introduce the 'yarn franchise' that made spinning for half-an-hour every day for Congress members compulsory, he was very unhappy with the way in which the new franchise came to function. The Congress office statistics show that the number of those who sent in their yarn in any single month in 1924 did not exceed 8,000 in the whole country.[45] With the intention of reinforcing the practice of spinning, Gandhi insisted at the Belgaum Congress meeting that only those who wore hand-spun and handwoven khadi could be members of the Congress committees or organization, or take part in political or Congress functions. Later when the CWC met in September 1925, Gandhi persuaded them to set up the AISA as an integral part of the Congress. At the end of 1925, the Congress did set up the association and Gandhi himself became its president. Jamnalal Bajaj, a devoted Gandhian, was appointed the treasurer. With a separate organization, Gandhi was now ready for the further promotion of the charkha and khadi throughout the country to teach the dignity of manual labour to the masses.

Apart from teaching Indians lessons in manual labour through the charkha, Gandhi also extended his leadership to the Vaikom Satyagraha in the early 1920s. This was the first systematically organized agitation to secure for the untouchables the right to walk on the roads around the Vaikom Temple in Travancore—a princely state in south India. Immediately after the Kakinada session, the Kerala Provincial Congress Committee (KPCC) took up the eradication of untouchability as an urgent issue. It also decided to launch an immediate movement to open Hindu temples and all public roads to the untouchables/Dalit. A beginning was made in Vaikom, a village in Travancore. There was a major temple there whose four walls were surrounded by temple roads which could not be used by the untouchables. The KPCC decided to start a satyagraha to open the roads for them. Gandhi was keenly observing every activity of the Vaikom Satyagraha and guiding it from his ashram. However, in early March 1925, nearly a year after the start of the Vaikom Satyagraha, Gandhi arrived at Vaikom and met the maharani, the trustees of the temple, the *Ezhavas*'s (members of a caste that was considered 'low') spiritual leader Narayana Guru, and British officials. His tour helped him arrive at a compromise. The roads around the temple were opened for untouchables but those in the *Sankethan* of the temple remained closed to them. Upon returning from Vaikom, Gandhi attended the INC's annual session in December 1925. By then, sick and tired of the high pitch of Indian politics, he decided to observe 1926 as a 'year of silence' which he would spend in his ashram.

But as soon as 1927 dawned, Nanda writes, Gandhi embarked on an extensive tour to spread the message of the spinning wheel. In January 1927, Gandhi visited Calcutta (now Kolkata) and Comilla in Bengal, Banaras, and Allahabad in the United Provinces, and Dhanbad, Jharia, Chapra, Muzaffarpur, Samastipur, Patna, and other places in Bihar. In February and March, he visited the Central Provinces and Maharashtra. However, the real changes in his methods, approaches, and writings on different important issues started appearing after the British government's announcement of the all-white Simon Commission (8 November 1927). While the changes occurring in Gandhi's attitude after the announcement of this commission will be explained in the next section, for now let us understand the changes occurring in his writings on the issues of untouchability, caste, varna, inter-dining, and inter-caste marriage for the period 1920–7.

Themes in Gandhi's Writings

It has been found that, starting from 1920, Gandhi very frequently speaks and writes on caste, untouchability, and other related issues. There is notable reference to these subjects in almost every important speech and writing by him. New themes now appear in his writings on caste, untouchability, and other related issues. With some themes, one can see a continuity in approach over these two time periods. The dual purpose of this section is to explain the different themes that appear in his writings of this period and to try and understand the continuity, if any, appearing in his writings on the subjects of caste, untouchability, and other related issues.

Themes in Gandhi's Writings on Untouchability

Gandhi's writings on untouchability during this period contain two major themes. One of them shows continuity with his writings of the previous period. As with the last period of Gandhi's writings, this period, too, shows that Gandhi kept insisting on the removal of untouchability not so much for removing atrocities against the untouchables but for saving Hinduism and for attaining swaraj. In 1920, Gandhi said:

> We may not cling to putrid customs and claim the pure boon of swaraj. Untouchability, I hold, is a custom, not an integral part of Hinduism. The world has advanced in thought, though it is still barbarous in action. And no religion can stand that which is not based on fundamental truths. Any glorification of error will destroy a religion as surely as disregard of a disease is bound to destroy a body.[46]

And again in 1925, he wrote in *Young India*:

> I want to remove untouchability because its removal is essential for swaraj and I want swaraj. But I would not exploit you for gaining any political ends of mine. The issue with me is bigger even than swaraj. I am anxious to see an end put to untouchability because for me it is an expiation and a penance. It is not the untouchables whose *shuddhi* I effect—the thing would be absurd—but my own and that of the Hindu religion. Hinduism has committed a great sin in giving sanction to this evil and I am anxious—if such a thing as vicarious penance is possible—to purify it of that sin by expiating for it in my own person.[47]

But there are two differences in the way Gandhi addressed the theme during this period and the previous one. First, the occurrence of this theme in Gandhi's writings was more frequent in this period than previously. Second, in the previous period, this theme was almost absent in Gandhi's writings relating to his local political struggles—in Champaran, Kheda, and Ahmedabad—as well as his national-level satyagraha against the Rowlatt Act. But in the current period, the theme became a part and parcel of every speech and writing related to his national political movement of non-cooperation.

The second theme in Gandhi's writings on untouchability during this period shows strategic development. In the previous period,

Gandhi's writings defined removal of untouchability as destroying the notion that one gets polluted by the physical touch of someone lower in caste. But his writings of the current period show him as moving one step ahead. For Gandhi, the removal of untouchability now also included equal treatment and status for the untouchables as the other four varnas. He said: 'I can generally answer the question by saying that removal of untouchability means disappearance of a fifth caste. It therefore does mean at least that mere touch of a man shall not be regarded as a pollution. The so-called untouchable should enjoy the same freedom that the touchables do.'[48] At another point, he said: 'The removal of untouchability means the abolition of the fifth caste. There should, therefore, be no objection to a *Panchama* boy drawing water from the common well of a village and to his attending its common school.'[49] From now onwards, he argued, the removal of untouchability meant destruction of the fifth caste—the so-called untouchables must have equal status in society.

While he kept insisting that all should have equal access to every public place like the temple, water well, and so on, his writings of this period show that he laid more emphasis on entry into schools for the untouchable children than on anything else. In December 1920 when the Congress discussed the different aspects of the Non-Cooperation Movement, Gandhi made it very clear that 'removal of untouchability is more certain, by actually having untouchable children in all the sixty national schools'.[50] And, at the time of moving the resolution on civil disobedience at the Bardoli taluka conference, he insisted on untouchables' entry into schools as one of the conditions on which the resolution would be passed. He said:

> If there are separate schools for the untouchables elsewhere, it may not matter, but here untouchability must positively be considered a sin. You cannot rest satisfied with having separate schools for *Antyajas*. It is your duty to persuade the *Antyajas* of those villages which have national schools to enrol their children in those schools

and you should let them sit with your children. Before we pass today's resolution, such villages ought to agree to this.[51]

He kept repeating the same point time and again, reminding people
that so long as there was even a single national school without the
so-called untouchables, swaraj was not possible, and the resolution
of the Bardoli conference could not be carried out. He wrote: 'I
have just learnt that *Antyaj* children have already been enrolled in
18 national schools. I was indeed very happy to hear this. As long
as there is a single national school without *Antyaj* pupils, it cannot
be said that the resolution of the *Parishad* has been carried out.'[52]

It needs to be remembered that before embarking on a national-
level appeal for removal of untouchability to mean admission of
untouchable students to all national schools, Gandhi did experiment
with admitting untouchables to the schools recognized by Gujarat
Vidyapith. Gujarat Vidyapith was established as a national university
without a government charter on 18 October 1920 by Gandhi. At a
meeting of its senate on 31 October 1920, under the presidentship
of Gandhi, it was resolved that the so-called untouchables would
not be excluded from any of the schools approved by the university. This resolution also said that the so-called untouchables could
not be excluded from any place which is open to other classes or
communities.[53] Gujarat Vidyapith was created as an example for
other national schools, and to play the role of an effective organization for execution of Gandhi's demand for admission of untouchable children to schools.

That Gandhi restricted his campaign at this time to access to
schools for untouchable children and did not extend it to cover
issues like temple entry or inter-caste marriage should not be seen
as a sign of orthodoxy or a lack of reformative attitude on his part.
It must be seen as a part of his long-term strategy to gradually
move from less contentious issues to highly controversial ones.
His methods can be best understood from what he had suggested
to T.K. Madhavan, the editor of *Deshabhimani* and a leader of

the Ezhava caste of Kerala, who were fighting for their right to enter the Vaikom Temple. When Madhavan asked Gandhi for his opinion on their movement to get public temples thrown open to all classes of Hindus, Gandhi said: 'Removal of untouchability assumes a concrete shape when you demand temple-entry. *On strategical grounds*, I would ask you to drop temple-entry now and begin with public wells. Then you may go to public schools.'[54] This response, like his views on Vallabhbhai Patel's Marriage Bill in the previous period, gives us a glimpse of the overall strategy that Gandhi had in mind for dealing with the whole issue of caste and untouchability.

Themes in Gandhi's Writings on Caste, Varna, and Sanatani Hindu

Gandhi's writings of this period contain two major themes on the issues of caste, varna, and sanatani Hindu. In the previous period, he had only appreciated some aspects of the caste system, but his writings of this period show that he defines and validates the caste system in its orthodox form. This acquires a new kind of theme. Probably for the first time, he shows faith in caste being hereditary in his writings and speeches in December 1920. He writes: 'I am inclined to think that the law of heredity is an eternal law and any attempt to alter that law must lead us, as it has before led, to utter confusion.'[55] And in 1921, he says: 'I believe that one acquires one's caste by birth.'[56] It is also the first time that he attached the notion of heredity to varna, and in October 1921, he is found saying: 'It does attach to birth. A man cannot change his Varna by choice.'[57] During this period, he also says, again probably for the first time ever, that 'I am prepared to defend, as I have always done, the division of Hindus into four castes'.[58] And, starting from 1920, the definition of caste or varna as hereditary occupation becomes a theme in Gandhi's writings. He clearly expresses his willingness to defend the fourfold division of Hindu society.

The second theme that emerges during this period is his claim of being a sanatani Hindu. This claim frequently occurs in his writings. For instance, in October 1920, he says: 'I claim to be a *sanatani* Hindu.' In 1921, he writes: 'In dealing with the problem of untouchability during the Madras tour, I have asserted my claim to being a *sanatani* Hindu with greater emphasis than hitherto....'[59] Indeed it is on the basis of his remarks on caste, on varna, and on being a sanatani Hindu, made in these six years from 1920 to 1926, that Gandhi acquired the reputation of being an orthodox Hindu who defended and validated the caste system more than anyone else in modern India. But Gandhi's writings of this period show that he had to assert his identity as an orthodox Hindu, because even this claim of his was rejected by some important and powerful groups of Hindus. In 1920, he says: 'At present I am engaged in a great dispute with the Hindus in Gujarat. They, especially the *Vaishnavas,* reject my claim to be called a *sanatani* Hindu, but I cling to it and assert that I am one.'[60]

In fact, he had to show his willingness to defend the division of Hindus into four castes because, in spite of his effort to be patient and careful in articulating his movement against the caste system in such a way that it appeared to be in continuity with tradition and not a movement for the destruction of tradition, Gandhi and his movement were suspect in the eyes of many orthodox Hindus. They believed that Gandhi had started his movement to destroy the caste system under the influence of his Christian friends or Western ideas. In January 1921, Gandhi wrote to his close Christian friend C.F. Andrews: 'The *Gujarati* is endeavouring to weaken my position on the question by saying that I have been influenced by *you* in this matter, meaning thereby that I am not speaking as a Hindu but as one having been spoiled by being under your Christian influence.'[61] At another juncture, he says: 'I am convinced that I am not a Westernized reformer. There are critics who say that I am an apologist of the Western ways. I consider them childish.'[62] It was to reject the accusation that he was distorting the Hindu religion and tradition by being influenced by Christianity and Western ideas that Gandhi asserted his identity as an orthodox Hindu, showing his willingness to defend the traditional notion of the division of Hindus into four castes.

A closer reading of Gandhi's writings of this period also reveals that Gandhi's frequent insistence on being a sanatani Hindu and his willingness to defend the division of Hindus into four castes or varnas was part of his continuous effort to project his movement as one that stood for the continuity of tradition. This would make it easier for him to be understood and accepted by the Hindu masses. For example, in Gandhi's writings of this period, almost every reference to his being a sanatani Hindu is accompanied by a request for abolishing untouchability. For example, in September 1921, at Srirangam, he says: 'As a *sanatani* Hindu I venture to assert that there is no warrant for untouchability in Hinduism.'[63] And in the same month at Dindigul, he says: 'I claim to be a *sanatani* Hindu with a due sense of my responsibility to my religion. I venture to say that there is no warrant in Hindu *Shastras* for untouchability.'[64] On another occasion, he says: 'Do not conclude that I am a polluted person, a reformer. A *rigidly orthodox Hindu*, I believe that the Hindu *Shastras* have no place for untouchability of the type practiced now.'[65]

Indeed his writings of this period show that he was effectively and pragmatically defending the fourfold division of Hindus to justify his two demands within the traditional discourse. The first was his demand that the removal of untouchability entail abolishment of the fifth division. He writes: 'There are four castes, and not five. The practice of untouchability is not evidence of self-restraint, it is not a restriction inherent in the caste system.'[66] At another time, he says: 'In Hinduism there is no such thing as a fifth or untouchable class.'[67] And on still another occasion, he says: 'It is a question purely and simply of removing untouchability, of abolishing the

unwarranted fifth division.'[68] The second demand was for uniting all sub-castes within the four major castes or varnas; he says:
'Like every other institution it (the caste system) has suffered from
excrescences. I consider the four divisions alone to be fundamental,
natural, and essential. The innumerable sub-castes are sometimes a
convenience, often a hindrance. The sooner there is fusion the better.'[69] He argues that 'the division, however, into innumerable castes
is an unwarranted liberty taken with the doctrine. The four divisions are all-sufficing.'[70] In 1925, he says: 'I would abolish all castes
and would keep the four divisions.'[71] Gandhi was not just seeking
the fusion of sub-castes but was also asking that each of the four
castes develop the qualities of all the four castes. He says at one time
that 'everyone, whatever his caste, should have the qualities of all the
four castes'.[72] He repeats this idea another time: 'Each of the four
castes must, in some measure, have the qualities of the others.'[73]

To some, all this might still sound as though Gandhi was holding an orthodox position. Though he was demanding equal status
for untouchables and persuading all sub-castes to merge into the
four major castes, he still upheld the traditional idea of the fourfold
division of society which, according to many scholars, was the chief
reason for the caste differences and hierarchies in Hindu society.
Their argument seems reasonable, but only if Gandhi's this particular position is taken in isolation and not seen as a part of his
long-term strategy. It needs to be remembered that during this time,
his movement was still in its early stages, but as early as in 1925, he
made clear what he was aiming at. He said: 'The best remedy is that
the *mahajans* of the various small communities should join together
and constitute a single caste, and that this big association should
merge with other associations and the four castes should become
a single caste. But in the present atmosphere of weakness such a
reform would be considered impossible.'[74]

Now, it is increasingly evident that Gandhi's frequent claim of
being a sanatani Hindu and his defence of the fourfold division of

Hindu society was not a sign of his orthodoxy; rather, it was part of his strategy to mollify both those who criticized him for destroying the fourfold caste system and those who opposed his movement against untouchability.

Themes on Inter-dining and Inter-Caste Marriage

Gandhi's writings of this period contain two different themes on the issues of inter-dining and inter-caste marriage. One theme shows continuity from Gandhi's previous writings, while the other shows strategic progress. Just as in the previous period, Gandhi's writings of this period, too, show him emphasizing that his movement against untouchability does not include removal of restrictions on inter-dining and inter-caste marriage. He writes: 'The reform contemplated in the untouchability movement does not obliterate the restriction as to inter-dining and inter-marriage.'[75] This is a theme that continues from the previous period, both his earlier and current writings carrying it. There are also a few occasions during the current period when he goes one step further and openly says he is against both inter-dining and inter-caste marriage, citing some specific grounds. For instance, in 1921, perhaps for the first and last time, Gandhi strongly and openly says that 'I am against both [inter-dining and inter-marriage] on hygienic and spiritual ground'.[76] But such quotes are very rare and do not acquire the dimensions of a major theme in his writings of this period.

Gandhi's writings of this period also show one theme on this subject as exhibiting strategic progress. He keeps repeating that restrictions on inter-dining and inter-caste marriage are not essential parts of Hinduism; neither would their violation destroy varnashrama dharma. He once says: 'The rules which people observe in regard to food, water and marriage are not essential features of Hinduism.'[77] And at another time, he writes: 'I do not believe, that inter-dining or even inter-marriage necessarily deprives a man of his status that his birth has given him.'[78] And, 1920 onwards, he kept emphasizing this point in most of his writings and speeches on the subject.[79] It appears that by propagating the idea that such restrictions are not an essential part of Hinduism and that they do not violate varnash-rama dharma, he was offering justification within the traditional discourse for promoting inter-dining and inter-caste marriage. It will be explained in the analysis of his writings of the next period that Gandhi goes on to argue in favour of inter-sub-caste marriage within the larger four divisions of Hindu society.

These themes that begin to appear in Gandhi's writings from 1920 onwards continue up to 1927. From 1927 onwards, his writings on caste, untouchability, and other related issues reveal some new themes. But as has been discussed earlier, Gandhi was not drawing up his campaigns in isolation; the changes that occurred in his writings were inextricably linked with the changes that were taking place in the political scenario of the nation. In the beginning of the next section, we first reflect on the changes taking place within the Indian political context, and then analyse the different themes that emerge in the writings of Gandhi on different issues during the period 1927–32.

Third Stage of Gandhi's Long-Term Strategy (1927–32)

The themes discussed earlier kept appearing in Gandhi's writings until the end of 1927. From then onwards, there are some very distinct changes in Gandhi's writings on untouchability, caste, and other related issues. These changes, however, cannot be properly understood or historically evaluated unless they are studied in their particular historical context. In the following subsection, the major political activities from 1920 to 1927 are described. These activi-ties paved the path for the new changes occurring in the writings of Gandhi.

Historical Background

As mentioned earlier, Gandhi spent the year 1926 in silence in his ashram and as 1927 dawned, he embarked on an extensive tour to spread his messages of removal of untouchability, spinning of the charkha, and Hindu–Muslim unity. However, his writings of this period reveal some new themes because in 1927, the situation and conditions were a little different from those existing in 1920. The Vaikom Satyagraha had created enough awareness about the issue of temple entry for untouchables in other parts of India. It was in 1927 that the Mahars (an untouchable caste from Maharashtra) launched their first movement to enter a temple, at Amravati, under the leadership of G.A. Gavai.[80] In 1927, Babasaheb Ambedkar also launched his famous Mahad Satyagraha to assert equal rights for untouchables by drinking water from the Chawdar tank. The Mahad municipality itself had already passed a resolution to open the tank to everyone, but this had not been implemented. All these changes must have played an important role in the emergence of the new themes in Gandhi's writings during this time. It appears that it was the British government's announcement of the all-white Simon Commission to study constitutional reform in British India and the resultant unity shown by India in its opposition to this commission that provided a catalyst for the changes that took place in Gandhi's writings.

The changes that started appearing from 1927 onwards in Gandhi's writings and attitude were not an innocent attempt to optimize people's enthusiasm to take his movement against the caste system one step ahead. This was also a demand of time. Near about 18 untouchable/Dalit organizations were consulted by the Simon Commission in Bombay Presidency alone. All of them had clearly expressed themselves in favour of separate representation for themselves. This was a great challenge for the Congress which claimed to represent the concern of all groups in India. It was

particularly more dangerous because in case of the political separation of untouchables/Dalit, upper-caste Hindus who dominated
the Congress might have found it difficult to justify their claim of
being a majority community. Therefore, it was becoming increasingly necessary for the Congress to take some serious steps to keep
these groups of people within their fold. Thus, the changes that
started appearing in the writings and attitude of Gandhi were also
a political necessity. These changes appearing from 1927 onwards in
Gandhi's writings are analysed in the next subsection. The analysis
will also provide us a considerable understanding of the political
scenario in India from 1927 to 1932.

Describing the political atmosphere of 1927, Sumit Sarkar writes:
'Prospects for Indian unity seemed bright towards the end of 1927,
as practically all established political groups (except the Justice Party
in Madras and the Punjab Unionists) decided to boycott the Simon
Commission.'[81] Wherever the commission visited in India, it was
greeted with a sea of black flags and the slogan 'Simon, go back'.
The Congress had resolved to boycott the Simon Commission at its
annual session in December 1927 at Madras and turned the boycott
into a popular movement. At this session, the Congress also accepted
Jinnah's offer to organize an all-parties' conference for preparing a
draft of a constitution for India as the country's answer to the Simon
Commission. Gandhi's response to the Simon Commission was
quite different: he neither participated in nor organized any protest
movement against the all-white Simon Commission; neither did
he appreciate the Congress and other parties' effort to organize an
all-parties' conference to prepare a draft of the Indian constitution.
In mid-1928, Gandhi wrote: 'I confess ... that neither the Statutory
Commission [Simon Commission] nor constitution-making interests me much.'[82] Brown informs us that Gandhi's voice was singu-
larly absent in the reaction from politicians to the all-white Simon
Commission, while the Congress and other parties attempted to
achieve an alternative plan (constitution) for India's future.[83]

Gandhi emphasized that *purna* swaraj will only come through constructive work in the villages, and hence tried to confine the Congress's activities between 1927 and 1929 to this kind of activity. While Gandhi continued to stress on the charkha, removal of untouchability, and Hindu–Muslim unity, this period finds him turning to the subject of sanitation too; he intended to take it up on a larger scale. This subject was not new to Gandhi; in fact, it was always one of his priorities. Scavenging was part of day-to-day life in Gandhi's ashrams and everyone, irrespective of their caste, gender, and religion, had to do scavenging. Gandhi had been giving lessons to people on sanitation in South Africa long before he returned to India. However, it appears that he began to emphasize its practice in India on a larger scale only towards the end of the 1920s.

For Gandhi, 'indifference to sanitation is ever a crime'[84] and hence he asked his Congress volunteers: 'What you have done to popularize the principles of sanitation and hygiene in the villages?'[85] In 1929, to bring the attention of the masses to the issue of sanitation, he wrote an article in *Young India* titled 'A National Defect'. In that article, he said: 'There is, I know, the custom of saying that these reforms must not be permitted to take the nation's attention away from the work of swaraj. I venture to submit that conservation of national sanitation is swaraj work and may not be postponed for a single day on any consideration whatsoever.'[86] At the end of the same year, we find him suggesting that 'during the long vacation the students will stay in the villages and offer to conduct classes for adults and to teach the rules of sanitation to the villagers'.[87] The next year, in 1930, we find Gandhi again involved in high-level politics. On 6 April 1930, by picking up a handful of salt in Dandi, Gandhi inaugurated the Civil Disobedience Movement against the British empire. Even at the height of the movement, he was saying: 'If there is true mass awakening, those who are not engaged in civil disobedience are expected to occupy themselves and induce others to be engaged in some national service, such as khadi work, liquor and opium picketing, foreign-cloth exclusion, village sanitation, assisting the families of civil resistance prisoners in a variety of ways.'[88]

However, this by no means meant that he ignored the charkha or the issue of removal of untouchability; these remained integral parts of his basic struggle to abolish caste differences and hierarchies. In fact, by 1927, these two issues had acquired the status of national priority and had become indisputable conditions for achievement of swaraj. Moreover, there were separate organizations set up to ensure that these conditions were fulfilled. As such, Gandhi's emphasis on sanitation must be seen as an extension of his movement to teach the Indian masses the importance of manual labour in achieving social equality. To this effect, his writings of this period amply confirm how he capitalized on the enthusiasm of the masses during the Civil Disobedience Movement to spread his messages of the charkha, removal of untouchability, sanitation, Hindu–Muslim unity, and so on.

Gandhi inaugurated the Civil Disobedience Movement by picking up a handful of salt at Dandi on 6 April 1930. Jad Adams writes:

> Gandhi made the march the occasion for promoting the messages in favour of spinning and against untouchability. At the village of Dabhan he walked past the temple to the untouchables' quarter, where he drew water from the 'untouchable' well and bathed. He then persuaded the high-caste Hindus of the welcoming committee to allow the untouchables to join the gathering.[89]

Following this, there was a countrywide mass participation in the movement from different sections of Indian society. The British government, however, arrested Gandhi soon after the inauguration of the programme and sent him to Yeravada Jail in Poona. Though incarcerated, Gandhi managed to spread the message of constructive programmes on removal of untouchability, the charkha, Hindu–Muslim unity, and now sanitation among the common people.

Soon Gandhi was released for talks with Lord Irwin. This resulted in what is known as the Gandhi–Irwin Pact of 5 March 1931.

Since the Gandhi–Irwin Pact was signed by Gandhi on behalf of the Congress and by Lord Irwin on behalf of the government, it placed the Congress on an equal footing with the government and projected Gandhi as its sole representative. Gandhi's public image was further strengthened when he was the sole representative of the Congress at the Second Round Table Conference held in the spring of 1931 in London. On the Civil Disobedience Movement and the subsequent events, Judith Brown writes: 'This man [Gandhi] whom contemporaries had considered a spent political force in the mid-1920s was now central to Indian politics, and had a public reputation unique in range and quality.'[90] It is a well-accepted fact that the Civil Disobedience Movement had enhanced Gandhi's public reputation and enabled him to demand more sacrifices from the masses. However, Gandhi's decision to go on a fast unto death against the MacDonald Communal Award for depressed classes (untouchables) caused an emotional stir among the caste Hindus; this was probably the chief catalyst for the changes that started to appear in Gandhi's writings from 1932 onwards. These changes will be analysed within their historical context in the next chapter. But for now, the different themes emerging in the writings of Gandhi for the period 1927–32 are analysed in the following section.

Themes in Gandhi's Writings

Themes in Gandhi's Writings on Untouchability

Gandhi's writings of this period contain three major themes on the issue of untouchability. One theme shows continuity over the last two periods of his writings, the second displays strategic development, and the third seems to be a new addition. As with the last two periods, the third period of his writings, too, sees Gandhi laying stress on the removal of untouchability as an essential condition for the attainment of swaraj and for purifying or saving Hinduism. He writes: 'For reform of Hinduism and for its real protection, removal of untouchability is the greatest thing.'[91] At another point, he writes: 'There is no swaraj without the removal of untouchability.'[92] He keeps arguing for removal of untouchability on the two aforementioned grounds.

The second theme—the one which shows strategic progress—relates to the definition of removal of untouchability. Gandhi's writings in the first period define removal of untouchability as 'abolishing an idea that one gets polluted by mere physical touch of one community'. The writings of the second period show that he articulated removal of untouchability to mean elimination of the unwanted fifth caste or equal treatment for untouchables, with equal emphasis on 'admitting untouchable children in all national schools'. His writings of the third period, however, show him extending his demand to temple entry for untouchables. On 7 October 1927, at a public meeting in Tinnevelly, he says:

> I therefore invite you all to join me in this crusade against untouch-ability in every form. Whilst I am glad to find from your addresses and the talk I had this afternoon that your municipal schools are open to untouchables, I ask you not to be satisfied with that alone. When untouchability is really removed from our midst you will not find any untouchable quarter. The untouchables will have the same rights as the tallest Brahmin to enter the inmost sanctuary of any temple to which any Brahmin can go.[93]

At another public meeting, he says: 'I would ask you to gird up your loins in order to fight this curse of untouchability and caste, and all the influence that you might have at your command in order to see that every temple is thrown open to all irrespective of caste.'[94] Before 1927, there were only occasional requests from him that untouchables not be denied temple entry, but that year onwards, his writings carry an increasing emphasis on this point. Temple entry for untouchables emerges as a strong and forceful theme in his writings. It is evident that, as it happened during the previous periods, this time, too, he extended his demands when caste Hindus among his supporters seemed ready for bigger sacrifices. In the previous period, he raised his demands during the Non-Cooperation Movement; this time, he does so during the boycott of the Simon Commission. Being a great strategist of mass movements, he could gauge when the time was ripe for demanding extreme sacrifices from critical sections of the public. He also knew that to make such demands acceptable, or for their effective implementation, there was a need for a separate organization fully devoted to such specific purposes. Therefore, in the previous period, before stretching his demand that 'untouchables must be permitted in every public school', he established the Gujarat Vidyapith. And while emphasizing temple entry for the so-called untouchables, he set up a committee for the removal of untouchability to actualize this appeal.

This committee was set up in 1929 by the CWC on the advice of Gandhi. One of its major objectives was to allow access to public temples for the untouchables.[95] According to Gandhi, this committee requested the trustees of different temples to throw open their temples to untouchables.[96] He also kept informing his readers about the progress of this committee and shared with them, with great joy, the fact that many temples were now permitting entry for Dalits due to the work of this committee.[97] During this time, he made an appeal to the municipalities of many towns suggesting that all restrictions which forbade anyone from entering public temples must be done away with.[98] Alongside, he kept educating the masses on the subject through his speeches and writings.[99]

There is yet another theme appearing in Gandhi's writings of this period regarding untouchability. Around 1927, he began saying that untouchability was dying very rapidly. He said in 1928: 'We get evidence from all parts of India which proves how untouchability is losing its hold.'[100] In 1929, he said: 'I see untouchability disappearing with the speed of a horse; I desire day and night that it should take on the speed of wind. And I have faith that some day it will,'[101] And in 1930, at the Round Table meeting he said: 'Thank God, the conscience of Hindus has been stirred, and untouchability will soon be a relic of our sinful past.'[102] It appears that by proclaiming that untouchability was dying very rapidly, he was preparing the ground for rejecting the notion and practice of caste itself in the next period of his writings.

Themes in Gandhi's Writings on Caste, Varna, and Sanatani Hindu

Gandhi's writings of this period on caste, varna, and sanatani Hindu show continuity in some themes from the previous periods. A few other themes show strategic progress. One can see the emergence of some new themes as well. The particular theme of his claiming to be a sanatani Hindu, very prominent in Gandhi's writings of the previous period, has now lost its force. In the previous period, Gandhi asserted his identity as sanatani Hindu many times, but during this period, this theme is almost absent. There may be a few occasions during this period when he evokes this idea, but it can be safely concluded that it was no longer as dominant a theme as it was in his earlier writings and speeches.

It is seen that in the previous period, Gandhi was using the term 'caste' almost like a synonym for varna. For instance, in 1925, he wrote: 'There are only four *varnas* or castes, not five.'[103] At the same time, he also expressed his faith in the caste system/ varnas and appreciated some aspects of it. But during this period, he very categorically says: 'I draw the sharpest distinction between *varnashrama* and caste.'[104] And on this ground, he criticizes caste as an excrescence on Hinduism or varnashrama dharma. He writes: '*Varna* has nothing to do with caste. Caste is an excrescence, just like untouchability, upon Hinduism. All the excrescences that are emphasized today were never part of Hinduism.'[105] It is found from his writings that as early as in 1926,[106] he rejected his faith in caste as practised during his time and criticized it for numerous reasons. This theme gains momentum and acquires a distinctive shape in his writings from 1927 onwards.

From that time onwards, he keeps emphasizing the differences between varna and caste.[107] During this time, he also keeps asserting that there is no endorsement of caste in any Shastra,[108] and keeps criticizing it at every public meeting and in all his writings. In 1929, he says: 'There can be no more castes than the four *varnas*. The Hindu *Shastras* do not authorize the existence of the innumerable castes found today. It may be that the multiplication of castes served some useful purpose. But today, castes serve no purpose and meet no need.'[109] At another public meeting, he says:'*Varna* dharma is not caste. As I have said in so many speeches in South India, and as I have written fairly exhaustively on *varna* dharma in *Young India*, I hold that there is nothing in common between caste and *varna*. Whilst *varna* gives life, caste kills it, and untouchability is the most hateful expression of caste.'[110]

However, Gandhi's rejection of the caste system in the writings of this period was not a rejection of the hereditary fourfold division of Hindu society. During this period, he rejects caste as 'practised during his time', but he kept writing in favour of the hereditary fourfold division of Hindu society. Furthermore, during this period, he refers to the fourfold division as varna and not caste. He writes: 'It is the excrescence of *varnashrama dharma* which has been misrepresented as the caste system with which, as seen in the multitudinous castes of latter-day Hinduism, the original four divisions have little to do.'[111] Because of this, scholars who argue that Gandhi's writings do not reflect any significant changes seem to be right, because in his writings and speeches, he continues to defend the hereditary fourfold division of Hindu society. In his classical work *Annihilation of Caste*, B.R. Ambedkar criticizes Gandhi precisely for this reason. He writes:

Some might think that the Mahatma has made much progress inasmuch as he now only believes in Varna and does not believe in Caste. It is true that there was a time when the Mahatma was a full-blooded Sanatani Hindu.... He believed in Caste and defended it with the vigour of the orthodox.... It is good that he has repudiated this sanctimonious nonsense and admitted that caste 'is harmful both to spiritual and national growth'.... But has the Mahatma really progressed? What is the nature of the Varna for which the Mahatma stands?.... The essence of the Mahatma's conception of Varna is the pursuit of ancestral calling irrespective of natural aptitude. What is the difference between Caste and Varna as understood by the Mahatma? I find none. As defined by the Mahatma, Varna becomes merely a different name for Caste for the simple reason that it is the same in essence—namely pursuit of ancestral calling. For making progress the Mahatma has suffered retrogression.... If the Mahatma believes as he does in every one following his or her ancestral calling, then most certainly he is advocating the Caste System and that is calling it the Varna System he is not only guilty of terminological inexactitude, but he is causing confusion worse confounded.... The Mahatma must be told that he is deceiving himself and also deceiving the people by preaching Caste under the name of Varna.[112]

Although it is a fact that Gandhi's writings during this period show no fundamental changes, it must be remembered that his adherence to the idea of varnashrama was only strategic and had no practical implication except to assure the Hindus that his reforms were not intended to destroy their religion but rather to purify it. It is explained earlier that in the previous period, Gandhi's defence of the fourfold division of Hindu society helped him, on the one hand, to explain that his movement for removal of untouchability was not an effort to destroy the Hindu religion and tradition but to purify it by giving up its excrescence; on the other hand, it also enabled him to criticize the numerous subdivisions of castes. Now, when in this period he says 'I do believe in varnashrama—a totally different institution from the modern castes' or 'I draw the sharpest distinction between varnashrama and caste', it again serves the same purpose. It helps him to stick to his position that his movement is not for distorting the traditional idea of the fourfold division of Hindu society, and at the same time gives him adequate reasons, which his political supporters can understand, to criticize the caste system. Hence, his adherence to the fourfold division of Hindu society or varnashrama dharma should not be viewed as a sign of his orthodoxy. As Rajmohan Gandhi metaphorically writes: 'I see the Varnashrama remark as sugarcoating for his pill for caste Hindus. He wants them to swallow his reforms.'[113]

It appears that during this period, by propagating the idea that 'untouchability is disappearing rapidly' and by defining 'caste as an excrescence of varnashrama', Gandhi was preparing the foundation for his next big step—that of rejecting the caste system itself. His writings of the next period reveal that whenever Gandhi got the opportunity, he moved ahead to do exactly that.

Themes in Gandhi's Writings on Inter-Dining and Inter-Caste Marriage

As explained earlier, during the first period Gandhi made it clear that his movement against untouchability did not promote inter-dining and inter-caste marriage. In the next period, he kept asserting the same idea that he did not expect people to either inter-dine or go to the extent of marrying the so-called untouchables, but at the same time he went a step ahead and strategically argued that these restrictions were not an essential part of Hinduism or varnashrama dharma. Based on this premise, during this period, he argued: 'It is very necessary that people should follow a new custom and enter into marriage alliances among the sub-divisions of the major castes of Brahmins, Kshatriyas, Vaisyas and Sudras. That is, marriages should be permitted in circles among which, under the rules of *Varnashrama* inter-dining is permitted.'[114]

But his propaganda for inter-caste marriage within the caste sub-divisions was not as intense as it was in the case of his promoting the opening of public schools, public temples, public wells, and so on to the untouchables. Most of the time, it was only at a personal level that he promoted inter-caste marriage[115] and even inter-provincial marriage.[116] In all likelihood, it may be the case that he found the masses not yet ready to accept or act on such a reform. However, there are references to argue that he, though not very forcefully, did in fact propagate the idea of inter-caste marriage within the caste subdivisions even among the masses during this period. An example of this is when he spoke on 24 January 1928, at a meeting of his own Modh caste people:

> I wish to carry forward this attempt of mine to break down caste barriers. Perhaps you do not know that I got one of my sons married outside my caste and have lost nothing by doing so.... I ask those belonging to the smaller castes to hand their daughters over to me, if the latter cannot be married off. I shall get them married to good upright boys belonging to other castes....[117]

There are a few other occasions when he wrote about promoting inter-caste marriage[118] and later, in 1932, he made it clear that he advocated inter-caste marriages because he desired the disappearance of sub-castes.[119]

However, these were not Gandhi's last words on inter-dining, inter-caste marriage, removal of untouchability, caste, and varna. Starting from 1932, his writings reveal some new themes on all these issues. Again, despite the changes, there was continuity and strategic evolution in the writings of Gandhi. And, it must be repeated again that his writings cannot be seen in isolation from the events that were taking place in India's political firmament.

The next chapter goes on to further analyse the correlation between the changes taking place in the Indian political context and the changes in Gandhi's writings, and how the former impacted the latter. But before embarking upon the journey of analysing the subsequent shifts in Gandhi's writings concomitant to the changes in Indian politics, it is only fair to mention that in 1926, in the beginning of this period, when his son Manilal Gandhi expressed his desire to marry a Muslim girl, Gandhi had refused him permission. The reason for rejecting this marriage, he wrote to Manilal, was that 'your marriage will have a powerful impact on the Hindu–Muslim question. Inter communal marriages are no solution to this problem. You cannot forget nor will society forget that you are my son.'[120] Later, on 6 March 1927, Gandhi got Manilal married to Sushilabehn, the niece of Kishorilal Mashruvala (Gandhi's colleague at *Young India* and *Navajivan*), who belonged to a different sub-caste of his varna. When his other son, Devdas Gandhi, wanted to marry Lakshami, the daughter of C. Rajagopalachari, a high-caste Brahmin and a source of political support for Gandhi from Tamil Nadu, Gandhi asked them to wait for five years. And in 1932–3, Gandhi allowed Devdas to marry Lakshmi who belonged to a different varna. It is also in the same period, in 1931, that Gandhi wrote to Dudabhai, the biological father of Lakshmi (a Dalit girl adopted by Gandhi), expressing his desire to get her married to a boy who was not an untouchable.[121] When he got Lakshmi married to Marutidas, a south Indian, orphaned Brahmin boy, on 14 March 1933, Gandhi seemed to have broken all barriers of caste, varna, and untouchability.

Notes

1. M.K. Gandhi, 'Letter to Lalchand', 29 January 1921, in *CWMG*, Vol. 19, p. 291.
2. M.K. Gandhi, 'Introduction to "Varnavyavastha"', 23 September 1934, in *CWMG*, Vol. 59, p. 62.
3. Dennis Dalton writes, 'If Gandhi's approach to the reform of caste changed in the early 1930s from cautious reform to radical opposition, his attitude toward the institution of untouchability remained

consistent: he was always unequivocally against it.' See Dennis Dalton, *Nonviolence in Action: Gandhi's Power* (New Delhi: Oxford University Press, 2011), p. 53. B.R. Nanda writes, 'While Gandhi's opposition to untouchability was consistent and uncompromising, his attitude to the caste system—of which untouchability was a morbid growth—seemed to be marked by a certain ambivalence in the early years after his return from South Africa.' See Nanda, *Gandhi and His Critics*, p. 25. R.K. Srivastava writes:

> In the earlier schedule of stages which we examined in case of Gandhi's conception of caste, we were struck by opposing tendencies and how he integrated them at successive levels, qualified by the fundamentals of his conception. Such a framework would not be relevant in reviewing Gandhi's views on untouchability question. What strikes one most in a chronological survey of his campaign against untouchability is his consistency of formulation, tenacity of purpose, and an abiding concern for reconstituting Hindu social order.

See R.K. Srivastava, 'Gandhi and the Problem of Caste and Untouchability', in Verinder Grover (ed.), *Mohandas Karamchand Gandhi: A Biography of His Vision and Ideas* (New Delhi: Deep & Deep Publications, 1998), p. 438.

4. M.K. Gandhi, 'Duty of Bread Labour', 29 June 1935, in *CWMG*, Vol. 61 (New Delhi: Publications Division, Government of India, 1975), p. 212.

5. Tendulkar, *Mahatma, Vol. 1*, p. 177.

6. Rizwan Kadri, 'When Gandhiji Was Graceful in Both Victory & Defeat', *DNA*, 2 October 2011, available at http://www.dnaindia. com/india/1594174/report-when-gandhiji-was-graceful-in-both-victory-and-defeat (accessed on 5 June 2013).

7. Tendulkar, *Mahatma, Vol. 1*, p. 158.

8. M.K. Gandhi, 'Speech at War Conference', 28 April 1918, in *CWMG*, Vol. 14, p. 376.

9. Kakasaheb Kalelkar, *Stray Glimpses of Bapu* (Ahmedabad: Navajivan Publishing House, 1950), p. 10.

10. The Kumbh Mela, a fair held at Haridwar once every 12 years, fell in 1915.

11. V.S. Naipaul, *An Area of Darkness: His Discovery of India* (London: Picador, 1995), p. 75.

12. Gandhi, *An Autobiography*, p. 381.

13. For details, see Tendulkar, *Mahatma, Vol. 1*, pp. 169–75.

14. M.K. Gandhi, 'Letter to Narandas Gandhi', 16 September 1930, in *CWMG*, Vol. 44, p. 149.

15. Lelyveld, *Great Soul*, p. 150.

16. Gandhi, *An Autobiography*, pp. 359–60.

17. Gandhi, *An Autobiography*, p. 360.

18. Gandhi's writings on the caste system during this period also give a glimpse of his reflection on how to deal with the issue of caste. Nine months before his first statement in favour of caste and just three months after the admission of the untouchable family into the ashram on December 1915, while giving a speech at Bhavnagar, Gandhi said, 'I do not believe in castes [but] I am always in quest of truth. For the sake of truth I have abandoned many of my ideas and acquired new ones. I have never hesitated to give up the old and accept the new and will never hesitate as long as I live.' See M.K. Gandhi, 'A Talk, Bhavnagar', on or after 7 December 1915, in *CWMG*, Vol. 15, p. 79. Gandhi gave another speech on 5 June 1916 about the caste system in Ahmedabad. In this speech, he said, 'I have devoted much thought to the subject of the caste system and come to the conclusion that Hindu society cannot dispense with it.' See M.K. Gandhi, 'Speech on Caste System, Ahmedabad', 5 June 1916, in *CWMG*, Vol. 13, p. 277. In October 1916, Gandhi, in an article published in *Bharat Sevak*, a Marathi monthly, wrote, 'The caste system has struck such deep roots in India that I think it will be far more advisable to try to improve it, rather than uproot it.' See Gandhi, 'The Hindu Caste System', October 1916, p. 303.

19. M.K. Gandhi, 'Speech at Gurukul Anniversary', 20 March 1916, in *CWMG*, Vol. 13, p. 260.

20. Gandhi, 'The Hindu Caste System', October 1916, p. 301. There is one statement found before it in December 1915 where he says, 'I do not believe in castes.' See M.A. Gandhi, 'A Talk', 7 December 1915, in *CWMG*, Vol. 15, p. 79.

21. Sumit Sarkar, *Modern India: 1885–1947* (New Delhi: Macmillan, 1983), p. 195.

22. Gandhi, 'Letter to C.F. Andrews', 29 January 1921, p. 289.

23. Gandhi, 'Speech at Ahmedabad', 2 August 1931, p. 246.

24. M.K. Gandhi, 'Speech at Weavers' Meeting, Dohad', 31 August 1919, in *CWMG*, Vol. 16 (New Delhi: Publications Division, Government of India, 1965), p. 81; emphasis in original.

25. M.K. Gandhi, 'Speech at Social Conference, Godhra', 5 November 1917, in *CWMG*, Vol. 14, p. 72.

26. Gandhi, 'Speech at Weavers' Meeting, Dohad', 31 August 1919, pp. 81–2. In 1915, Gandhi wrote, 'The subject of physical contact [whether it is rightly prohibited] is a large one. I think we are committing a great sin in treating a whole class of people as untouchables and it is owing to the existence of this class that we have still some revolting practices among us. Not to eat in company with a particular person and not to touch him are two very different things. No one is an untouchable now. If we don't mind contact with a Christian or a Muslim, why should we mind it with one belonging to our own religion?' See M.K. Gandhi, 'Fragment of Letter to Mathuradas Trikumji', 26 July 1915, in *CWMG*, Vol. 13, p. 120.

27. M.K. Gandhi, 'Miscellaneous Issues', 30 May 1920, in *CWMG*, Vol. 17, p. 471.

28. M.K. Gandhi, 'Off the Rails', 25 January 1920, in *CWMG*, Vol. 16, p. 505. Gandhi also wrote, 'This movement [removal of untouchability] will not cause the system of *Varnashrama* to disappear. It aims at saving it by doing away with its excesses.' See M.K. Gandhi, 'A Stain on India's Forehead', 5 November 1917, in *CWMG*, Vol. 14, p. 76.

29. Gandhi, 'A Stain on India's Forehead', 5 November 1917, p. 73.

30. M.K. Gandhi, 'Preface to "Antyaj Stotra"', 17 April 1918, in *CWMG*, Vol. 14, p. 345.

31. Gandhi, 'Letter to C.F. Andrews', 25 May 1920, p. 534.

32. Gandhi, 'The Hindu Caste System', October 1916, p. 301.

33. Gandhi, 'The Caste System', 8 December 1920, p. 83.

34. M.K. Gandhi, 'Hindu–Mohammedan Unity', 25 February 1920, in *CWMG*, Vol. 17, p. 44.

35. Gandhi, 'The Hindu Caste System', October 1916, p. 302.

36. M.K. Gandhi, 'Speech at Khilafat Meeting, Banaras', 23 February 1920, in *CWMG*, Vol. 17, p. 41.

37. M.K. Gandhi, 'Letter to "The Indian Social Reformer"', 2 March 1919, in *CWMG*, Vol. 15, p. 123.

38. This is evident in the *Bombay Chronicle* report on the Ahmedabad Congress session, December 1921, that was titled 'Mahatma—The Dictator, Vested with All Congress Authority'. See http://www.mkgandhi.org/biography/nnviolnt.htm (accessed on 5 January 2017).

39. H.L. Polak, H.N. Brailsford, and Lord Pethick-Lawrence, *Mahatma Gandhi* (London: Odhams Press Ltd, 1949), pp. 141–2.

40. See Sarkar, *Modern India*, pp. 206–10.

41. B.R. Nanda, *In Gandhi's Footsteps: The Life and Times of Jamnalal Bajaj* (New Delhi: Oxford University Press, 2003), p. 57.

42. Sarkar, *Modern India*, p. 209.

43. M.K. Gandhi, 'Speech at Public Meeting, Godhra', 2 January 1925, in *CWMG*, Vol. 25, p. 536; emphasis added.

44. Sarkar, *Modern India*, p. 228.

45. Nanda, *In Gandhi's Footsteps*, p. 119.

46. M.K. Gandhi, 'More Difficulties', 24 November 1920, in *CWMG*, Vol. 19, p. 20.

47. M.K. Gandhi, 'Speech at Untouchability Conference, Belgaum', 22 January 1925, in *CWMG*, Vol. 25, p. 514.

48. M.K. Gandhi, 'Notes', 1 December 1921, in *CWMG*, Vol. 21, p. 509.

49. M.K. Gandhi, 'The Congress and After', 5 January 1922, in *CWMG*, Vol. 22 (New Delhi: Publications Division, Government of India, 1966), p. 136.

50. M.K. Gandhi, 'Bardoli's Decision', 30 January 1922, in *CWMG*, Vol. 22, p. 296.

51. M.K. Gandhi, 'Speech at Bardoli Taluka Conference', 29 January 1922, in *CWMG*, Vol. 22, p. 287.

52. M.K. Gandhi, 'Appeal to People of Bardoli', 5 February 1922, in *CWMG*, Vol. 22, p. 336.

53. Gandhi writes, 'The resolution, to the effect that the *Antyajas* cannot be excluded from any place which is open to members of other classes or communities, is not mine but that of the senate as a whole. I welcome the resolution. Had the senate not passed it, it would have been guilty of *adharma*.' See M.K. Gandhi, 'To "Vaishnavas"', 5 December 1920, in *CWMG*, Vol. 19, p. 73. At another place, Gandhi writes, 'An innocent resolution of the Gujarat Vidyapith has created a commotion in Ahmedabad, Bombay and elsewhere. The resolution is to the effect that no school which excludes Antyajas will be recognized.' See M.K. Gandhi, 'Conditions for Swaraj and Practice of Untouchability', 21 November 1920, *CWMG*, Vol. 19, p. 7.

54. M.K. Gandhi, 'Interview to "Deshabhimani"', 23 September 1921, in *CWMG*, Vol. 21, p. 186; emphasis added.

55. Gandhi, 'The Caste System', 8 December 1920, p. 84.

56. M.K. Gandhi, 'Who Is a "Sanatani" Hindu?', 6 February 1921, in *CWMG*, Vol. 19, p. 329.

57. Gandhi, 'Hinduism', 6 October 1921, p. 246.

58. Gandhi, 'The Caste System', 8 December 1920, p. 85.

59. Gandhi, 'Hinduism', 6 October 1921, p. 245.

60. M.K. Gandhi, 'Speech at "Antyaj" Conference, Nagpur', 25 December 1920, in *CWMG*, Vol. 19, p. 149.

61. Gandhi, 'Letter to C.F. Andrews', 29 January 1921, p. 289.

62. M.K. Gandhi, 'Speech at Marwari Agrawal Conference, Calcutta', 24 July 1925, in *CWMG*, Vol. 27, p. 412.

63. M.K. Gandhi, 'Speech at Meeting, Srirangam', 20 September 1921, in *CWMG*, Vol. 21, p. 157.

64. M.K. Gandhi, 'Speech at Public Meeting, Dindigul', 21 September 1921, in *CWMG*, Vol. 21, p. 160.

65. Gandhi, 'Speech at Bardoli Taluka Conference', 29 January 1922, p. 292; emphasis added. Viewed against his earlier statements and practice, this cannot be taken at face value as being truthful, but makes sense only if seen as a strategic attempt to persuade upper-caste Hindus that Hindu orthodoxy as such would not permit untouchability.

66. M.K. Gandhi, 'Untouchability', 21 August 1921, in *CWMG*, Vol. 21, p. 1. He also said, 'There is no such thing as a fifth caste in Hinduism. Untouchability is a sin against God and humanity.' See M.K. Gandhi, 'Speech to Labourers, Madras', 16 September 1921, in *CWMG*, Vol. 21, p. 132. 'The four *Varnas* do not regard one another's touch as defiling or sinful. We should treat *Antyajas* in the same way.' See M.K. Gandhi, 'My Notes', 20 April 1924, in *CWMG*, Vol. 23, p. 465. 'The removal of untouchability means the aboliton of the fifth caste.' See M.K. Gandhi, 'The Congress and After', 5 January 1922, p. 136. 'I recognize only four *varnas*. There is to me no fifth *varna* called the untouchables. See M.K. Gandhi, 'To Remove a Misgiving', 16 July 1925, in *CWMG*, Vol. 27, p. 284. 'Do your duty manfull and I undertake to show to you that this fifth class from Hinduism entirely eradicated.' See M.K. Gandhi, 'Speech in Reply to "Ezhavas" Address, Varkalai', 16 March 1925, in *CWMG*, Vol. 27, p. 299. 'There are four classes among the Hindus and I recognize no fifth one.' See M.K. Gandhi, 'Interview at Dinajpur', 23 May 1925, in *CWMG*, Vol. 27, p. 143. 'But I am not asking you to violate any social barriers as regards eating and drinking. I expect only one thing from you, namely, that you should not create a fifth caste. God has cast men in a fourfold structure of society. I can understand that; but please do not create a fifth caste of untouchables.' See M.K. Gandhi, 'Opening Speech at Kathiawar Political Conference, Bhavnagar', 18 January 1925, in *CWMG*, Vol. 25, p. 568.

67. M.K. Gandhi, 'The Canker of Superiority', 5 November 1925, in *CWMG*, Vol. 28, p. 436.

68. M.K. Gandhi, 'Difficulties in the Way', 21 August 1924, in *CWMG*, Vol. 25, p. 25.

69. Gandhi, 'The Caste System', 8 December 1920, pp. 83–4.

70. Gandhi, 'Hinduism', 6 October 1921, p. 246. 'The doctrine of caste cannot be extended. I would restrict it to four divisions. Any multiplication would be an evil.' See M.K. Gandhi, 'TO M.V.N.', 12 March 1925, in *CWMG*, Vol. 26, p. 289. '*Varnashrama* is useful, but a plethora of sub-castes can only do harm.' See M.K. Gandhi, 'My Notes', 11 May 1924, in *CWMG*, Vol. 24, p. 34. 'I believe in the

four castes only. It is necessary to merge the sub-castes. But that will take time.' See M.K. Gandhi, 'Infanticide of Girls', 13 July 1924, in *CWMG*, Vol. 24, p. 382.

71. M.K. Gandhi, 'Pertinent Questions', 5 February 1925, in *CWMG*, Vol. 26, p. 64.

72. M.K. Gandhi, 'Test', 13 November 1921', in *CWMG*, Vol. 21, p. 426.

73. M.K. Gandhi, 'My Notes', 17 July 1921, in *CWMG*, Vol. 20, p. 384. He also writes, 'Members of all the four castes should have the virtues of a Kshatriya, though in a Kshatriya they should be prominent and it is his business in life to cultivate them.' See M.K. Gandhi, 'My Notes', 1 May 1921, in *CWMG*, Vol. 20, p. 52. 'People of all the four castes and all religions should become Kshatriya enough to protect themselves.' See M.K. Gandhi, 'Understanding as Distinct from Literacy', 30 October 1912, in *CWMG*, Vol. 21, p. 268.

74. M.K. Gandhi, 'Invasion in the Name of Religion', 7 June 1925, in *CWMG*, Vol. 27, p. 208. Gandhi also writes:

There are only four castes, whether communities number four or forty thousand. The merger of sub-divisions in communities is something to be actually welcomed. Small social circles with rigid barriers have done great harm to Hinduism. Why should not a Vaisya try to enter into marriage alliance with another Vaisya in any part of the country? Why should a Brahmin of Gujarat not look for a son-in law or daughter-in-law in any Brahmin family of the same level of culture as his? If we lack the courage even for this reform, Hinduism will be in danger of becoming a religion of extremely narrow outlook. A Gujarati girl marrying in Bengal or a Bengali girl marrying in Gujarat is not altogether a calamity. If those who wish to preserve the division of society into four castes also try to preserve the present sub-divisions into communities, the former will disappear along with the latter, which are already disappearing. Today, even the division into four castes has lost its sanction. Thinking men and women ought to consider this problem. As a first step, if the various castes in Gujarat meet and decide to enlarge the boundaries of social intercourse within them, will not that be great progress? Can they not decide to merge the communities which form their sub-divisions? If the heads of these communities have no desire even to think over this problem, it is very necessary that individuals should take the lead.

See M.K. Gandhi, 'If Expelled from One's Community', 11 October 1925, in *CWMG*, Vol. 28, pp. 313–14.

75. In the same speech, he also says, 'I cannot recommend wholesale abolition of these restrictions to the public, even at the risk of being charged with hypocrisy and inconsistency.' See M.K. Gandhi, 'Speech at Untouchability Conference, Belgaum', 27 December 1924, in *CWMG*, Vol. 25, p. 513.

76. Gandhi, 'Interview to "Deshabhimani"', 23 September 1921, p. 187.

77. Gandhi, 'Who is a "Sanatani" Hindu?', 6 February 1921, p. 330.

78. Gandhi, 'Hinduism', 6 October 1921, pp. 246–7.

79. Gandhi writes:

> Though therefore *varnashrama* is not affected by inter-dining or inter-marriage, Hinduism does most emphatically discourage inter-dining and inter-marriage between divisions. Hinduism reached the highest limit of self-restraint. It is undoubtedly a religion of renunciation of tile flesh so that the spirit may be set free. It is no part of a Hindu's duty to dine with his son. And by restricting his choice of a bride to a particular group, he exercises rare self-restraint.'

> See Gandhi, 'Hinduism', 6 October 1921, p. 247. 'Restrictions about marriage and inter-dining may be undesirable and may require modification. But I do not regard them as a blot upon Hinduism, as I do untouchability. The latter puts a class of human beings beyond the pale of social service and therefore is an inhuman institution.' See M.K. Gandhi, 'Notes', 1 December 1921, in *CWMG*, Vol. 21, p. 507.

80. Jaffrelot, *Analysing and Fighting Caste*, p. 50.

81. Sarkar, *Modern India*, p. 262.

82. M.K. Gandhi, 'Letter to Arthur Moore', 10 June 1928, in *CWMG*, Vol. 36 (New Delhi: Publications Division, Government of India, 1970), p. 391.

83. Brown, *Gandhi*, p. 219.

84. M.K. Gandhi, 'Third-class Travelling', 14 February 1929, in *CWMG*, Vol. 39 (New Delhi: Publications Division, Government of India, 1970), p. 437.

85. M.K. Gandhi, 'Speech at Bardoli', 12 August 1928, in *CWMG*, Vol. 37, p. 165.

86. M.K. Gandhi, 'A National Defect', 25 April 1929, in *CWMG*, Vol. 40 (New Delhi: Publications Division, Government of India, 1970), p. 283.

87. M.K. Gandhi, 'Definite Suggestions', 26 December 1929, in *CWMG*,Vol. 42, p. 316.

88. M.K. Gandhi, 'Remember 6th April', 3 April 1930, in *CWMG*, Vol. 43 (New Delhi: Publications Division, Government of India, 1971), p. 171.

89. Adams, *Gandhi*, p. 190.

90. Brown, *Gandhi*, p. 239.

91. M.K. Gandhi, 'Notes', 6 January 1927, in *CWMG*,Vol. 32, pp. 515–16. Gandhi writes, 'They have either to leave Hinduism or to make good the claim that untouchability is no part of it but that it is an excrescence to be rooted out.' See M.K. Gandhi, 'Untouchability', 17 April 1930, in *CWMG*, Vol. 46, p. 266.

92. Gandhi, 'Untouchability', 17 April 1930, p. 264. Gandhi also writes, 'The fact is that the foundations of swaraj are being laid by those who regard communal unity, equality of rights and opportunity and removal of untouchability as articles of faith.' See Gandhi, 'Untouchability', 17 April 1930, p. 265. 'I believe that unity between Hindus, Mussalmans, Sikhs, Parsis, Jews, Christians and others is essential for the attainment of swaraj. I believe the removal of untouchability to be equally essential for our purpose.' See M.K. Gandhi, 'My Limitations', 12 September 1929, in *CWMG*, Vol. 41 (New Delhi: Publications Division, Government of India, 1970), p. 378. 'For the fulfilment of this object to conduct the *Navajivan,* through it to carry on propaganda for peaceful attainment of swaraj; and particularly (a) to propagate the spinning-wheel and khadi; (b) to propagate for the removal of untouchability; (c) to propagate for unity between the Hindus and Mussalmans and the various communities who have settled in India.' See M.K. Gandhi, 'Declaration of Trust', in *CWMG*, 1 December 1929, Vol. 42, pp. 211–12.

93. M.K. Gandhi, 'Speech at Public Meeting, Tinnevelly', 7 October 1927, in *CWMG*, Vol. 35, p. 95.

94. M.K. Gandhi, 'Speech at Public Meeting, Rajapalayam', 4 October 1927, in *CWMG*, Vol. 35, p. 82.

95. M.K. Gandhi, 'Committee for Removal of Untouchability', 2 June 1929, in *CWMG*, Vol. 41 (New Delhi: Publications Division, Government of India, 1970), p. 3.

96. Gandhi writes:

Sjt. Jamnalalji in his capacity as Hon. Secretary, Anti-untouchability committee of the Indian National Congress, has addressed the following forcible appeal to the trustees of public Hindu temples…. It is to be hoped that the Hindu public will support these appeals by calling meetings and otherwise. Perhaps the most effective way is to organize local meetings in places where there are important temples and take deputations to the trustees. After all they are not owners, but agents of the public, and if the public demand freedom of entry for the "untouchables" into a particular temple, the trustees concerned have to carry out their desire irrespective of their own opinions.

See M.K. Gandhi, 'Appeal to Temple Trustees', 9 September 1929, in *CWMG*, Vol. 41, p. 349.

97. Gandhi writes: 'Sjt. Jamnalalji, the Secretary of the Congress Anti-untouchability Committee, has succeeded in having the famous Dattatreya temple of Elichpur, the former capital of Berar, thrown open to the so-called untouchables.' See M.K. Gandhi, 'Notes', 29 August 1929, in *CWMG*, Vol. 41, p. 335. Gandhi further writes: 'I have therefore just read with great joy the news that Ramchandra temple in Bombay has been thrown open to the suppressed classes by Sjt. Thakordas Nanabhai, a trustee of the temple. I hope that there will be no relaxation in the effort initiated in Bombay.' See M.K. Gandhi, 'Temples for "Untouchables"', 28 November 1929, in *CWMG*, Vol. 42, p. 223. He also wrote:

This delusion of untouchability has assumed monstrous and terrible proportion among the Hindus. Shri Jamnalal is striving hard to eradicate it. His success in getting the temples thrown open to the untouchables is no mean achievement. Events like the opening of the eight temples to the untouchables at Jabalpur and the participation of distinguished citizens, etc., are quite hopeful signs. The best way to remove this delusion of untouchability is that those who have overcome it should by their actions convince others still laboring under it that untouchability has no connection with religion.

See M.K. Gandhi, 'Our Delusion', 5 December 1929, in *CWMG*, Vol. 42, p. 243.

98. See M.K. Gandhi, 'Khaddar and Untouchability: Duty of Indian Municipalities Camp Hardoi', 12 October 1929, in *CWMG*, Vol. 41, pp. 548–50.

99. For example, in one of his speech, he says, 'Schools and temples must be thrown open to them and they should be allowed to draw water from the wells.' See M.K. Gandhi, 'Speech at Public Meeting, Banaras', 26 September 1929, in *CWMG*, Vol. 41, p. 478.

100. M.K. Gandhi. 'Letter to W.H. Pitt', 19 August 1928, in *CWMG*, Vol. 37, p. 189.

101. M.K. Gandhi, 'What Should the Antyajas Do?', 24 March 1929, in *CWMG*, Vol. 40, p. 176.

102. M.K. Gandhi, 'Speech at Minorities Committee Meeting', 8 October 1931, in *CWMG*, Vol. 48 (New Delhi: Publications Division, Government of India, 1971), p. 119. Gandhi writes: 'Whilst there is no doubt that public opinion against untouchability has been strengthening day by day, public action still remains weak.' See M.K. Gandhi, 'Remember the Untouchables', 5 April 1928, in *CWMG*, Vol. 36, p. 184. He writes: 'The untouchability question in Travancore is still hanging fire. But untouchability, it is undoubtedly going steadily though ever so slow.' See M.K. Gandhi, 'Letter to W.H. Pitt', 26 October 1928, in *CWMG*, Vol. 37, p. 401. Another statement by him is: 'And so while I deplore occurrences such as happened at Tanuku, the fact cannot be gainsaid that untouchability is fast dying of exhaustion.' See M.K. Gandhi, 'Untouchability', 16 May 1929, in *CWMG*, Vol. 40, p. 382.

103. M.K. Gandhi, 'Speech at Villagers' Meeting Pudupalayam', 21 March 1925, in *CWMG*, Vol. 26, p. 349.

104. Gandhi, 'Speech at Public Meeting, Rajapalayam', 4 October 1927, p. 81.

105. Gandhi, 'Brahmin–Non-Brahmin Question', 24 November 1927, p. 519.

106. He writes: 'I do not believe in caste as it is at present constituted.' See M.K. Gandhi, 'A Student's Questions', 25 February 1926, in *CWMG*, Vol. 30 (New Delhi: Publications Division, Government of India, 1968), p. 47.

107. Gandhi writes, 'There is nothing in common between *varnashrama* and caste.' See M.K. Gandhi, 'Speech at Trivandrum', 10 October 1927, in *CWMG*, Vol. 35, pp. 106–7. Gandhi also writes: '*Varna* considered in the manner above indicated has nothing in common with caste as we know it today.' See M.K. Gandhi, 'Varnashrama and its Distortion', 17 November 1927, in *CWMG*, Vol. 35, p. 261. 'Thus conceded, varnashrama dharma has nothing in common with castes as we know them today.' See M.K. Gandhi, 'Speech at Public Meeting, Coimbatore', 16 October 1927, in *CWMG*, Vol. 35, p. 152. 'There is not even a trace of castes in the *varnadharma*.' See M.K. Gandhi, 'Speech at Morvi', 24 January 1928, in *CWMG*, Vol. 35, p. 487. 'In the first place, varnashrama has nothing to do with untouchability or with castes as we know them today.' See M.K. Gandhi, 'The Thousand-headed Monster', 3 October 1929, in *CWMG*, Vol. 41, p. 495. 'I do believe in varnashrama—a totally different institution from the modern castes.' See M.K. Gandhi, 'Letter to R. Sankaranarayana Iyer', 24 December 1932, in *CWMG*, Vol. 52 (New Delhi: Publications Division, Government of India, 1972), p. 277.

108. Gandhi writes: 'In the true Shastras there is no reference to castes; there is a reference only to the four *varnas,* God has washed his hands off after creating these four *varnas.*' See Gandhi, 'Speech at Morvi', 24 January 1928, p. 487.

109. Gandhi, 'A Few Questions', 20 July 1929, p. 69.

110. Gandhi, 'Speech to Ceylon Hindus, Jaffna', 27 November 1927, p. 336.

111. Gandhi, 'Khaddar and Untouchability: Duty of Indian Municipalities Camp Hardoi', 12 October 1929, p. 549.

112. B.R. Ambedkar, 'Annihilation of Caste with a Reply to Mahatma Gandhi', in *Selected Works of Dr BR Ambedkar*, p. 142, available at http://drambedkarbooks.wordpress.com (accessed on 14 June 2013).

113. Gandhi, *The Good Boatman,* p. 237.

114. M.K. Gandhi, 'Hardship Suffered by a Worker Serving "Antyajas"',
4 April 1926, in *CWMG,*Vol. 30, p. 312.

115. Gandhi writes:

> Jamna believes that you now wish to get married or are willing to consider
> a proposal.... If I am to choose for you, tell me whether you wish to respect
> the restrictions of caste or Province.You know my own views in the matter.
> We wish to do away with such restrictions but in a matter like marriage I
> would certainly not insist on my own ideas being followed.

See M.K. Gandhi, 'Letter to Purushottam Gandhi', 23 August 1931,
in *CWMG*, Vol. 47, p. 354.

116. Gandhi writes, 'We must encourage, within certain limits, inter-
provincial marriages. I would regard it as essential that the husband
and the wife should learn each other's language.' See M.K. Gandhi,
'Letter to Chhaganlal Joshi', 14 October 1929, in *CWMG*, Vol. 41,
p. 562. On the day of Shankarlal Agrawal and Umiya's marriage at
the ashram, Gandhi says, 'In this marriage we have gone one step
further. In Manilal's marriage we broke the caste barrier; in this
we blast the provincial prejudices. From Gujarat we have come to
Mewar. This is a good sign.' See M.K. Gandhi, 'Speech at Prayer
Meeting, Sabarmati Ashram', 4 December 1929, in *CWMG*, Vol. 42,
p. 236.

117. Gandhi, 'Speech at Morvi', 24 January 1928, p. 488.

118. Gandhi writes:

> When Hindus were seized with inertia, abuse of *Varna* resulted in innumer-
> able castes with unnecessary and harmful restrictions as to intermarriage
> and interdining. The law of *Varna* has nothing to do with these restrictions.
> People of different varnas may intermarry and interdine. These restrictions
> may be necessary in the interest of chastity and hygiene. But a Brahmin
> who marries a Sudra girl or *vice versa* commits no offence against the law
> of varna.

See M.K. Gandhi, 'Caste and Communal Question', 6 June 1931, in
CWMG, Vol. 46, p. 303. Gandhi also writes, 'We now insist that the
Ashram will not help to arrange a marriage between members of

the same subcaste, and everyone is encouraged to seek his mate out-side his own subcaste.' See M.K. Gandhi, 'History of the Satyagraha Ashram', 11 July 1932, in *CWMG*, Vol. 50, p. 213.

119. Gandhi writes, '... I advocate inter-caste marriages because I desire the disappearance of sub-castes.' See M.K. Gandhi, 'A Letter', 24 May 1932, in *CWMG*, Vol. 49 (New Delhi: Publications Division, Government of India, 1972), p. 478.

120. M.K. Gandhi, 'Letter to Manilal Gandhi', 3 April 1926, in *CWMG*, Vol. 30, p. 229.

121. Gandhi writes, 'I have decided to give Lakshmi in marriage to a non-Antyaja. It seems necessary to me to do that. Let me know what you think in the matter. It will do if you send your reply to the Ashram.' See M.K. Gandhi, 'Letter to Dudabhai', 18 May 1931, p. 170.

Gandhi's evolving strategy to abolish the caste system: Part II

4

Maybe you are not acquainted with my views as they have progressed. *They were of course implicit in all my writings but of late they have become more explicit....* What I believe is that if we want to preserve whatever is good in varnashrama every Hindu has to become not only a Shudra but an atishudra, and regard himself as such. And as a true indication of it marriages should really take place only between atishudras and the so-called other varnas.

—M.K. Gandhi[1]

As mentioned earlier, this and the previous chapter together aim to give an account of how Gandhi's strategy to abolish the caste system evolved. The previous chapter identifies and analyses the various changes that occurred in Gandhi's attitude towards the caste system and in his writings on the subject. It chronologically studies them under three different time spans, starting from 1915 and going up to 1932. It argues that the changes that occurred in the attitude and writings of Gandhi were indeed strategic developments meant to direct his struggle against the caste system to its logical end. This chapter undertakes a chronological analysis of the changes occurring in the attitude and writings of Gandhi from 1932 to his death in 1948.

This chapter is divided into various sections. There is a section that deals with the period '1932–45' and another that deals with '1945–8'. As with the previous chapter, each of the sections contains two subsections. The first subsection deals with the historical background, highlighting some of the major changes occurring in Indian politics during the period under review. Exposition and analysis of the historical events during each of these periods reveal how the prevailing political scenarios paved the path for the changes that occurred in Gandhi's writings. The second subsection, in each of the period under review, deals with the different themes that appear in Gandhi's writings on issues like caste, varna, untouchability, inter-dining, and inter-caste marriage. An attempt is also made to show the consistency in and strategic relations between Gandhi's differing views on the aforementioned issues during the identified time periods. There is also a section in this chapter, titled 'Overview of Gandhi's Strategy', that reflects on Gandhi's long-term strategy against the caste system. It tries to explain how Gandhi's evolving strategy in its entirety worked to undermine the existing caste system.

However, before all this, an effort must be made to understand a landmark event in Gandhi's struggle against the caste system. This was his 1932 fast against the MacDonald Communal Award that assured separate electorates for untouchables. Many scholars have identified this as an important event not only in Gandhi's struggle against the caste system but also in the Dalit movement. Jad Adams writes that the fast marked the turning point for Gandhi's struggle against untouchability.[2] Therefore, it seems only appropriate to delve deeper into the significance of this event before analysing how it critically affected the attitude and writings of Gandhi on caste and related issues and, subsequently, his whole strategy.

Gandhi's Fast against Separate Electorates
(MacDonald Communal Award) for Depressed Classes[3]

In India, it was the Muslim community that was first given separate electorates by the British government through the Indian Councils Act 1909, commonly known as the Morley–Minto Reforms. From 1919 onwards, many untouchable leaders including Ambedkar had been time and again demanding either reservation or separate electorates for the untouchables.[4] Ultimately, the Simon Commission, in its report, suggested that the depressed classes must be granted reserved seats. However, its recommendations could not be implemented as the Congress had taken no part in its drafting. To resolve the problem, the British government announced the Round Table conferences that were to be held in London. The First Round Table Conference, in 1930, was attended by representatives of Muslims, Sikhs, Christians, untouchables, and the Hindu Mahasabha, along with many other participants. Again, this conference could not produce any results as it was boycotted by the Congress. However, in 1931, Gandhi participated as the sole representative of the Congress in the Second Round Table Conference organized by the British government to discuss constitutional reforms in India. The conference, starting in September and going up to November, was held in London. At the conference, Ambedkar supported separate electorates or reserved seats for untouchables, while Gandhi opposed both for them, though he accepted this arrangement for Muslims and Sikhs. The two leaders failed to find any common ground and this conference, too, ended inconclusively. In the end, the representatives, including Gandhi, left the matter of separate electorates for untouchables to the British prime minister to decide.

Consequently, on 17 August 1932, the British prime minister Ramsay MacDonald announced separate electorates for untouchables and some other minority groups in India. Gandhi decided to go on a fast unto death to oppose the government's move. The

British government made it clear that though it was not going to change its decision, it would, however, accept any suitable changes that were agreed to by both the caste Hindu and the untouchable leaders. Gandhi's fast began inside the Yerwada prison in Poona on 20 September 1932. The next day, Gandhi outlined, in an interview, his immediate reform expectations to caste Hindus and his position on the matter to Ambedkar. He said:

> If I had my way I would insist on temple-entry and the like being included in any pact that may be concluded. I would invite all reformers and the untouchables to do so.... I would accept any pact that has not a tinge of separate electorate about it. I would, with utmost reluctance, tolerate reservation of seats under a joint electorate scheme. But I should insist on what is to me that vital part of the pact, the social and religious reform.[5]

Both the upper-caste Hindu leaders and Ambedkar responded positively in their own way. Sympathetic Gandhi biographers, like Louis Fisher, B.R. Nanda, Tendulkar, and Ravinder Kumar, say that his fast led to a spontaneous upsurge of feeling among the caste Hindus. These scholars feel that in response to Gandhi's fast, many upper-caste Hindus began to fraternize with the untouchables in the streets, and the doors of Ram Mandir in Banares and Kalighat Temple in Calcutta, which represented the centres of Hindu ortho-doxy, were thrown open to the untouchables.[6] This was besides the opening up of many other temples all over the country. They also write that during this time, at many places throughout the country, untouchables and Brahmins ate together at public places.

The caste Hindu leaders convened a conference in Bombay to show commitment towards Gandhi's movement for removal of untouchability, which was presided over by Pandit Madan Mohan Malaviya. At this conference, where Ambedkar was in attendance too, a resolution was passed. It said: 'No Hindu should be regarded as untouchable because of his birth, and that all those who had once been untouchables would now have equal access with other Hindus to all public institutions, including wells, roads, and schools.'[7] Some important Congressmen who were caste Hindus, like Sapru, Jayakar, and Birla, visited Poona to discuss with Ambedkar the terms of a new electoral arrangement for the untouchables in place of separate electorates.

In the beginning, Ambedkar took a tough stand and questioned Gandhi's intent to fast unto death. He argued that when Gandhi did not go on such a fast to oppose the British and press for independence or to protest Muslims being given separate electorates, why was he doing it now to deprive the depressed classes of a benefit they were getting from the government? He, more than anyone else, knew the importance of constitutional safeguards to the untouchables for advancement of their social, economic, and political life, and he, by no means, would be a part of any agreement that would deprive the untouchables a life-saving protection. However, he also understood very well that Gandhi's fast had made it almost impossible for him to continue pressing for a separate electorate. Later he expressed his difficulty in the following words:

> No man was placed in a greater and graver dilemma than I was then. It was a baffling situation. I had to make a choice between two different alternatives. There was before me the duty, which I owed as a part of common humanity, to save Gandhi from sure death. There was before me the problem of saving for the Untouchables the political rights which the Prime Minister had given them.[8]

He understood, perhaps correctly, that he was left with a little or no choice at all, and an agreement of some sort was unavoidable. However, he was not such a man who would let things go out of his hand that easily. He vigorously debated with Gandhi and other upper-caste Hindu leaders for the rights of his people and pressurized them to agree to an arrangement that would provide enough space to give the untouchables real political force. He made Gandhi and other upper-caste leaders accept a system which is known as 'reserved seats in joint electorates'. Under such an arrangement, a two-tier system of voting would allow the untouchables, first, to select a panel of four untouchable candidates and then the general constituency (including caste Hindus) would select one among them. Following this, Ambedkar took up the issue of number of seats, because what the Communal Award by the British government offered was small in proportion to the untouchable population. Therefore, Ambedkar demanded more reserved seats for untouchables in the centre than what the government had given them through the Communal Award. First, Ambedkar demanded 197 reserved seats in place of 78 that the award gave, but finally the number was settled at 148 seats, which 'were nearly equivalent to their proportion in the population'.[9]

The issue that created a deadlock in the negotiation was the duration of the award. Ambedkar wanted that seats should be reserved for 25 years, and for longer if a referendum after 25 years showed that the untouchables wished to retain them. However, Gandhi wanted referendum on the question in five years, for which Ambedkar did not agree. After long discussions, Gandhi said, '[F]ive years or my life.'[10] Ambedkar said he could not agree to anything less than 10 years. Finally, it was Rajaji (Chakravarti Rajagopalachari) who saved the negotiation; he proposed that the duration of the award may be decided by mutual agreement in future, which was accepted by both Gandhi and Ambedkar. Ultimately, the new electoral arrangement—'148 reserved seats in joint electorates' in place of '78 sets of separate electorates'—was accepted and signed by Ambedkar, other untouchable leaders, and caste Hindu leaders. This new electoral arrangement, which came to be known as the Poona Pact, was also accepted by the British government. Gandhi ended his fast against the MacDonald Communal Award on 26 September 1932.

While referring to the Poona Pact, Dhananjay Keer, in his biography of Ambedkar, writes, 'So effective and crushing was the victory of Gandhi that he deprived Ambedkar of all the life-saving weapons and made him a powerless man as did Indra in the case of Karna.'[11] And Kanshi Ram, in his small tract *The Chamcha Age: The Era of Sycophants* writes, '*Poona Pact made dalits helpless. By rejecting separate electorate, dalits were deprived of their genuine representation in legislatures. Several and various kind of chamchas were born in the last fifty years.*'[12] If such are the consequences of Poona Pact, how can Gandhi's act to fast unto death be justified from the untouchables' perspective? Many sympathetic Gandhian scholars often justify it by evoking an idea of Hindu unity or national unity; they argue that Gandhi's concern was the unity of Hindus or 'Indian' during the struggle for political independence. For them, Gandhi believed that separate electorate would destroy the much-needed unity among Hindus or Indian nation. For untouchables and Dalit scholars, such justification has no value at all. They argue, 'Gandhi who feared a political division ... ignored the division that already existed.'[13] Moreover, for them the real issue was upper-caste Hindus' monopoly over economic, social, and political power, and not as such the unity of Hindus or nation. They argue that Gandhi's aim was to deprive the untouchables of the little they had got through the Communal Award of 1932, thereby maintaining the monopoly of upper-caste Hindus over economic and social power. Consequently, scholars who accept that Gandhi had risked his life to save the unity of 'nation' or Hindu community glorify Gandhi's fast as a 'second crucifixion'[14] or 'epic fast',[15] and scholars who accept that Gandhi's fast had deprived the untouchables their vital interests equally decry Gandhi as 'unfair',[16] the 'biggest enemy'[17] of untouchables, and so on. However, from the works of these scholars, it appears that in the rush to glorify or vilify Gandhi and his fast, most of them forget to examine the other arugment. Therefore, let us first examine the justifications before rejecting or accepting any one of them as the appropriate explanation of Gandhi's motive to fast unto death against the MacDonald Communal Award.

Dalit scholars' main argument is that the Poona Pact deprives the untouchables of an opportunity to select their own genuine representatives, thereby constituting themselves into a real political force. The basic assumption of their argument is that the difference between a separate electorate and reserved seats in joint electorate is of kind and not degree. It means they believe that a separate electorate has potential enough for the untouchables to constitute their own separate political identity, thereby transforming themselves into a real political force. On the other hand, reserved seats in joint electorate or reserved seats leave no space for them to construct their own separate political identity and thereby transform into a real political force. However, while explaining the consequences of separate electorate in relation with Muslims, Bipan Chandra reminds us that there is not much difference between both systems and they produce similar consequences. He writes that in a separate electorate, the voters were exclusively the followers of one religion or community and the candidates did not have to appeal to voters belonging to other groups. They could, therefore, make blatantly communal appeals and voters as well as others who listened to these appeals were gradually trained to think and vote communally and express their socio-economic grievances in communal terms. 'The system of reservation of seats and weightage in legislatures ...' Chandra adds, 'also had the *same consequences*.'[18]

If we look at the history of constitutional safeguards for the untouchables in India in terms of difference between 'separate electorate' or 'reservation of seats', it appears that there was not any period of time when separate electorate and reserved seats in joint electorate were considered as two entirely different kinds of system that produce entirely different consequences, that is, one (separate electorate) could help the minority in constituting themselves into a real political force and the other (reserved seats or reserved seats in joint electorate) would wipe out such a possibility bringing great dangers for the minority. Even Ambedkar, starting from 1919 until his death, saw both the options as equally valid and explained differences between both only in terms of degree. In 1919, in his testimony to the Southborough Committee, the body which had been entrusted with redefining electoral franchise within the framework of the constitutional reform, Ambedkar recommended 'either to reserve seats ... for those minorities that cannot, otherwise, secure personal representation or grant communal electorates'.[19] In 1928, whereas 16 out of 18 untouchable organizations consulted by the Simon Commission in Bombay Presidency had clearly expressed themselves in favour of separate electorates,[20] Ambedkar argued in favour of granting universal franchise and a quota of seats for the untouchables rather than of separate electorates. Later, during his speech before a delegation of the Simon Commission at Poona (now Pune), he explained that in case universal suffrage was not being granted for the untouchables, he would campaign for separate electorates.[21] Ambedkar justified his demand for reserved seats in place of a separate electorate in the following words:

> With separate electorates the minority gets its own quota of representation and no more. The rest of the house owes no allegiance to it and is therefore not influenced by the desire to meet the wishes of the minority. The minority is thus thrown on its own resources and as no system of representation can convert a minority into majority, it is bound to be overwhelmed. On the other hand, under a system of joint electorates and reserved seats the minority not only gets its quota of representation but something more. For, every member of the majority who has partly succeeded on the strength of the voters of the minority if not a member of the minority will certainly be a member for the minority.[22]

In the Nagpur Conference of Depressed Classes in 1930, just before leaving for the First Round Table Conference, Ambedkar stated publicly that he would be satisfied with reserved seats as long as there was adult suffrage.[23] And in the first round of the conference, Ambedkar spoke 'for a unitary state and adult suffrage with reserved seats and safeguards for untouchables'.[24] Some Dalit scholars remind us that it was only during the Second Round Table Conference that Ambedkar strongly favoured a separate electorate: 'perhaps because Gandhi would not even concede that reserved seats for Untouchables were necessary, Ambedkar came out strongly for separate electorates for the Depressed Classes....'[25] However, in the Second Round Table Conference also, while bitterly clashing with Gandhi, Ambedkar did not completely reject the possibility of joint electorate with reserved seats for the untouchables.[26] Even 13 years after the Poona Pact, when Ambedkar reflected on the incident in his great work *What Congress and Gandhi Have Done to the Untouchables*, it was with a sense of regret. And though he acknowledged that there was no gain in Poona Pact for the untouchables, he did not seem to argue that a separate electorate could have converted the untouchables into a political force. He considered the latter as being relatively better. He wrote, 'The Untouchables were worse off under the Poona Pact than they would have been under the Prime Minister's Award.'[27]

Moreover, though it is a fact that in a separate electorate, the minority community (that is, the untouchables) gets a greater opportunity to select its own genuine representatives, it may be erroneous to think that this by itself generates the opportunity for them to become a great political force in a parliamentary democracy. Just by the virtue of being able to elect genuine representatives by themselves, a minority community cannot assure greater benefits for themselves in a parliamentary democratic system; greater benefits in such a system can be assured if they are in a position to either form their government, or participate in it, or have powerful control over it. Since there is, typically, no way a separate electorate could turn the minority community into a majority, to form their own government, the only way left for them is a kind of coalition government, for which they have to depend on the support of other political parties. It is needless to say that other political parties would form coalitions with such individuals or parties of a minority community only if they can control them easily. It means that if reserved seats in a joint electorate had produced many chamchas, separate electorates would not have produced much greater consequences. Therefore, the Dalit scholars' claim that Gandhi's fast deprived them a life-saving instrument for transforming themselves into a political force seems problematic. And it may not be appropriate to say that *only* a separate electorate has potential enough to constitute the untouchables into a real political force, whereas a joint electorate with reserved seats would completely terminate such a possibility. From the given discussion, it appears that both the systems are helpful in making minority groups think of their socio-economic problems in communal terms. However, both the systems are weak enough to turn minority representatives (that is, the untouchables) into chamchas and the difference between both is only of degree and not of kind.

Let us now examine the validity of Gandhian scholars' claim. Most of the sympathetic Gandhian scholars argue that Gandhi went on a fast to save the unity of nation or Hindus. Their argument is based on the assumption that the system of a separate electorate for untouchables alone was/is harmful for the unity of 'nation' or Hindus. However, if we look at the history, it appears that during the 1920s and early 1930s, a separate electorate for untouchables was not considered such a great threat to the unity of nation or Hindu society by any community, though since the beginning 'any kind of separate representation' for any minority was criticized by Hindu nationalists as being supportive of the British policy of divide and rule. Sardar Patel, Jawaharlal Nehru, and other prominent Congress leaders also did not perceive separate electorates as such a dangerous thing. On the other hand, far from seeing a separate electorate of the untouchables as dangerous for the unity of nation or Hindus, Nehru saw Gandhi's fast as a diversion from the goal of political independence of India. Reacting from the Dehradun Jail, Nehru expressed his great annoyance with Gandhi

> ... for choosing a side-issue for his final sacrifice—just a question of electorate. What would be the result on our freedom movement? Would not the larger issues fade into the background, for the time being at least? ... And was not his action a recognition, and in part an acceptance, of the Communal Award.... After so much sacrifice and brave endeavour, was our movement to tail off into something insignificant.[28]

Many other leaders also felt the same. For instance, E.M.S. Namboodiripad, a Marxist leader, saw it not simply as a diversion from the goal of political independence of India, but as a great blow to India's struggle for political independence. He wrote, 'However, this [Gandhi's fast] was a great blow to the freedom movement. For this led to the diversion of the people's attention from the objective of full independence to the mundane cause of the upliftment of the Harijans.'[29]

Even the Hindu Mahasabha, which claimed to be a custodian of Hindu interests, did not believe that a separate electorate necessarily divides Hindu society. As Dr B.S. Moonje, the then president of the Hindu Mahashaba, explained, separate electorates did not necessarily mean that the untouchables constituted non-Hindu communities; in fact, the Mahasabha saw them similar to Sikhs who were considered Hindus but had been granted separate electorates.[30] If we accept Ambedkar's testimony, Dr Moonje, in the speeches he had been delivering since his arrival in India from the Second Round Table Conference, was insisting that the Communal Award did not create any separation between the depressed classes and the Hindus.[31] Even Gandhi, in 1925, expressed his agreement with a correspondent who said, 'The untouchables have even stronger case than the Mussalmans for separate representation.'[32]

Moreover, when Gandhi accepted, 'with utmost reluctance',[33] reserved seats in joint electorate, it means that he had already accepted the separate status of the untouchables and that he recognized them as an oppressed minority. It looks only absurd to say that he fasted to save the unity of nation or Hindus. Therefore, the interpretation of Gandhian scholars that Gandhi risked his life to save the unity of nation or Hindus seems to be problematic, because there are no good reasons to accept why only a separate electorate poses such a great threat to the unity of Hindus or nation, whereas reserved seats in a joint electorate abolish any such possibility.

Let us now look at the whole episode a little closely. During the Second Round Table Conference, Gandhi said that 'it will create a division in Hinduism' and 'I cannot possibly tolerate what is in store for Hinduism if there are two divisions set forth in the villages'.[34] And he vehemently added, 'I want to say with all the emphasis that I can command that if I was the only person to resist this thing I would resist it with my life.'[35] He was not referring to separate electorate alone; he was referring to any kind of special arrangements or any kind of separate political representation for the untouchables, that is, a separate electorate, a joint electorate with reserved seats, or reserved seats. And if Gandhi had gone on a fast to deny any kind of special arrangements or any kind of separate political representation for the untouchables, then both Dalit and Gandhian scholars' explanations can be better justified. Denial of any kind of political representation must have ruined all possibility of converting the untouchables into a political force, and if Gandhi would have fasted against it (any kind of separate political representation for the untouchables) it would have some sense to say that he put his life in danger to save the unity of Hindus, if not national unity. Gandhi, however, did not fast to deny all kind of separate political representation to the untouchables. Therefore, the justification seems to be problematic.

If the whole episode is analysed purely from the point of political calculation, it makes no sense as to why Gandhi decided to risk his life for something that would yield nothing but some minor relative benefits either to upper-caste Hindus or to the untouchables. Ambedkar was also surprised and said that if the Mahatma had agreed for a joint electorate in reserved seats at the Second Round Table Conference, 'it would not have been necessary for him [Gandhiji] to go through "this ordeal".'[36] Dhananjay Keer agrees with Ambedkar and argues that 'Ambedkar was justified in saying that had Gandhi shown enough resilience at the Round Table Conference in the matter of the problem of the Depressed Classes, the Mahatma would not have been required to go through the ordeal'.[37] However, it still remains unanswered that why Gandhi decided to go through the ordeal deliberately.

There can be many answers to the question, and one of them, according to Judith Brown, is that 'Willingdon and the Bombay government thought it was designed to revive the failing civil disobedience movement and reassert Gandhi's political authority'.[38] There was another issue too. It seems that Gandhi could understand the growing political status of Ambedkar and his growing influence on the untouchables. He might have seen this as a threat to his well-established and long-standing position of an all-India leader, which is why he took the MacDonald Award as an opportunity to reassert his political position as an all-India leader.

Joseph Lelyveld suggests another possible answer to the question. He writes, 'The fight against separate electorates could be justified only if it were part of a larger reformation of Hindu values and society, the one on which Gandhi had been insisting practically since his return from South Africa.'[39] And if Gandhi's fast against separate electorates is understood in relation to his long-term strategy to fight the caste system, it may be possible that Gandhi's deliberate act to go through the ordeal can be explained as part of his continued effort to bring social awakening or consciousness among the caste Hindus and to drive his anti-caste movement deeper into Hindu society.

Bhikhu Parekh also suggests that 'perhaps he [Gandhi] was look-ing for the right moment to launch a dramatic and decisive attack on untouchability and to shake up the Hindus'.[40] Gandhi's own writings also indicate that he saw his fast against separate electorates for the untouchables as an opportunity to take his fight against the caste system one step ahead. In a letter to Kedarnath Kulkarni, he discusses his decision to go on the fast. He says:

> The Prime Minister's decision was only the immediate cause. It pro-vided me with an opportunity to undertake the fast. However, the aim of my fast is not merely to get the decision changed but to bring about the awakening and self-purification which are bound to result from the effort to get the decision changed. In other words this was an opportunity to strike at the very root of untouchability.[41]

This suggests that if Gandhi's fast against separate electorates is understood in relation to his long-term strategy to fight the caste system, then the fast is a likely part of Gandhi's old strategy to move the common people emotionally and prepare them for a move-ment that would strike at the caste system. The idea that Gandhi was being a strategist in his decision to undergo fast unto death to move the common people can make better sense if it is seen as similar to his decision to organize the Dandi March to mobilize common people against the British government. Many historians have argued that Dandi March was very strategically conceived by Gandhi to challenge the British hegemony. They argue that taking salt tax as a symbol of protest, the route of the march, the time of the march, and even the members of the march were very strategically decided by Gandhi. Suchitra argues that even to go on a march to oppose the British government was part of Gandhi's strategy to create propaganda to mobilize the common people. She writes:

Though Gandhi had decided on salt after much deliberation, he realised that people would not automatically rally around him. He needed to make a dramatic appeal. So he decided to go on a march. A march would give him the opportunity to rouse the people in the countryside through which he passed. It would be a live drama generating press publicity in India and the world. If on the other hand, he were to simply take a train to some place on the coast, arriving there the next day, the event would be too fleeting and have no propaganda value.[42]

Borrowing Suchitra's expression, it can be argued that Gandhi's decision to go on fast unto death can be understood as part of his strategy to create 'live drama' to strike an emotional chord with the common people and prepare them for a movement that would attack the caste system. It is in this context that the changes occurring in Gandhi's attitude towards, and writings on, caste, varna, and other related issues of this period need to be examined and understood.

From 1932 to 1945

Historical Background

Gandhi ended his fast on 26 September 1932 and decided to work from prison for the removal of untouchability. Initially, the government refused to let him do this as a prisoner. However, in November, he was granted permission.

Very soon into his work, Gandhi felt that a movement aimed at abolishing untouchability would require an all-India organization exclusively devoted to that purpose. He had discussed this issue with some of his coworkers and as a result, a new organization called the All India Anti-Untouchability League, later renamed as the Servants of Untouchables Society, but popularly known by its Hindi equivalent—the Harijan Sevak Sangh—came into existence. Gandhi appointed Ghanshyamdas Birla as its president and Amritlal

Thakkar (Thakkar Bapa) as its secretary. Gandhi also decided to start a new journal exclusively devoted to the same cause. In February 1933, he launched *Harijan*, a weekly English journal, from prison. Soon, *Harijan Bandhu* in Gujarati and *Harijan Sevak* in Hindi were launched and for some time the Urdu, Bengali, and Tamil editions of the journal were also published. These Harijan journals became Gandhi's voice; through these publications, he guided his movement against untouchability while he was still in prison.

However, dissatisfied with the progress of work and unhappy with the lack of real interest among his fellow workers, Gandhi announced a 21-day fast from 8 May to 28 May 1933 for self-purification as well as purification of his associates. The government released him on the day of the commencement of this fast, which Gandhi completed at Lady Vithaldas Thackersey's bungalow in Poona.

After this fast, Gandhi went on to arrange an inter-caste/varna marriage between his son Devdas Gandhi and Lakshami, the daughter of Rajaji, a well-known Brahmin leader from Tamil Nadu.[43] However, Gandhi was arrested soon afterwards and sent back to Yerwada Jail before he could offer satyagraha against the British government along with his ashramites. Gandhi again demanded to be allowed to work from prison for the removal of untouchability. This time the government was not ready to give a free hand to Gandhi and instead their permission came with restrictions. Gandhi wrote to the government that if his request to resume his movement for removal of untouchability on the same terms as before was not granted, he would go on a fast. The government was unrelenting and Gandhi embarked on his fast. On the fifth day of the fast, he was shifted to a hospital. Eventually, the government released him unconditionally. Gandhi declared that he would not participate in the Civil Disobedience struggle until his one-year prison sentence was over and decided to spend this time working against untouchability.

For the next nine months, Gandhi travelled extensively across India in what is popularly known as the Harijan Yatra, in an attempt to speed up his fight for removal of untouchability. This Harijan Yatra started on 5 November 1933 and continued up to 2 August 1934. During this period, Gandhi travelled around 12,500 miles across the country. The objective of this tour was to educate the masses and collect money for his struggle for the removal of untouchability. Writing about Gandhi's Harijan Yatra, Nanda says: 'Starting from Wardha and the Central provinces, the Mahatma went to Delhi, Andhra, Mysore, Malabar, Travancore and Cochin. Early in 1934 he toured Tamil Nadu, Orissa and Bengal, from where he went to Assam, Bihar, Punjab and western India. He wound up his tour with Maharashtra and Deccan in July.'[44]

It is difficult to say how far Gandhi's Harijan Yatra was successful in removing from Hindu society the caste prejudices and hierarchies based on ideas of purity and pollution, but it certainly made Gandhi acutely aware of the gravity of the issue. Lelyveld writes that Gandhi received a reminder of the rock-like durability of the customs he was trying to crack when he invited 10 members of a local untouchable group called Bauris, along with one bhangi, to have their meals in his tent at a place called Satyabhamapur in the eastern state of Orissa (now Odisha). Lelyveld writes: 'None of Mr. Gandhi's party, however, dined with these guests' and 'the Bauris refused to dine with the sweeper'.[45] Lelyveld also notes that during the Harijan Yatra, Gandhi learnt that caste Hindus were critical of the aims and objectives of his tour and made many attempts to disturb his meetings. He writes:

> Soon it became routine for batteries of orthodox Hindus to intercept him at his rallies or along his route, zealously chanting anti-Gandhi slogans and waving black flags. In Nagpur, where the tour started, eggs were thrown from the balcony of a hall in which he was speaking; in Benares, where it ended, orthodox Hindus, called sanatanists, burned his picture. A bomb went off in Poona, and an

attempt was made to derail the train on which he travelled from Poona to Bombay. At a place called Jasidih in Bihar, his car was stoned. Scurrilous anti-Gandhi pamphlets appeared at many of these places, targeting him as an enemy of Hindu dharma....[46]

On this tour, Gandhi appears to have understood the limitations of his methods and also the factors inhibiting the progress of his struggle against the caste system. The changes that were occurring in his attitude and in his writings on caste and other related issues during this period must be the result of his personal experiences during the Harijan Yatra.

In September 1934, one month after completing this yatra, Gandhi decided to stay on at Wardha on the request of Jamnalal Bajaj. This was because Gandhi had declared, before setting off on the Dandi March in 1930, that he would not return to Sabarmati Ashram until swaraj was won. In 1933, Gandhi had consulted his closest colleagues and wealthiest benefactors and permanently converted Sabarmati Ashram into a colony for Harijans. In October 1934, Gandhi travelled to Bombay to attend the annual session of the INC. In this session, Congress leaders debated the issue of what course the national movement should take in the immediate aftermath of the withdrawal of the Civil Disobedience Movement. Bipan Chandra informs us that there were two traditional responses. A section of Congressmen advocated the revival of the constitutional method of struggle and participation in elections to the central legislative assembly to be held in 1934. Gandhi, as expected, laid emphasis on constructive work in the villages.[47] Convinced that he was out of tune with the powerful themes running in the party, Gandhi resigned from the Congress in 1934. However, before he withdrew, he gained approval from the CWC for a new organization called All India Village Industries Association (AIVIA) at Wardha, and involved himself in the process of uplifting the life of villagers through constructive work. During this period, he kept himself away from all activity related to elections. And though he walked from village to village promoting the AIVIA programmes, he made no political speeches during this period. Meanwhile, the Congress leaders were engaged in canvassing for the forthcoming elections. The Congress fought both elections—in 1934 and 1937—doing especially well in the 1937 polls.

From the end of 1934, and until 1939, Wardha and Shegaon became the centres of Gandhi's activities. Maganwadi in Wardha was where the AIVIA was headquartered, and Shegaon, a small village populated mainly by untouchables, was the site of Gandhi's new ashram known as Sevagram. For the next five years, Gandhi exhausted himself in the process of reviving village industries with the help of AIVIA. He proposed the name of Joseph Cornelius Kumarappa for the secretary; he would help the new organization focus on improving science and technology related to paddy-husking, flour-grinding, oil pressing, bee-keeping, palm-*gur*-making, papermaking, soap-making, village pottery, and paint- and ink- making. Gandhi was keenly observing the progress of all these activities and was also promoting newly developed products and technologies brought in by the organization by arranging exhibitions in different parts of India. Explaining the importance of development of village industries, Gandhi wrote in the *Harijan*: 'Any problem connected with the welfare of villages as a whole must be intimately related to the Harijans, who represent over a sixth part of India's population.'[48] It appears that his experiences during the Harijan Yatra convinced him that without improving the economic condition of the untouchables, there was no hope for them to realize self-autonomy. It was after the yatra that Gandhi started laying intense emphasis on the overall development of village industries—and not just on the charkha, sanitation, and tanning—which, he believed, would ultimately help to improve the economic condition of the Dalits.

On 30 April 1936, Gandhi walked five miles from the Maganwadi headquarters of the AIVIA at Wardha to Shegaon.

Balvant Sinha, who accompanied Gandhi, writes that while addressing the Shegaon villagers at the evening prayer, Gandhi said: 'I have removed untouchability completely from my mind.... I shall not thrust my opinions on you. I shall try to remove untouchability, as well as the difference between high and low by argument, persuasion and best of all, by my own example.'[49] He walked his talk; in the coming decade, we find him trying hard to win over the villages by example, persuasion, and argument. A coworker and follower described Gandhi in the village: 'One of my earliest memories of Bapu is seeing him trudge along the tracks sweeping up the excrement that the villagers had left around like dogs, even by the well. This was his way of setting an example.'[50] In Sevagram, Gandhi had adopted a local Dalit boy Govind as his son. Govind used to render personal services to Gandhi, including preparation of his food. Explaining Gandhi's inimitable way of helping villagers to overcome their traditional caste prejudices, Mark Thomson writes: 'When the village barber refused to cut the hair of a *harijan* boy, who Gandhi had adopted as his sixth son. Gandhi responded by refusing the barber's services until he agreed to serve the *harijans*.'[51]

The untouchables were an integral part of almost all activities at Sevagram Ashram. At the ashram, the charkha remained one of Gandhi's priorities. He spun regularly and religiously, and expected the same of each of his coworkers. He also started a tanning centre at Nalwadi and, from time to time, arranged tanning classes where the skinners were taught improved methods and a variety of ways to use the flesh and bones of dead animals. Gandhi also recruited some local Harijan youths to help him and Dr Sushila at the ashram dispensary. It was not just the ashram where Gandhi was active in working to remove caste differences and hierarchies. There were several of his coworkers in the nearby villages who were helping villagers to overcome their caste prejudices in Gandhian ways. At the national level, although Gandhi had officially resigned from his primary membership of the Congress, he was determined to teach dignity of manual labour to every Congress worker.

In 1936, Gandhi persuaded the Congress to hold its annual session in a village. The Faizpur Congress session of 1936 was thus held in one of the most backward villages of Maharashtra. Gandhi also insisted that sanitation work should be done by Congress volunteers and that no paid bhangi should be employed for this work. During the session, the sanitation work was done by 200 Congress volunteers under the guidance of P.S. Patwardhan, popularly known as Appasaheb Patwardhan. While talking to Congress volunteers who voluntarily did the sanitation work, or 'scavenging' as it was called, at the Congress camp at Faizpur, Gandhi said:

> Do not forget what you have learnt here. I would ask you to make it your duty wherever you are and wherever you go to be ministers of cleanliness. You did creditable work, but you might have done better. What about the villages in our vicinity like Faizpur, Khiroda and Savda? They are as filthy as ever. The Congress in future will have to be a permanently civilizing influence so far at least as sanitation is concerned, in the whole of the area where it is held.[52]

It thus seems evident that Gandhi was determined to make sanitation and scavenging issues of national priority, for he saw them as important means to end caste prejudices. Explaining the importance of sanitation and scavenging work in his struggle, Gandhi said:

> I have discussions here with my co-workers about the scavenging work we are doing. 'Why can't we do it after swaraj? They say. 'We may do it better after swaraj'. I say to them, 'No. The reform has to come today, it must not wait for swaraj; in fact the right type of swaraj will come only out of such work.' Now I cannot show you, as perhaps I cannot show some of my co-workers, the connection between swaraj and scavenging.[53]

In 1937, when the Congress formed the government in many provinces of British India under the Act of 1935, Gandhi saw an opportunity to attack caste prejudices based on the idea of purity and pollution through education. This was because health and education were among the portfolios that came under the responsibility of these governments. Gandhi knew that education could be a very effective way to teach Hindu society lessons in manual labour in order to break caste prejudices. He organized an All India Education Conference in Wardha on 22 and 23 October 1937. At this conference, Gandhi proposed that there should be free, universal, and compulsory education for all boys and girls between the ages of 7 and 14. He also suggested education should be craft-centred and that all the subjects to be taught were to be integrally related to crafts in accordance with the local needs. Gandhi wanted this craft education system, popularly known as 'Nayee Talim' or 'basic education system', to become the top priority for the Congress governments in the provinces. Congress ministers also tried their best to implement the basic education system wherever it was possible.

With the outbreak of the Second World War and withdrawal of Congress rule in the provinces,[54] Gandhi's public role changed drastically. As tension increased in Europe as well as in the country, Gandhi could no longer afford to avoid direct participation in high-level political activities. The Ramgarh Congress in March 1940 talked of civil disobedience 'as soon as the Congress organisation is considered fit enough for the purpose',[55] but left the timing and structure of the movement entirely to the personal discretion of Gandhi. With some hesitation, Gandhi at last sanctioned a civil disobedience movement, but of a peculiarly limited and deliberately ineffective kind. The issue he took up was freedom of speech; more specifically, the right to make public anti-war pronouncements. It was decided that initially, only individual Congressmen nominated by Gandhi himself would defy the law by making public anti-war pronouncements and go to jail. Later Gandhi permitted defying of the law on a more general scale. At the height of this movement in June 1941, about 20,000 had gone to jail, but the movement petered out by the autumn of 1941, with most prisoners released. This was by far the weakest and least effective of all the Gandhian national campaigns and could not bring much change in the Indian political situation of the time.

The event that transformed the Indian situation during this period was the Japanese drive through Southeast Asia which started in December 1941, and which, in four months, swept the British out of Malaya, Singapore, and Burma (now Myanmar) and threatened to bring their empire in India to a sudden end. To discuss the situation and the role of the Congress, its working committee decided to meet in Bardoli in the last week of December. Gandhi also set off to participate in it, but even during those difficult times, he did not forget his objective of swaraj and ways to realize it. Brown writes: 'Significantly it was during the train journey from Wardha to Bardoli that Gandhi first drafted his manifesto on the constructive movement and its fundamental significance for Swaraj, thereby indicating how his mind was working and where his priorities lay.'[56] In the basic draft letter, written in 1945, Gandhi listed a comprehensive and constructive 18-point programme to achieve purna swaraj. The programme included removal of untouchability, promotion of khadi and village industries, and so on. It was designed along the lines of Gandhi's concept of an ideal society in which every individual would have equal opportunity to realize self-autonomy. However, at Bardoli, Gandhi discussed the present political crisis with the CWC, emphasizing that the party should work towards retaining its unity.

In view of the international developments, the British, at long last, felt obliged to make some gestures to win over Indian public opinion. The British government sent Cripps to India; he met with Indian leaders on 23 March 1942. Even though Cripps announced that the aim of British policy in India was 'the earliest possible realization of self-government in India', negotiations between Cripps and the Congress broke down. The failure of the Cripps mission in April made Gandhi increasingly sure of the inevitability of a struggle against the British government for political independence of the country. A fortnight after Cripps's departure, Gandhi drafted a resolution for the CWC calling for Britain's withdrawal from India. It was at the working committee meeting in Wardha on 14 July 1942 that the Congress, after some disagreement and argument, first accepted Gandhi's idea of struggle.

The famous 'Quit India' resolution was passed on the night of 8 August 1942, at the AICC meeting held in Bombay, after Gandhi delivered his memorable speech. However, in the early hours of 9 August, all the top leaders of the Congress were arrested and taken to unknown destinations. As news of this spread in the rural areas, there was a spontaneous and tremendous mass upsurge all over the country. The British government also used brutal methods to suppress the movement.

The political situation in India changed after the announcement of post-war elections in England in 1945. With British elections just a month ahead, on 14 June, Wavell, the viceroy of India, ordered the release of all CWC members and proposed talks to set up a new executive council which would be entirely Indian except for the viceroy himself and the commander-in-chief. Known in Indian history as the Simla Conference, the meeting, which was held from 25 June to 14 July 1945, dissolved without yielding any agreement between the two parties.

The massive victory of the Labour Party in the July 1945 elections in England was a good sign for the Indians, and especially for the Congress. Reflecting on the victory of the Labour Party, Wavell initially expressed some nervousness: the majority was 'too big' and Labour might try to hand over 'India to their Congress friends as soon as possible'.[57] Wavell's fears were genuine. He knew that Lord Pethick-Lawrence, the new secretary of state for India, was an old friend of Gandhi's. Congratulating Pethick-Lawrence on his appointment, Gandhi wrote: 'If the India Office is to receive a decent burial and a nobler monument is to rise from its ashes, who can be a fitter person than you for the work?'[58]

It was now obvious to everyone that political independence for India was just a matter of time. The optimism that this generated in political circles paved the way for further changes in Gandhi's attitude and writings. The political situation from 1945 until Gandhi's death and the changes that can be seen in Gandhi's writings from 1945 onwards, will be analysed in the next section.

In the following subsection, an attempt is made to explain the changes that took place in the writings of Gandhi from 1932 to 1945. This subsection also aims to examine the continuity and strategic development in Gandhi's writings, if any.

Themes in Gandhi's Writings (1932–45)

New Themes in Gandhi's Writings on Untouchability

In the previous chapter, it was explained how Gandhi, from a very young age, condemned the practice of untouchability. It was only on returning to India from South Africa in 1916 that he systematically began to attack the practice. It was also explained that from 1916, Gandhi's writings on the issue of untouchability reveal certain themes, some of which remained consistent until 1932 and some of which showed gradual strategic development. It may be recalled, for instance, that Gandhi's writings from 1916 to 1932 show him justifying his demand for the abolition of untouchability on two grounds: first, to save Hinduism; and second, as a primary condition to attain swaraj. At the same time, his writings from that period also show a gradual strategic development in his emphasis on what he meant by removal of untouchability. For example, the writings from 1916 to 1920 show that during this period, his idea of removal of untouchability meant only that one should not believe that one can get polluted merely by someone's physical touch. This was the least that he could demand at that time in order to abolish the notion of purity and pollution. However, from 1920, he began to say that it was not enough to just abolish the notion that one gets polluted by someone's physical touch; removal of untouchability meant the untouchables should have equal rights as other caste Hindus. But again, his writings show that rather than being in a hurry to achieve this goal, he preferred to move gradually and steadily towards it. Hence, from 1920 to 1927, he laid more emphasis on school entry for untouchable children than on anything else. His writings from 1927 to 1932 show him move a step further. Now he argued that one should not be satisfied by just allowing untouchable children into schools; untouchables must have the same right as caste Hindus to enter temples. During the period 1927–32, for Gandhi, removal of untouchability meant temple entry for the untouchables.

The period 1932–45 also saw certain themes emerge in Gandhi's writings. One of them appeared to show continuity with a theme that appears in his writings right from the beginning. Another theme echoed one that started appearing only in the writings of the immediate previous period. A third theme represented a logical and strategic development in Gandhi's writings on untouchability.

The first theme runs across Gandhi's writings and across different time periods. This was his emphasis that removal of untouchability was an essential condition both for saving Hinduism and for obtaining swaraj for India. He said on one occasion: 'I must repeat for the thousandth time that Hinduism dies, as it will deserve to die, if untouchability lives.'[59] On another occasion, he wrote: 'For so long as the incubus of untouchability remains, our efforts to win swaraj will be like looking for flowers in the sky.'[60] One can find numerous such instances of Gandhi's emphasis on both points during the 1932–45 period as well.

The second theme on untouchability in Gandhi's writings of this period is his emphasis on temple entry for untouchables. This emphasis began in the previous period. In 1936, he wrote: 'No workers, whether men or women, can rest in peace as long as all the temples are not thrown open to Harijans, hypocrisy, wickedness and filth are not banished from all the temples and untouchability is not eradicated from the very marrow of Hinduism.'[61] However, Gandhi's writings of 1932–45 show that his emphasis on temple entry for the untouchables was different in one sense from his emphasis on it during the previous period. Now, on some conditions, he was ready to take help from the state to ensure temple entry for the untouchables; this he never agreed to in the previous period. This point will be discussed in detail later.

The theme on untouchability that showed strategic and logical development during the period under discussion relates to what Gandhi meant by removal of untouchability. As was the case earlier, during this period, too, Gandhi wrote on the necessity of temple entry for the untouchables, but he went further and talked about 'a combined effort by the caste Hindus to improve their [the Harijans'] material and educational state'.[62] He put forth a new demand that students from Harijan background should be given financial assistance to complete their studies at every level. It appears that most of the schools run by the Harijan Sevak Sangh used to make arrangements for school dress, books, and other necessary things for untouchable students. They also had a range of scholarships for these students.[63] In 1933, Gandhi said: 'We are bound to give scholarships and other help to those Harijan boys and girls who attend the established schools.'[64] In short, during this period, he insisted on the economic upliftment of untouchables through education. He also started the David Scheme for helping untouchable students to pursue higher education. This programme was named after one of Gandhi's Jewish merchant friends, M.I. David, who had first suggested this idea to Gandhi and offered the first scholarship as well. The total amount of the scholarship was Rs 2,500 and its duration was for five years.[65]

Gandhi's writings of this period also show that his activities pro-gressed in two other ways in relation to removal of untouchability. The first was at the organizational level. Whereas during the previous period a committee for removal of untouchability was established by the CWC on Gandhi's suggestion, this time the Harijan Sevak Sangh was established as an independent organization with its own constitution and funds. Gandhi himself drafted the constitution of the sangh, which was registered under the Societies Registration Act of 1860 in 1932. To collect funds for the sangh and to give momentum to the propaganda against untouchability and caste prejudices, Gandhi set out on a countrywide tour, covering almost 12,500 miles between November 1933 and August 1934. During this tour, he visited hundreds of villages and educated people about the evils of untouchability. He also collected roughly Rs 0.8 million for the Harijan Sevak Sangh fund. For greater publicity for the works of the sangh, Gandhi founded, in February 1933, a weekly publication called *Harijan* in English and Hindi in place of *Young India*.[66] Branches of the Harijan Sevak Sangh were opened in almost every province of British India and in many districts. Some branches were also opened in some of the princely states. Sources say that within three to four years, the Harijan Sevak Sangh had a standing army of devoted volunteers who would sacrifice their lives for the removal of untouchability.

The second noticeable change at the activity level was that Gandhi readily took help from the state for any campaign for removal of untouchability. As early as in 1932, Gandhi said that the removal of untouchability undoubtedly would be one of the fundamental rights in the new constitution of India. He added that it should be considered a *criminal offence* to treat anyone as untouchable.[67] His writings from 1942 onwards reveal that he now not only wished to make untouchability a form of criminal offence but also wanted to secure political power for the untouchables. In 1942, he wrote: 'The constitution which I could influence would contain a provision making the observance of untouchability in any shape or form an offence. The so-called "untouchables" would have seats reserved for them in all elected bodies according to their population within the electoral area concerned.'[68]

During this period, he also personally took interest in advocating the Temple Entry Bill for the untouchables. He wished that it should be passed only after taking caste Hindu leaders into confidence. He used all his forces and resources to lobby for Ranga Iyer's Temple Entry Bill of 1934 and even asked Ambedkar to support it. However, after realizing that the majority of caste Hindu leaders were not in its favour, Gandhi gave up this effort temporarily. In 1934, in a press interview, he made his position on the Temple Entry Bill clear:

> As to the Temple-entry Bill, I hold that it is a legal necessity. But I have declared times without number that I would be no party to forcing the Bill through the Assembly by the vote of a mixed majority. It is, therefore, that Mr. C. Rajagopalachari is ascertaining independently Hindu sentiment in the legislature and if Hindu sentiment is against the Bill, so far as I am concerned, it will be withdrawn.[69]

Finally, due to the apathetic attitude of the Congress and the government, Iyer had to withdraw the bill. Gandhi wrote in the *Harijan:* 'The temple entry battle has to continue. The promise made to Harijans must be redeemed and the temples have to be flung open.... The hasty withdrawal of the Bill teaches its own lesson. There is no cause for disappointment. Redoubled effort is required.'[70]

Although Gandhi did not want the Temple Entry Bill passed without assurance of support from the majority of the upper-caste Hindu leaders, he did not insist on the same condition for the Anti-Untouchability Bill. In 1935, while addressing a meeting of Members of Legislative Assembly (MLAs) in Delhi, he said he would advise that the Anti-Untouchability Bill be pursued to the end. It concerned the civic rights of the Harijans and so could be taken up by all legislators, whether Hindu, Muslim, or any other. He also said that even if the whole body of Hindu opinion were against the removal of untouchability, he still would advise a secular legislature like the assembly not to tolerate that attitude.[71]

With respect to removal of untouchability, his views show continuity and strategic development during the period under discussion. The following subsection looks for continuity and strategic development in Gandhi's views on caste and varna.

Themes in Gandhi's Writings on Caste and Varna

As mentioned in the previous chapter, Gandhi did not believe in caste or varna except in some of its idealized forms, and for strategic reasons alone, he emphasized some of their positive aspects. For the same reason, he defined and redefined what he meant by caste, varna, and the relation between them. For instance, from 1916 to 1920, he appreciated caste as a 'useful institution if properly regulated' and argued that 'I am one of those who do not consider caste to be a harmful institution.' His writings from 1920 to 1927 reveal that during this period, he kept defining both caste and varna in terms of hereditary occupation; at the same time, he kept stressing on the need for merging all the subdivisions of castes within the fourfold division of varna. His writings from 1927 to 1932 show him drawing 'the sharpest distinction between *varnashrama* and caste', though until 1927, he had used both synonymously. One also finds that during 1927–32, he kept defining caste as 'an excrescence, just like untouchability, upon Hinduism' and criticizing it for several reasons.

His writings of 1932–45 show him continuing his efforts to explain and highlight the differences between varna and caste. He still criticized caste as an excrescence upon Hinduism and upon the original idea of varna. However, during this period, he logically

and strategically moved forward, progressing from mere criticism
of caste to straightaway asking people to abolish the caste system.
This he never did in the earlier periods. After condemning the caste
system as an excrescence for almost six to seven years, it was only
in 1934, in a discussion with the Harijan Sevak Sangh, that Gandhi,
probably for the first time, explicitly said that 'castes are a human
manufacture, are daily weakening and have to go'.[72] And in 1935,
in response to an open letter from a former judge of the Bombay
High Court who appealed to Gandhi and other Hindu leaders to
give a clear and a courageous lead on this issue, Gandhi wrote an
article for the *Harijan* titled 'Caste Has to Go'. In this article, Gandhi
wrote: 'The present caste system is the very antithesis of *varnashrama*.
The sooner public opinion abolishes it the better.'[73]

Gandhi's writings of this period on varna also reveal two different themes that show strategic and logical development in his
writings. One relates to how, until now, he had placed heredity as
the central defining factor of varna. During this period, though he
did not reject it altogether, he defined his idea of varna in such a
way that heredity loses its meaning entirely. He wrote:

> Varna is determined by birth, but can be retained only by observ-
> ing its obligations. One born of Brahmin parents will be called a
> Brahmin, but if his life fails to reveal the attributes of a Brahmin
> when he comes of age, he cannot be called a Brahmin. He will have
> fallen from Brahminhood. On the other hand, one who is born not
> a Brahmin but reveals in his conduct the attributes of a Brahmin will
> be regarded as a Brahmin.[74]

Another theme on varna which appears in Gandhi's writings
and speeches during this period also renders the idea of heredity
almost redundant. This theme, too, shows strategic development in
Gandhi's writings. From 1932, Gandhi started arguing and mobilizing the masses to say that true varna does not exist in today's world
and that since there is confusion about varna, everyone should call

himself or herself a Shudra. He wrote: 'My own opinion is that the varna system has just now broken down. There is no true Brahmin or true Kshatriya or Vaishya. We are all Shudras, i.e., one varna. If this position is accepted, then the thing becomes easy.'[75] And yet again, he wrote:

> I have come to see now clearly, namely, that the four varnas are no longer in actual working order, even as the four Ashrams are not. Hence at the present moment there is only one varna in existence. We are all Shudras and if we can bring ourselves to believe this, the merger of the Harijans in *Savarana* Hindus becomes incredibly simple.[76]

It is found that from 1932 onwards, these two ideas keep occurring in Gandhi's speeches and writings,[77] but it was only in 1934, after the publication of the booklet *Varnavyavastha*, that they acquired the status of a theme in Gandhi's writings and speeches. After his famous fast of 1932 and the Harijan Yatra, Gandhi, for the first time, decided to publish whatever he had written and spoken on varna and other related issues over the last 15 years. He asked one of his associates to collate all his writings and speeches and publish them in a booklet titled *Varnavyavastha*. He offered to write an introduction for this booklet to express his current views. In his introduction, he clearly elaborated on the two aforementioned ideas, going by which the hereditary concept of varna would lose all meaning. First, he said that one can obtain his or her varna by birth but can retain it only by his or her virtue. The second idea was that the varna system does not exist in the present-day world and, therefore, everyone could call themselves Shudras. He suggested to the reader that 'wherever he finds that what I have said or written before runs contrary to what I am writing now, he should without hesitation reject the former. I do not claim omniscience'.[78] In this way, Gandhi tried to reject all his early writings and speeches which supported and appreciated varna or caste as a hereditary division of society. These were Gandhi's dominant views on the issues of caste, varna, and related matters during the period.

The following subsection analyses Gandhi's writings of this period in order to see whether there was similar strategic development in his views on inter-dining and inter-caste marriage.

New Themes in Gandhi's Writings on Inter-Dining and Inter-Caste Marriage

In the previous chapter, it was explained that Gandhi, in his writings from 1916 onwards, appreciated caste restrictions on food and marriage on certain grounds. He also made it clear to the masses that his movement against untouchability did not include encouragement of inter-dining or inter-caste marriage. His writings of the subsequent period show an evolution of this thought. Now he was saying that though not propagating inter-dining and inter-caste marriage, he did believe that such restrictions on food and marriage were neither an integral part of Hinduism nor against the rules of varna. He also started to advocate inter-marriage among the subdivisions of the four varnas, saying he wanted these unhealthy subdivisions to disappear.

Gandhi's writings on inter-dining and inter-caste marriage during the 1932–45 period, as previously, continued to convince the masses that restrictions on food and marriage were not an integral part of varna or Hinduism. One theme during his early writings of this period was that inter-dining and inter-caste marriage are not an integral part of his movement against untouchability; this was, of course, present in the writings of every one of the previous periods too.[79] However, his later writings of this period show him step up his challenge to tradition. First, though he agreed he did not want to propagate inter-dining and inter-caste marriage as part of his movement against untouchability, he now admitted that he was not opposed to inter-dining per se, and considered it *adharam* for anyone to refuse to eat in the company of a person out of contempt for him or on account of his birth.[80] Second, he was explicit in his writings in appreciating restrictions on inter-dining and inter-caste marriage on certain grounds; he did this only because he found the masses were not yet ready for such radical reforms. In 1937, during a discussion in which Gandhi suggested that members of the Harijan Sevak Sangh should take all possible steps to develop more active social intercourse with Harijans, Vallabhbhai Patel asked Gandhi: 'This proposal justifies the fear of the sanatanists. From removal of untouchability you want to proceed step by step to intermarriage.' Gandhi said:

> The Hindu masses still follow quite a few restrictive practices in the matter of inter-dining and intermarriage.... That is the reason why I have not spoken to the masses about these. But if I suggest to you that you should go to the extent of inter-dining and intermarrying with Harijans I would not be violating truth.... You should certainly not bring compulsion on your children in this matter.[81]

Third, he also explained that while he appreciated restrictions on inter-dining and inter-caste marriage on certain grounds, his notion of inter-caste marriage was very different from the popular idea of inter-caste marriage. Defining his idea of inter-caste marriage, he wrote:

> Today we hardly come across any true Brahmins or true Shudras. Therefore what you do not regard as a mixed marriage is likely to be one and what, if I accepted the popular parlance, would be a mixed marriage may not actually be such. For instance, if a so-called Shudra girl possessing the qualities of a Brahmin girl marries a real Brahmin I would not call it a mixed marriage, whereas you would regard it as such. On the other hand, if a so-called Brahmin boy with the qualities of a Shudra marries a so-called Shudra girl with Brahmin-like qualities it would be a mixed marriage in my view. You would also regard it as one. Both of us will, however, do it for different reasons.[82]

During this period, he also explained that he was not immediately insisting on inter-dining and inter-marriage in his movement because 'it would be unwise in a hurricane campaign to be over-weight and thus endanger the main issue'. He also added that 'it may even amount to a breach of faith with the masses to call upon them suddenly to view the removal of untouchability in a light different from what they have been taught to believe it to be.' But he said he would not have objections if inter-dining happened where the public was itself ready for it.[83] It appears that on the matters of inter-caste marriage and inter-dining, he still wanted to wait for some more time to educate the masses about their need and importance. He also kept telling the masses that these reforms were going to happen sooner than expected.[84] Replying to some students who criticized him for advocating inter-dining and inter-caste marriage, he made it clear that he was not immediately taking up the issue, but would do so at a later date. He wrote: 'At the moment I am not at all canvassing for inter-dining and mixed marriage. We shall see about it when I start advocating them. It is neither scientific nor moral to condemn, because of faults you find in me, the noble work that I happen to be doing.'[85]

He also advanced his position on the issue of inter-dining and inter-caste marriage in the sense that he not only privately advocated inter-caste marriage but also started appreciating it publicly. In the previous period of study, Gandhi's advocacy of inter-marriage was done only on a personal basis. When he came to know that Shri Radhamadhab, a caste Hindu boy, had married an untouchable girl, he congratulated him in the *Harijan*. He wrote: 'I congratulate Shri Radhamadhab on his courage in breaking through the rock of caste superstition. I hope his example will be copied by other young men.'[86] It seems that during this period, Gandhi had made up his mind to encourage inter-dining and inter-caste marriage, but he still wanted to be slow and steady in his approach. Therefore, he spent a lot of time clarifying some misunderstandings regarding his views on the subject and also preparing the masses for radical reform.

These themes on inter-dining, inter-caste marriage, caste, varna, and untouchability keep appearing in his writings until 1945. From that year onwards, there were some distinct changes in his emphasis on what he meant by removal of untouchability, caste, varna, and the interrelations among these issues. However, the changes occurring in Gandhi's writings were not independent or isolated from the changes that were taking place in India's political scenario. Indeed the changes in his writings were determined by a whole range of complex forces, of which the political developments of that period were the most crucial. Hence, the next section not only analyses the new themes that began to appear in Gandhi's writings from 1945 onwards, but also the political background which paved the path for such changes.

From 1945 to 1948

Historical Background

It became evident in early 1945 that it would be difficult for Britain to keep control over India given the post-war circumstances. The massive victory of the Labour Party in the July 1945 elections in England confirmed that its leaders would have to hand over power to their friends in the Congress as soon as possible. During the same period, Gandhi said, 'India is on the march to Independence, it is coming....'[87] The realization that India was about to get political freedom brought tremendous and cumulative changes in the attitude and writings of Gandhi on different issues. Now Gandhi was increasingly moving towards his own original stand on key issues. For instance, during this period, he suggested winding up of the AISA as a centralized organization for the production and distribution of khadi. And Gandhi suggested that all possible effort should be made to stop the spinning of yarn for commercial purposes.

Instead, now people should be encouraged to *spin for their own use*.[88] Partha Chatterjee, commenting on the radical changes in Gandhi's views on khadi during this period, wrote: 'Thus Gandhi was now quite explicitly moving away from his "practical" argument about the economic necessity of Khadi with which for more than two decades he had sought to persuade those who did not share his moral presuppositions. Now he was reasserting the primacy of the moral objectives.'[89]

During the same period, when the top leaders of India were busy in discussions with British authorities on the terms and conditions for transfer of power, Gandhi was engaged in discussions on his vision of swaraj for India with Nehru, whom he called his political successor. He tried to convince Nehru that India needed the kind of swaraj he envisaged in his famous booklet *Hind Swaraj*. He wrote to Nehru:

> I still stand by the system of Government envisaged in Hind Swaraj. These are not mere words. All the experience gained by me since 1908 [*sic*] I wrote the booklet has confirmed the truth of my belief. Therefore if I am left alone in it I shall not mind, for I can only bear witness to the truth as I see it.[90]

The new themes reflected in Gandhi's writings on untouchability, caste, varna, inter-dining, and inter-caste marriage actually did not represent an evolution in his position over time; they are a reassertion of his primary or basic positions that were deliberately watered down for a period of time due to strategic reasons. In 1945, Gandhi again showed his desire to bring out another book on his views on varna and related issues. On 15 May 1945, he wrote a letter to Kishorilal Mashruwala saying, '[I]t would certainly be good if my articles on varna, etc, are published.' He added that 'no omissions and additions should be made before getting them published. Even if I had the time I would make no changes. However, I would explain my present stand in detail.'[91] Within

15 days, Gandhi wrote a foreword to *Varnavyavastha* (a booklet of collections of his writings on varna), in which he ultimately rejected, in his own way, heredity as the defining factor of one's caste or varna. He suggested that the reader reject his early views if they are contradictory to his current views as published in the introduction to the booklet.

The charkha and sanitation remained Gandhi's basic instruments with which to restore the dignity of manual labour in Indian society. But in 1945, Gandhi also brought out his 18-point constructive programme for the overall development of Indian villages. The points included Hindu–Muslim unity, removal of untouchability, khadi, village development, sanitation, and education. During this period, we find Gandhi repeatedly saying that swaraj had never been mere political freedom from the British government; for him, it meant developing the capacity of self-reliance in every individual who would work with the others to create a harmonious society in which everyone had equal opportunity for self-realization. This was his message to the people of India before the country's political independence. His message remained so until his death. To actualize his vision of swaraj, we find Gandhi, during the period, preaching the need for radical constructive work. Brown reminds us that for years Gandhi had periodically tried to reform the Congress into a body of dedicated constructive workers. Now, in the last months of his life, he reverted to his old hope of creating a body of servants of the country.[92] And it is known that in his last will and testament, he proposed to transform the INC into an organization dedicated to constructive programmes. But before he could actualize his desire, Gandhi was assassinated on 30 January 1948.

The following subsection tries to analyse the themes on untouchability, caste, varna, inter-dining, and inter-caste marriage that appeared in Gandhi's writings during the period under discussion. The themes are seen as part of his basic strategy to abolish the caste system. As has been done for the earlier periods, the subsection first examines the continuity of these themes and then their strategic relation to his writings of the earlier periods of study.

Themes in Gandhi's Writings (1945–8)

New Themes in Gandhi's Writings on Untouchability

It has been mentioned both in the previous chapter and in this one that though, from the very beginning of his movement, Gandhi defined removal of untouchability as abolition of the differences between non-untouchable and untouchable Hindus, he still endured as a strategist, for he emphasized certain themes during certain periods of time. For instance, his writings between 1916 and 1920 defined removal of untouchability merely as destruction of the notion that one gets polluted by the physical touch of someone. But his writings from 1920 to 1927 emphasized on school entry for untouchable children. For the period 1927–32, he again extended his demand and argued that untouchability cannot be removed unless untouchables get the right to enter the innermost part of any temple. From 1932, he started emphasizing that removal of untouchability meant a combination of efforts by the caste Hindus to improve the economic and educational status of Dalits. And from 1945, as new favourable political circumstances started emerging, he again shifted his emphasis and some new themes emerged in his writings.

There were two major themes that dealt with the issue of removal of untouchability. First, as in the previous period, Gandhi kept insisting that one of the important ways to raise the social and economic condition of the untouchables was to give them education. In a letter to Shyamlal, the secretary of the Kasturba Gandhi National Memorial Trust, he wrote: 'There are two ways of serving the Harijans. First, by raising them through education, etc., and secondly by rooting out untouchability from among the caste Hindus. The first course always bears fruit and it is desirable to pursue it however little one can.'[93]

The second theme showed a kind of strategic progress in its emphasis on what Gandhi meant by removal of untouchability. Initially, Gandhi kept arguing that inter-dining and inter-caste marriage were not an integral part of his movement for removal of untouchability. Later he explained that he hesitated to include such reforms because he found that the masses were not yet ready for radical reforms.[94] His writings of the period under discussion went further and stressed that inter-dining and inter-caste marriage were part of his movement against untouchability. This acquired the nature of a theme in his writings from 1945 onwards, after the marriage of Indumati Gunaji, an untouchable girl, and G. Tendulkar, a Brahmin. The wedding was held on 19 August 1945 at Wardha, in the presence of Gandhi and was conducted by Prabhakar, a follower of Gandhi from an untouchable background.[95] In 1946, in a discussion with the Harijan Sevak Sangh, Gandhi made it very explicit that, for him, removal of untouchability means inter-dining and inter-caste marriage. This discussion deserves to be quoted at length because it not only helps us understand Gandhi's insistence on inter-dining and inter-caste marriage being part of his movement for removal of untouchability, but also contains fascinating insights into Gandhi's long-term strategy against untouchability.

Q. Can the members of the Sangh refuse to interdine with the untouchables? Have your views on this question undergone any change?

A. At one time I did say that inter-dining was not an essential part of the campaign for the removal of untouchability. *Personally, I was for it.* Today I encourage it. In fact, today I even go further, as a perusal of my recent preface to which I have already referred[96] would show.

... But can the members of the Harijan Sevak Sangh truthfully claim to have eradicated the last trace of untouchability from their own hearts? Are their professions altogether on a par with their practice?

A member asked what his criterion was in that respect.

G. Are you married?

THE MEMBER: I happen to be.

G. The [sic] have you an unmarried daughter? If you have, get for her a Harijan bridegroom, not to satisfy her lust but in a purely religious spirit and I shall send you a wire of congratulations at my expense.[97]

This discussion reveals that during this period, Gandhi insisted that inter-dining and inter-caste marriage were part of his movement for removal of untouchability. It also helps us understand that even when Gandhi did not include many practices like inter-dining and inter-caste marriage in the early years of his movement against untouchability, he was still personally for them. He just did not insist on them because he neither had the capacity to persuade the masses to reform so radically nor was himself convinced that the masses were indeed ready for such reforms. But now, in 1945, when he was hailed as the father of the nation and had carried out intense propaganda against untouchability for roughly 30 years, he was indeed in a position to persuade the masses to his point of view and also to include these practices as part of his movement against untouchability.

From 1945 onwards, he made it a practice to not be present at, or give his blessings for, any marriage unless one of the parties was an untouchable.[98] There were indeed a few occasions when he refused to give his blessings at the marriage of his very intimate coworker's son or daughter[99] because one of the parties was not an untouchable. While explaining Gandhi's purpose in doing so, Narayan Desai, the son of Mahadev Desai, the personal and faithful secretary to Gandhi, wrote: 'Gandhiji supported the Varnashrama. But, during the last twelve years of his life, he attended marriages only when either the groom or the bride was untouchable. He made no exception to this practice even in the case of young men and women who were particularly close to him. This was his form of abandoning the Varnashrama.'[100] Thus, we find Gandhi preaching that a marriage can be considered as ideal if 'one of the contracting parties in a marriage should be Harijan'. And we also find him saying: '[T]he practical attainment of which [inter-caste marriage between upper-caste Hindu and Harijan] it is our duty to strive for as speedily as possible.'[101]

During this period, yet another theme that ran strong in his writings was his support to the idea of a direct state-led assault on the practice of untouchability. As mentioned earlier, as early as in 1932, Gandhi started saying that untouchability in any shape or form was an offence. A little later, he also strongly advocated 'reservation for so-called untouchables in all elected bodies according to their population within the electoral area concerned'.[102] During this period, he was also convinced that the untouchables needed political power for their overall development. He thus gave full support to the policy of reservation of seats for Dalits in elections. In 1946, he was asked, 'Should not the Harijan Sevak Sangh try to secure for the Harijans political power by demanding due representation for them on *gram* panchayats, municipalities and legislatures?' To this, he answered, 'Certainly it ought to. No effort can be too great for it.'[103] Some scholars like Bhikhu Parekh and David Hardiman also believe that it was Gandhi who insisted that Nehru appoint Ambedkar, an untouchable, as the law minister in the new government, even though he was not a member of the Congress.[104]

During the last years of his life, Gandhi was advocating education, economic development, and political power for the upliftment of the untouchables. In doing this, he gradually came to accept what was proposed by Ambedkar for the same purpose. However, the basic difference between their approaches remained. For Gandhi, the demand for all these real sources of higher status for the untouchables was the last stage of a long-term process. He believed that before demanding such things for the untouchables, upper-caste Hindus must be educated and taken into confidence. For Ambedkar, such a precondition was unnecessary and since the

Dalits had been deprived of such basic requirements for realizing their potential, he felt they must be compensated irrespective of upper-caste Hindus' opinion.

New Themes in Gandhi's Writings on Caste and Varna

From 1945 to 1948, the changes that show in Gandhi's writings were not confined to the subject of untouchability. There were also marked changes in his emphasis on what he meant by caste or varna and the relation between the two. Like his writings on untouchability, his writings on caste and varna, too, revealed conclusive changes in his views. However, these changes did not represent an evolution in his position over a long period of time; on the other hand, they represent a reassertion of his primary or basic positions that were deliberately sidelined for a period of time due to strategic reasons.

As mentioned earlier, Gandhi's writings of the period 1932–45 emphasized that caste was an antithesis to varna and to Hinduism, and must go; he asked members of the Harijan Sevak Sangh to work for its abolition. Also, during this period, though he did not reject heredity as the defining feature of varna, he did articulate his concept of varna in such a way that heredity lost all significance. He also insisted that varnashrama dharma had disappeared and only one varna was functional and that was Shudra. Hence, every Hindu must consider himself or herself a Shudra. However, from 1945 onwards, he once again redefined caste and varna and the relation between the two. This led to the emergence of new themes in his writings on caste and varna.

Gandhi's writings of this period, as in the previous two periods of study, kept describing caste as 'an excrescence, just like untouchability, upon Hinduism' and urged the Hindu masses to abandon their faith in the doctrine of the caste system and the different practices based on it. He said, very explicitly: 'The caste system as it exists today in Hinduism is an anachronism. It is one of those ugly things which will certainly hinder the growth of true religion. It must go if both Hinduism and India are to live and grow from day to day.'[105] During this period, he also emphasized that castes must be eradicated if untouchability is to be abolished.[106] This is something that brings him closer to Ambedkar's analysis of the caste system which argues that untouchability is a by-product of the caste system and it cannot be abolished without annihilating the caste system.[107]

Gandhi had written an introduction to a booklet that had been published during the previous period under study. In that publication, he advanced two ideas on caste and varna. The first was that since varnashrama dharma does not exist in its pure form, we should all call ourselves Shudra. The second was his definition of varna, which was explained in such a manner as to suggest that heredity makes no sense, though he did not reject the idea of heredity explicitly.

During this period, too, Gandhi wrote an introduction to another book which contained his writings and talks. Here, he rejected the idea of heredity explicitly and extended the argument that we should call ourselves *atishudra*. He wrote: 'Varna is entirely different from caste. There are numerous castes. I know of no authority for caste in the *Gita* or any other scripture. The *Gita* has prescribed four varnas and they are based on one's *aptitudes and karma*'. He added that 'there can be more or less varnas than that. But there prevails only one varna today, that is, of "Shudras", or, you may call it, "Ati-Shudras", or "Harijans" or untouchables.' After that, he wrote: 'The reader is therefore requested to discard anything in this book which may appear to him incompatible with my views given above.'[108]

From this stage onwards, there were two changes in Gandhi's writings and speeches on varna. The first was that when asked his views on the subject, he said that he no longer had any interest in it, and that if anyone was interested to know his views on varna, he should read the introduction to *Varnavyavastha*.[109] The second was that he started mobilizing the masses by propagating the idea that if varnashrama is to be preserved, every Hindu should convert himself or herself into an atishudra, and it can happen only when marriages are arranged only between atishudras and the so-called other varnas. From 1945 onwards, he started mobilizing caste Hindus to become atishudra, or Harijan, or bhangi in their thoughts, words, and actions, and propagated inter-dining and inter-caste marriage to actualize the possibility of such a Hindu society.[110]

This was Gandhi's way of not only simply rejecting varnashrama in theory but also trying to abolish prejudices of caste or varna hierarchy and differences in practice from Hindu society. It was exactly what Ambedkar had proposed for abolition of the caste system and untouchability. In 1936, Ambedkar said: 'The real remedy is inter-marriage. Fusion of blood can alone create the feeling of being kith and kin, and unless this feeling ... becomes paramount, the separatist feeling—the feeling of being aliens—created by caste will not vanish.'[111] However, as the course of Gandhi's evolving strategy revealed, this was, for Gandhi, one of the steps, perhaps the last and decisive step of his long-term strategy to abolish the caste system. He also tried to remove prejudices arising from the ideas of purity and pollution from every aspect of human life and restore the dignity of manual labour that was traditionally assigned to the untouchables. In this way, he developed and applied a comprehensive plan to abolish the caste differences and hierarchies from Hindu society.

However, neither caste differences and hierarchies nor untouchability was eradicated from India. Even today, untouchability, caste differences, and hierarchies are present despite Gandhi's struggles and reform movements over three decades. It is even more difficult to say how much Gandhi and his movement contributed to whatever little progress has been achieved in this direction. But the main objective of this study is neither to find out whether Gandhi's movement had completely eradicated the caste system, nor to assess the contribution of Gandhi and his movement to whatever little progress has been achieved in this direction. The main objective of this study is to understand Gandhi's strategies that are often explored in the context of his struggle against the British colonial power but largely ignored and unexplored in the context of his struggle against the caste system.

The following section gives an overview of Gandhi's strategy and tries to understand how it was designed to achieve abolition of the caste system.

Overview of Gandhi's Strategy

As explained in the previous chapters, for Gandhi, the problem with the caste system was not just that it deprived one group of people, symbolically (the right to wear the sacred thread) or in real terms (political power and economic benefits), of equal status in society as the other groups. The real problem with the caste system was that it created a false consciousness of hierarchies and differences in the minds of Hindus. He believed that this false consciousness obstructs every individual's path to self-autonomy. Gandhi felt that since this false consciousness is internalized by everyone irrespective of their status in the caste hierarchy, everybody needs to be redeemed from it. However, this does not mean that he was unaware of the miserable social, economic, and political conditions of the untouchables. Rather, he believed that ensuring better social, economic, and political conditions was necessary but not sufficient to abolish the caste system. He believed that in order to abolish the caste system, this false consciousness of caste hierarchies and differences also needed to be eradicated. With this in mind, Gandhi implemented the following strategies in the course of his three-decade-long struggle against the caste system.

The first strategy on his part was to create the image of his being an orthodox Hindu and to articulate his struggle against the caste system as being in continuity with tradition. He wanted the excrescence to be removed but with the acceptance and support of the upper-caste Hindus. We find that starting from 1916, Gandhi asserted his identity as a sanatani Hindu, a genuine, orthodox Hindu, and not a social reformer adamant to alter Hinduism. He seemed to argue that he was a revivalist and a committed tradition-alist who was trying to save Hinduism by giving up its excrescences. It is evident from his course of struggle that he propagated every reform as an effort to save Hinduism or to purify varnashrama dharma and not as a new or modern value or practice to be adopted. In fact, one of the most radical social reforms, that of inter-caste marriage, that he propagated was to save whatever good remained in the varnashrama dharma and thereby save Hinduism itself.

His second strategy was to gradually remove caste prejudices related to the notion of purity and pollution by educating the masses by practice and personal example. From the very inception of his struggle against the caste system, Gandhi appears to have understood that the false consciousness of caste hierarchies and dif-ferences was created and justified by the notion of purity and pollu-tion. Therefore, the main objective of Gandhi's second strategy was to erode the notion of purity and pollution from the minds of every Hindu and from every area of their lives. Gandhi was gradually mobilizing and educating the Hindu masses to reject their faith in the notion of purity and pollution in every form, and also persuad-ing them to abandon the various practices based on it. The strategy he adopted was to move from less contentious issues like the notion of a polluting physical touch, to highly contentious ones like inter-caste marriage, by educating the masses through propaganda and personal example.

The third strategy adopted by Gandhi in his struggle against the caste system was to salvage the dignity of manual labour. He believed that the division between manual labour and intel-lectual activities had created this false consciousness about caste hierarchies and differences in Hindu society. He argued that by restoring the dignity of manual labour, this false consciousness can be extinguished. His course of struggle reveals that in order to restore the dignity of manual labour, Gandhi, at the appropriate political opportunity, introduced the charkha as a means to achieve real swaraj. He used all possible ways to persuade every individual, irrespective of their caste, gender, religion, and economic status, to learn the art of spinning. Until the end of his life, he argued that everyone should spin regularly and religiously to learn the art of self-rule. In order to restore the dignity of manual labour, he also tried to persuade the masses to learn sanitation and scavenging practices; the methods he used for this were the same—argument, propaganda, and personal example.

Though Gandhi consistently employed these strategies until the end of his life and did not abandon any of them at any point of time, it appears that he understood his methods were limited. Therefore, we find that from 1934 onwards, he also tried to ensure that the untouchables got the necessary financial aid to pursue education at every level. He also accepted that the untouchables must have reserved seats in every elected body so that they may obtain political power and proper representation. Though he remained sceptical until the end of his life about the role of the state in social reform and believed that it was largely the responsibility of the upper-caste Hindus to provide the basic facilities that the untouchables were deprived of, from 1934 onwards, he also accepted help from the state to secure basic civil rights for the untouchables.

While there is no doubt that all of the aforementioned strategies were developed and applied by Gandhi during his three-decade struggle against the caste system, there was something more in his approach that made his strategy different from that of other similar movements that aimed to abolish the caste system in India. The strategy's uniqueness lay in its being free of the 'logic of Sanskritization' which justifies caste differences and hierarchies. M.N. Srinivas defined Sanskritization as the process by which 'a *low* or *middle* Hindu caste, or tribal or other group, changes its customs, ritual ideology, and way of life in the direction of a high and frequently *twice-born* caste. Generally such changes are followed by a claim to a higher position in the caste hierarchy than that traditionally conceded to the claimant class by the local community.'[112] He explained that this becomes active when a dominant lower caste or other caste wants to move up in the local hierarchy through Sanskritization.[113] Perhaps it was only Gandhi among the modern social reformers and anti-caste leaders, including Ambedkar, who could diagnose the danger of the process of Sanskritization and could make himself and his struggle free from it right from the very beginning. Even Ambedkar, the greatest anti-caste leader, could not shake himself free of this in the beginning of his struggle against the caste system. While writing about Ambedkar, Christophe Jaffrelot writes:

> On the whole, Omvedt's analysis is a convincing one but it ignores the early phase of Ambedkar's public career, at which point he appeared in many respects as an heir to movements inspired by the *bhakti*; more importantly, he subscribed openly for some time to certain aspects of Sanskritisation. It was during the 1920s that he evolved towards a radical rejection of the Hindu socio-religious system.[114]

Other great social reformers like Swami Dayananda and Vivekananda, and their methods, were not free from the 'logic of Sanskritization', which ultimately justifies caste differences and hierarchies in place of eradicating them. Both these men suggested that the untouchables should learn Sanskrit and adopt the customs, rituals, and beliefs of the great Sanskrit tradition to empower themselves. Both also suggested that the untouchables should be like Brahmins for their spiritual, moral, social, and economic development.

Gandhi was very hostile to such methods and the course his strategy took clearly indicates that he very categorically rejected this 'logic of Sanskritization' or upward mobility. In 1932, Gandhi wrote: 'I remember a learned Shastri in 1915 suggesting ... that there was confusion of varnas and that as originally there was only one varna, viz., that of Brahmins, we should all now call ourselves Brahmins. I could not reconcile myself to that proposition then and I could do so less now.'[115] Gandhi rejected it because it only promised a change in hierarchical position for particular castes or subsections of castes and failed to actually bring about any definite structural changes within the caste system. On the other hand, Gandhi was asking every Hindu to be like a bhangi—the lowest among the low in the caste system—in thought, word, and action. It was something very radical, for by doing so, Gandhi was refusing to accept the superiority of Brahminical tradition, culture, and customs from which the justification for caste differences was derived. By rejecting the superiority of Brahminical culture, Gandhi indeed attacked the very root of the caste system, and perhaps better than any other social reform movement or anti-caste movement did.

Dalit Critique of Gandhi's Movement

Any study that intends to understand Gandhi and his movement against the caste system cannot ignore the powerful Dalit critique of Gandhi's life and his movement. While explaining the course of Gandhi's strategy, only a few references have been made until now on Dalit scholars' critique. In this section and the next chapter, an attempt is made to engage with the overall Dalit critique of Gandhi's movement, including the differences with Ambedkar's anti-caste movement.

One of the important Dalit critiques of Gandhi and his movement is that Gandhi was one among them who upheld Brahminism as a philosophy of life and social order. Another important Dalit critique of Gandhi's movement is that he was set against everything which assured economic and political benefits to the untouchables.

Both critiques are very well captured in the following quote of G. Aloysius. He writes:

> Gandhi was upholding precisely this ascriptive social order [Brah-
> minism as the philosophy of life and as social order] by dubiously point-
> ing out the impracticality of radical economic equality. Admittedly
> Gandhi's views on caste changed from time to time, but only within
> the extremely narrow spectrum of untouchability, interdining and
> intermarriage. (D. Dalton 1967: pp. 159). These issues were marginal
> to the existential life struggles of the lower caste masses. The agenda
> was the attempt to escape the humiliating ascriptive social identity
> by diversifying occupations and assuming a new anonymity of mem-
> bership within a large whole through competition and achievement.
> Gandhi was set against exactly this....[116]

Let us discuss Dalit scholars' critique one by one. First, they argue that Gandhi upheld, validated, and defended Brahminism as a philosophy of life and social order. Generally, the enigmatic relation between Gandhi's seemingly religious, simple, and disciplined life and his claim of being an orthodox Hindu in some of his writings led to the erroneous conclusion that Gandhi upheld and defended Brahminism as a philosophy of life and social order. In fact, there was no connection between the two. On the one hand, Gandhi's effort to live and experiment with a simple life was part of his ethical commitment which he developed through his personal experiences and by reading different scholars' work and different religious books, and on the other hand, his claim of being a sanatani Hindu was part of his strategy to develop his movement against the caste system in such a way that it may appear in conti-nuity with tradition. Therefore, neither his practice nor his writings can be taken as a sign of his belief in Brahminism as a philosophy of life and social order. As was explained in the first chapter, in his personal practices, Gandhi challenged and dared to violate all the practices and beliefs that constitute the core of Brahminism as a philosophy of life and social order. From his practices, it is difficult to come to the conclusion that he was in reality a defender of Brahminism.

Moreover, Gandhi's evolving strategy also reveals that he, more than anyone else, could understand that the caste differences and hierarchy in Hindu society were not established, maintained, and sustained by force alone; they also drew their justification from Brahminical cultural hegemony. Hence, for him, the real enemy to be tackled was the latter. This chapter and the previous one have explained that Gandhi developed a strategy to erode the hegemony or ideological influence of Brahminical culture from the minds and hearts of every Hindu inch by inch and in every area of life. In Gramscian terminology, Gandhi's struggle can be viewed as a hegemonic struggle, meaning a struggle that aimed to erase the hegemony or ideological influence from the minds and hearts of common people. Therefore, it is exactly contrary to what Dalit scholars have been arguing.

However, this explanation leads us to another challenge from Dalit scholars that is related to Gandhi's method. Some Dalit scholars identify a problem in relation to Gandhi's extensive use of Brahminical symbols that stand for caste differences and hierarchy. Gail Omvedt writes that for Gandhi, the great symbol of Hindu nationalism was 'Ram-Rajya' who 'represents a ruler whose support of the orthodox caste system involved the killing of a Shudra boy, Shambuka, for the sin of trying to follow a Brahman path to self-improvement'.[117] And D.R. Nagaraj also writes, 'This was one of the areas where Dr. Ambedkar clashed bitterly with Gandhiji. The latter's use of Hindu symbols is heavily dependent on mainstream Hinduism and the method he used to invest them with radical energy could hardly inspire the non-initiate.'[118]

The argument presented in this study might seem to be paradoxical, given that Gandhi did use extensively Hindu Brahminical symbols that are generally associated with caste differences and hierarchy even while trying to fight such hierarchy using counter-hegemonic methods. This also puzzles some scholars who could comprehend this dichotomy in Gandhi's method. For instance, Bhikhu Parekh explains his difficulty in understanding such contradiction in Gandhi's method in the following words: 'Strange as it may seem, while Gandhi kept hankering after the ancient *varna* system, his moral theory undercut its very basis.'[119] On the other hand, some scholars who could only notice Gandhi's extensive use of Hindu traditional symbols, like Gail Omvedt, argue that due to Gandhi's repeated use of these symbols, many untouchables, along with Muslims, felt alienated in Gandhi's concept of swaraj or *Ram Rajya*. However, both groups of scholars seem to forget what Ronald J. Terchek writes about Gandhi's style of communication. He writes: 'It is helpful to remember that he [Gandhi] wants to address the ordinary people of India. To do so, he writes in an idiom that his audience readily understands. The language, metaphors, and symbols he uses are not always ours, and *if we read Gandhi literally, we run the danger of sometimes reading him incompletely.*'[120]

It is also equally important to remember that though Gandhi borrowed the language, metaphors, and symbols from Hindu traditions, the connotation in which he used them is strictly his own and did not necessarily correspond to their traditional/common uses. For instance, Terchek argues that Gandhi uses the traditional idea of Advaita—in which transcendental and metaphysical unity of human being is assumed—to argue equality of human beings in a fully modernist sense.[121] It is also argued earlier that it was part of Gandhi's strategy to articulate his movement against the caste system in such a way that it may appear as continuity with tradition. His extensive use of traditional Hindu symbols and metaphors must also be understood in this direction and must be seen as his effort to explain problems and remedy of the caste system in such a way that can be readily understood by the audience.

Let us now look at another Dalit critique of Gandhi's movement. In Aloysius's words, Gandhi's approach worked against the Dalit attempt to escape their humiliating ascriptive social identity by diversifying occupations and assuming new anonymity of member-ship within a larger whole through competition and achievement. In Mani's words, 'Gandhi's approach was to create an "ideal bhangi" who would continue to clean the excreta of others with the status of a Brahman whereas Ambedkar's approach was to integrate the untouchables into mainstream society by giving them education and political rights.'[122]

But this critique also appears unconvincing given that Gandhi never in his life, during any period of time, opposed education for the untouchables. Rather, in South Africa, he started a school which was open to children of all Indians belonging to any caste or religion. And in 1917, he started a national school at his ash-ram in India, which was also open to everyone, including the untouchables. There are also several other instances that can be pointed out to support the view that Gandhi was actively engaged in promoting equal social status for Dalits. It must, therefore, be acknowledged that Gandhi worked towards assuring education, a fair share in economic development, and political power for the untouchables/Dalits. However, he could not achieve as much success in this direction as he hoped to with regard to removal of false consciousness of caste differences and hierarchy from the minds of Hindus.

Moreover, Gandhi's emphasis on removing false consciousness of caste prejudices from the minds of Hindus must not be seen as a deviation from the Dalit effort to escape a humiliating identity and assume a new respectful membership within the larger Indian society. In fact, it must be understood as part of the same process because, in orthodox Hindu society, a Dalit cannot escape from his traditional identity just by receiving good education, job, money, or political power; in spite of all achievements, he will remain untouchable for orthodox Hindus. Therefore, in order to assure respectful membership of the untouchables/Dalits in Hindu society, it was, and is, equally important that prejudices of caste differences and hierarchy should also be removed from the mind of every Hindu. In this respect, Gandhi's movement can be interpreted as part and parcel of the process to assure new respectful membership for the untouchables/Dalits within a larger whole.

Dalit scholars also find another problem with Gandhi's way of dealing with the issues of caste system. For them, Ambedkar defined the problem in terms of building an independent political identity for Dalits, whereas for Gandhi, it was purely a religious question, and that, too, an internal one for Hinduism.[123] D.N. explains it in a much more explicit way. He writes that the objective of Gandhi was to force the Dalits, under Ambedkar, to accept their position of being subordinated to the politically dominant sections of Hindus.[124] There are two issues involved in this argument. First, for Gandhi, the problem of untouchability and caste system was purely a religious problem and he was not ready to treat it as an issue of civil rights, equal opportunities in economic matters, and social intercourse. Second, he opposed political separation of Dalits from Hindus that would help them secure their civil rights, equal opportunities in economic matters, and would facilitate social intercourse with other communities. Gandhi, without any doubt, on many occasions defined the problem of the caste system primarily in terms of religion, that is, as a great threat to the very existence of Hinduism, a moral failure on the part of upper-caste Hindus, a great sin of Hindus, and so on. However, in practice, he took up issues which were civic in nature—like school entry for the untouchables/Dalit children, temple entry, and scholarship to facilitate higher education for the untouchables/Dalit youth—and political in nature, like reservation in every elected body, and also encouraged upper-caste Hindus to have active social intercourse with the untouchables/Dalits.

Moreover, it is also erroneous to argue that Gandhi was against the political separation of Dalits from Hindus because he wanted to accept their position of being subordinated to the politically dominant sections of upper-caste Hindus. If it is a fact that Gandhi 'in principle' was against separate political representation of 'any community', it is also a fact that for Ambedkar, 'the true representative character of the political process was something to be achieved by overcoming the caste and class structure'.[125] In principle, both seem to be in agreement with each other. Suhas Palshikar suggests that the issue of separate electorates should not be taken seriously while understanding Ambedkar because '"separate electorates" do not form the core of Ambedkar's thought'.[126] In another article, Palshikar writes that Ambedkar's demand of separate electorates was a response to the colonial–communal situation.[127] In the same fashion, it can be argued that Gandhi's opposition to any kind of separate political representation for Dalits during the Second Round Table Conference was part of his strategy, on the one hand, to emotionally motivate Hindus to take his movement one step ahead and, on the other hand, was a response to the colonial–communal situation.

* * *

This book began by attempting a question: was there a strategy in Gandhi's fight against the caste system? Towards the end of the fourth chapter, it now seems to be clear that Gandhi implemented several different strategies in the course of his long struggle against the caste system. However, while Gandhi's strategies had considerable merit, they also had limitations. Therefore, the next chapter tries to critically examine Gandhi's contribution and his strategies in order to understand their relevance in the upliftment of the untouchables during our time.

Notes

1. M.K. Gandhi, 'Letter to Vallabhram Vaidya', 4 December 1945, in *CWMG*, Vol. 82 (New Delhi: Publications Division, Government of India, 1980), p. 162.
2. Adams, *Gandhi*, p. 206.
3. The official term used by the British government for untouchables/Dalits.
4. Separate electorates and reservation are two important systems in a democracy to protect the rights and privileges of any minority community. In the reserved seats system, the candidates could only be members of the minority community, that is, the untouchables, in a certain number of constituencies (proportionate or not to the minority community's demographic weight). However, they may never be in a majority in any one constituency and in this case, in any constituency, a coalition of majority, that is, caste Hindus, could then elect a member of the minority community, that is, an untouchable, of their choice for whom the local minority community, that is, the untouchables, themselves would not have voted. On the contrary, in the separate electorates system, only the minority community, that is, the untouchables, could vote for the minority community.
5. M.K. Gandhi, 'Interview to S.M. Mate, P.N. Rajbhoj and Limaye', 21 September 1932, in *CWMG*, Vol. 51, p. 125.
6. Sankar Ghosh, *Mahatma Gandhi* (Calcutta: Allied Publishers Ltd., 1991), p. 229.
7. See Brown, *Gandhi*, p. 267.
8. B.R. Ambedkar, 'What Congress and Gandhi Have Done to the Untouchables', in *Selected Works of Dr B.R. Ambedkar*, p. 941, available at file:///D:/documents%20for%20book/to%20send/correction/selected-work-of-dr-b-r-ambedkar.pdf (accessed on 25 December 2016).
9. Gail Omvedt, *Dalits and the Democratic Revolution: Dr. Ambedkar and the Dalit Movement in Colonial India* (New Delhi: SAGE, 2010), p. 174.

10. Gandhi quoted in D. Keer, *Dr. Ambedkar: Life and Mission* (Mumbai: Popular Prakashan, 1962), p. 214.

11. Keer, *Dr. Ambedkar*, p. 216.

12. Ram quoted in Abhay Dubey, 'Anatomy of a Dalit Power Player: A Study of Kanshi Ram', in Ghanshyam Shah (ed.), *Dalit Identity and Politics* (New Delhi: SAGE, 2001), p. 205.

13. Omvedt, *Dalits and the Democratic Revolution*, p. 172.

14. Bhikhu Parekh, 'Strengths and Weaknesses of Gandhi's Concept of Nonviolence', p. 2, available at http://www.civilresistance.info/files/19-bhikhu.pdf (accessed on 5 August 2013).

15. Pyarelal Nayyar, 'The Epic Fast (1932)', in Jack Homer (ed.), *Gandhi's Reader* (Madras: Samata Books, affiliated to East-West Press, 1989).

16. Mani, *Debrahmanising History*.

17. Biswas, *Gods, False Gods and the Untouchables*.

18. Bipan Chandra, 'Communalism—the Liberal Phase', in *India's Struggle for Independence*, p. 419; emphasis added.

19. Ambedkar quoted in Christophe Jaffrelot, 'Dr. Ambedkar's Strategies against Untouchability and the Caste System', Working Paper Series, Vol. III, No. 4, Indian Institute of Dalit Studies, New Delhi, 2009, p. 3, available at www.dalitstudies.org.in/wp/0904.pdf (accessed on 10 May 2013).

20. Ambedkar quoted in Jaffrelot, 'Dr. Ambedkar's Strategies against Untouchability', p. 17, note 9.

21. Ambedkar quoted in Jaffrelot, 'Dr. Ambedkar's Strategies against Untouchability', p. 3.

22. Ambedkar quoted in Jaffrelot, *Analysing and Fighting Caste*, p. 55.

23. Bharat Patankar and Gail Omvedt, 1979, 'The Dalit Liberation Movement in Colonial Period', *Economic and Political Weekly*, 14(7 and 8): 409–24.

24. Omvedt, *Dalits and the Democratic Revolution*, p. 169.

25. H.C. Sadangi, *Emancipation of Dalits and Freedom Struggle* (Delhi: Isha Books, 2008), p. 203; see also Patankar and Omvedt, 'The Dalit Liberation Movement in Colonial Period'.

26. See Keer, *Dr. Ambedkar*, p. 188.

27. Ambedkar, 'What Congress and Gandhi Have Done to the Untouchables', p. 4207. (Therefore, even Ambedkar did not appear to view this as a great deprivation as many Dalit scholars have been arguing.)

28. Nehru quoted in Aditya Nigam, 2000, 'Secularism, Modernity, Nation: Epistemology of the Dalit Critique', *Economic and Political Weekly*, 35(48): 4258.

29. Namboodiripad quoted in Nigam, 'Secularism, Modernity, Nation', p. 4258.

30. Moonje quoted in Gail Omvedt, *Ambedkar: Towards an Enlightened India* (New Delhi: Penguin, 2008), p. 131.

31. See B.R. Ambedkar, 'B.R. Ambedkar on Gandhi's Fast', in *Selected Works of Dr. B.R. Ambedkar*, p. 4454, available at file:///D:/documents%20for%20book/to%20send/correction/selected-work-of-dr-b-r-ambedkar.pdf (accessed on 25 December 2016).

32. M.K. Gandhi, 'Hindu–Muslim Question', 19 February 1925, in *CWMG*, Vol. 26, p. 162.

33. Gandhi, 'Interview to S.M. Mate, P.N. Rajbhoj and Limaye', 21 September 1932, p. 126.

34. M.K. Gandhi, 'Speech at Minorities Committee Meeting, London', 13 November 1931, in *CWMG*, Vol. 48, (New Delhi: Publications Division, Government of India, 1971), p. 298.

35. Gandhi, 'Speech at Minorities Committee Meeting, London', 13 November 1931.

36. Ambedkar quoted in S.R. Sharma, *Life and Mission of B.R. Ambedkar* (New Delhi: Sublime, 2010), p. 44.

37. Keer, *Dr. Ambedkar*, p. 216.

38. Brown, *Gandhi*, p. 266.

39. Lelyveld, *Great Soul*, p. 232.

40. Parekh, *Colonialism, Tradition and Reform*, p. 236.

41. M.K. Gandhi, 'Letter to Kedarnath Kulkarni', 20 September 1932, in *CWMG*, Vol. 51, p. 114.

42. Suchitra, 'What Moves Masses', p. 744.

43. As mentioned earlier, this couple had waited for their marriage for five years as per Gandhi's suggestion.

44. Nanda, *In Gandhi's Footsteps*, p. 208.

45. Lelyveld, *Great Soul*, p. 244.

46. Lelyveld, *Great Soul*, p. 243.

47. Bipan Chandra, 'The Gathering Storm', in *India's Struggle for Independence*, p. 311.

48. M.K. Gandhi, 'Expansion of "Harijan"', 21 December 1934, in *CWMG*, Vol. 60 (New Delhi: Publications Division, Government of India, 1974), p. 15.

49. Sinha, *Under the Shelter of Bapu*, p. 80.

50. Mehta quoted in Adams, *Gandhi*, p. 208.

51. Thomson, *Gandhi and His Ashrams*, p. 220.

52. M.K. Gandhi, 'Talk to Congress Volunteers', 29 December 1936, in *CWMG*, Vol. 64, p. 200.

53. M.K. Gandhi, 'Interview to Prof. Mays', 10 January 1937, in *CWMG*, Vol. 64, p. 223.

54. On 3 September 1939, Viceroy Linlithgow unilaterally associated India with Britain's declaration of war on Germany, without bothering to consult the provincial ministries or any Indian leader. To discuss this matter, the CWC met in Wardha on 23 October 1939. It condemned the viceroy's statement as reiteration of the old imperialist policy and called upon the Congress ministries to resign in protest. With this, in October 1939, a 28-month-long Congress rule in different provinces came to a sudden end.

55. *India Annual Register*, 1940, Vol. 1 quoted in R.C. Dutt, *Socialism of Jawaharlal Nehru* (New Delhi: Abhinav Publications, 1981), p. 142.

56. Brown, *Gandhi*, p. 333.

57. Sarkar, *Modern India*, p. 358.

58. M.K. Gandhi, 'Letter to Lord Pethick-Lawrence', 3 August 1945, in *CWMG*, Vol. 81, p. 69.

59. M.K. Gandhi, 'Temple-Entry', 23 September 1939, in *CWMG*, Vol. 70, p. 184.

60. M.K. Gandhi, 'To the Readers', 14 September 1940, in *CWMG*, Vol. 72 (New Delhi: Publications Division, Government of India, 1978), p. 450. He also wrote, 'As long as the curse of untouchability pollutes the mind of the Hindu, so long is he himself an untouchable

in the eyes of the world, and an untouchable cannot win non-violent swaraj.' See M.K. Gandhi, 'Implications of Constructive Programme', 13 August 1940, in *CWMG*, Vol. 72, p. 379.

61. M.K. Gandhi, 'One Enemy Alone', 29 November 1936, in *CWMG*, Vol. 64, p. 92.

62. M.K. Gandhi, 'A Common Platform', 10 November 1933, in *CWMG*, Vol. 56, p. 209.

63. See M.K. Gandhi, 'For Harijan Teachers', 10 November 1933, in *CWMG*, Vol. 56, pp. 210–11; 'Reply to Depressed Classes Deputation', 22 December 1933, in *CWMG*, Vol. 56, pp. 375–81; 'Maharashtra Harijan Sevak Sangh', 28 September 1934, in *CWMG*, Vol. 59, p. 92; 'Harijan Work in Assam', 14 December 1934, in *CWMG*, Vol. 59, pp. 446–7; 'Bengal Harijan Sevak Sangh', 4 January 1935, in *CWMG*, Vol. 60, pp. 53–4; 'Harijan Conference', 6 July 1935, in *CWMG*, Vol. 61, pp. 231–2; 'Letter to S. Ranganayaki', 19 June 1941, in *CWMG*, Vol. 74 (New Delhi: Publications Division, Government of India, 1978), p. 119.

64. Gandhi, 'For Harijan Teachers', 10 November 1933, pp. 210–11.

65. See M.K. Gandhi, 'Higher Education for Harijans', 25 February 1933, in *CWMG*, Vol. 53, pp. 392–4; 'Letter to G.D. Birla', 2 March 1933, in *CWMG*, Vol. 53, pp. 445–6; 'The David Scheme', 4 March 1933, in *CWMG*, Vol. 53, p. 456; 'Letter to M.I. David', 5 March 1933, in *CWMG*, Vol. 53, p. 478.

66. After Gandhi's arrest in January 1932, *Young India* was discontinued, its last issue being that of 14 January 1932. As the movement against untouchability grew stronger, Gandhi decided to bring out another journal, *Harijan*, to propagate his views. The first issue of *Harijan* appeared from Poona on 11 February 1933, under the editorship of R.V. Shastri. On 13 April 1935, Mahadev Desai became its editor.

67. M.K. Gandhi, 'Statement on Untouchability–VII', 16 November 1932, in *CWMG*, Vol. 52, pp. 1–4.

68. M.K. Gandhi, 'Five Questions by a Harijan M.L.A.', 19 July 1942, in *CWMG*, Vol. 76, p. 314.

69. M.K. Gandhi, 'Interview to the Press', 3 August 1934, in *CWMG*, Vol. 58, p. 289.

70. M.K. Gandhi, 'That Ill-Fated Measure', 30 August 1934, in *CWMG*, Vol. 58, p. 382.

71. M.K. Gandhi, 'Speech at M.L.A.s' Meeting, Delhi', 27 January 1935, in *CWMG*, Vol. 60, p. 171.

72. Gandhi, 'Letter to Harijan Workers', 12 January 1934, p. 429.

73. M.K. Gandhi, 'Caste Has to Go', 11 November 1935, in *CWMG*, Vol. 62, pp. 121.

74. Gandhi, 'Introduction to "Varnavyavastha"', 23 September 1934, p. 65.

75. M.K. Gandhi, 'Letter to Haribhau Phatak', 6 October 1932, in *CWMG*, Vol. 51, p. 199. Gandhi also writes: 'If we must talk in terms of varna, there is only one varna today for all, whether men or women; we are all Shudras.' See M.K. Gandhi, 'Women and Varna', 12 October 1934, in *CWMG*, Vol. 59, p. 146. According to Gandhi, 'Today there is only one varna. Call it the Shudravarna. We cannot say Atishudra since we do not believe in untouchability. We do not believe in a fifth varna. Hence only the fourth varna, that is, Shudra is left. Let all of us consider that we are Shudras.' See M.K. Gandhi, 'Answers to Questions at Gandhi Seva Sangh Meeting, Brindaban–II', 6 May 1939, in *CWMG*, Vol. 69, p. 220.

76. M.K. Gandhi, 'Letter to Motilal Roy', 9 November 1932, in *CWMG*, Vol. 51, p. 389.

77. For instance, Gandhi writes, 'Today, however, varnashrama is a lost treasure and there is utter confusion. Therefore so far as I can see there is only one varna and that is Shudra. That there is confusion of varnas is humiliating. That we should call ourselves Shudras is no humiliation, for in religion there is none high and none low.' See M.K. Gandhi, 'Letter to Satis Chandra Das Gupta', 5 November 1932, in *CWMG*, Vol. 51, p. 350.

78. Gandhi, 'Introduction to "Varnavyavastha"', 23 September 1934, p. 62.

79. Gandhi writes, 'In any case, removal of untouchability as we have defined it today does not include inter-dining and intermarriage.' See M.K. Gandhi, 'Five Questions by a Youth', 28 April 1933, in *CWMG*, Vol. 55, p. 55.

80. Gandhi, 'Letter to Hanumanprasad Poddar', 5 November 1932, pp. 353–5.

81. M.K. Gandhi, 'Speech at Gandhi Seva Sangh Meeting, Hudli–IV', 20 April 1937, in *CWMG*, Vol. 65 (New Delhi: Publications Division, Government of India, 1976), p. 135.

82. M.K. Gandhi, 'Letter to a College Student', 17 January 1933, in *CWMG*, Vol. 53, p. 77.

83. M.K. Gandhi, 'Statement on Untouchability–I', 4 November 1932, in *CWMG*, Vol. 51, p. 344.

84. Gandhi, 'Statement on Untouchability–I', 4 November 1932, p. 344.

85. Gandhi, 'Letter to a College Student', 17 January 1933, p. 78.

86. M.K. Gandhi, 'Caste Hindu Marries Harijan Girl', 16 June 1940, in *CWMG*, Vol. 72, p. 179.

87. M.K. Gandhi, 'Talk with an English Journalist', 24 September 1946, in *CWMG*, Vol. 85, p. 370.

88. Gandhi quoted in Partha Chatterjee, *Nationalist Thought and the Colonial World: A Derivative Discourse*, The Partha Chatterjee Omnibus (New Delhi: Oxford University Press, 1999), p. 118.

89. Chatterjee, *Nationalist Thought and the Colonial World*, p. 118.

90. Gandhi, *Hind Swaraj*, p. 150.

91. M.K. Gandhi, 'Letter to Kishorelal G. Mashruwala', 15 May 1945, in *CWMG*, Vol. 80 (New Delhi: Publications Division, Government of India, 1980), p. 142.

92. Brown, *Gandhi*, p. 373.

93. M.K. Gandhi, 'Letter to Shyamlal', 23 July 1945, in *CWMG*, Vol. 81, p. 24.

94. In 1942, while discussing with the Harijan Sevak Sangh, Gandhi made it clear that 'when I said that removal of untouchability did not include the removal of restrictions on inter-dining and intermarriage, I had the general Hindu public in mind, not the Congress workers or Congressmen. These have to abolish untouchability from every part of their life.' See M.K. Gandhi, 'Discussion with Harijan Workers', 8 January 1942, in *CWMG*, Vol. 75, p. 207.

95. See Gandhi, 'Letter to Indumati Gunaji', 10 August 1945, p. 103; M.K. Gandhi, 'Letter to Bhagwaticharan Shukla', 11 November 1945, in *CWMG*, Vol. 82, p. 62.

96. Gandhi means his foreword to his new booklet *Varnavyavastha*, in which he explained his present stand on caste, varna, and other related issues.

97. Gandhi, 'Talk with Members of Harijan Sevak Sangh', 28 July 1946, pp. 23–8; emphasis added. For the matter of convenience, some change has been made in the order of questions and not all the questions and answers are quoted here.

98. *Amrita Bazar Patrika*, in its 3 January 1946 edition, states that while discussing with Congress workers, Gandhi said that so far as he understood the mind of the Congress he knew there was no difference of opinion about inter-dining, but he thought that so long as one could not think himself one of the Harijans the poison of untouchability could not be removed. If anybody was not prepared to marry a Harijan he found no occasion of giving his blessings to that marriage. The question of marrying a Harijan was not so difficult but the difficulty was only mental. See M.K. Gandhi, 'Discussion with Congress Workers', 1 January 1946, in *CWMG*, Vol. 82, p. 326.

99. Gandhi writes:

I have your letter. You must be aware that ordinary marriages no longer have any interest for me. I am interested, if at all, in a caste Hindu marrying a Harijan. For, if we wish to observe *Varnashrama* dharma, we should all belong to one caste, i.e., of Harijans. And how else can we prove that we have really become Harijans? But what if marriage between a Bhangi and a Brahmin is not for observing dharma but for indulgence? All the same you have my blessings if your marriage is for the service of the people and if both of you live a life of self-restraint.

See M.K. Gandhi, 'Letter to N. Vyasatirth', 16 November 1945, in *CWMG*, Vol. 82, p. 86. Gandhi also writes, 'Write and tell him that my blessings are given only when one of the parties to the marriage is a Harijan.' See M.K. Gandhi, 'Note to Munnalal G. Shah', 24 April 1946, in *CWMG*, Vol. 84, p. 56. At another place, Gandhi writes, 'I receive a large number of requests for blessings on the occasion of marriages which I am hesitant to send. I have already stated publicly that my blessings should be asked for only such marriages where one of the contracting parties is a Harijan.' See M.K. Gandhi, 'To Correspondents', 19 May 1946, in *CWMG*, Vol. 84, p. 106.

100. Narayan Desai, *My Life Is My Message: Satyapath (1930–1940)*, Vol. 3, Tridip Suhrud (tr.), (New Delhi: Orient Blackswan, 2009), p. 197.

101. M.K. Gandhi, 'Question Box', 21 February 1946, in *CWMG*, Vol. 83 (New Delhi: Publications Division, Government of India, 1981), p. 160.

102. M.K. Gandhi, 'Question Box', 2 August 1942, in *CWMG*, Vol. 76, p. 314.

103. Gandhi, 'Talk with Members of Harijan Sevak Sangh', 28 July 1946, p. 25.

104. Parekh writes, 'It would seem that it was Gandhi who had been largely instrumental in encouraging Nehru to appoint Ambedkar as Law Minister in his 1947 Cabinet.' See Parekh, *Colonialism, Tradition and Reform*, p. 221; see also Hardiman, *Gandhi in His Time and Ours*.

105. M.K. Gandhi, 'Answers to Questions', 16 April 1945, in *CWMG*, Vol. 79, p. 384.

106. Gandhi, 'Letter to Shyamlal', 23 July 1945, p. 25.

107. Ambedkar writes, 'The outcaste is a by-product of the caste system. There will be outcastes as long as there are castes. Nothing can emancipate the outcaste except the destruction of the caste system. Nothing can help to save Hindus and ensure their survival in the coming struggle except the purging of the Hindu faith of this odious and vicious dogma.' See B.R. Ambedkar, 'Statement', 7 February 1933, in *CWMG*, Vol. 53, p. 260.

108. M.K. Gandhi, 'Foreword to "Varnavyavastha"', 31 May 1945, in *CWMG*, Vol. 80, p. 222; emphasis added.

109. Gandhi writes, 'I have gone through your letter. I am no longer interested in that subject. I have expressed my views in the introduction to *Varnavyavastha*. Only those who are well versed in the subject can give their opinion.' See M.K. Gandhi, 'Letter to Bhai Hemendra Shah', 6 September 1945, in *CWMG*, Vol. 81, p. 232. According to Gandhi, 'Castes must go if we want to root out untouchability. Read my preface to *Varnavyavastha*.' See Gandhi, 'Letter to Shyamlal', 23 July 1945, p. 25. Gandhi also writes, 'A collection of my articles

has also been published. I have expressed my present views in the foreword. The gist of it is that it is the duty of every Hindu to regard himself as a Harijan, that is, the lowest among the Shudras. Thus alone can Hinduism be purified and saved.' See M.K. Gandhi, 'Letter to Paltu Jha', 22 December 1945, in *CWMG*, Vol. 82, p. 255.

110. Gandhi writes, 'That even among converts there are castes is a reflection upon Hinduism and should set every Hindu thinking and make him become, with me, a Bhangi.' See M.K. Gandhi, 'We are All Indians', 23 August 1946, in *CWMG*, Vol. 85, p. 195. Gandhi also writes, '[A]nd in this they should bear in mind the opinion the speaker had often expressed that all caste distinctions should be abolished, and there should be only one caste, namely, Bhangis, and all Hindus should take pride in being called Bhangis and nothing else.' See M.K. Gandhi, 'Speech at Prayer Meeting', 23 February 1947, in *CWMG*, Vol. 87, p. 11.

111. Ambedkar, *Annihilation of Caste with a Reply to Mahatma Gandhi*, p. 116.

112. M.N. Srinivas, *Social Change in Modern India* (New Delhi: Orient Blackswan, 2009), p. 6.

113. M.N. Srinivas, *The Cohesive Role of Sanskritization and Other Essays* (New Delhi: Oxford University Press, 1989), p. 35.

114. Jaffrelot, *Analysing and Fighting Caste*, p. 44.

115. Gandhi, 'Letter to Satis Chandra Das Gupta', 5 November 1932, p. 350.

116. G. Aloysius, *Nationalism without a Nation in India* (New Delhi: Oxford University Press, 1997), pp. 208–9.

117. Gail Omvedt, 1971, 'Jotirao Phule and the Ideology of Social Revolution in India', *Economic and Political Weekly*, 6(37): 1969–79.

118. D.R. Nagaraj, 'Self-purification versus Self-respect: On the Roots of the Dalit Movement', in A. Raghuramraju (ed.), *Debating Gandhi* (New Delhi: Oxford University Press, 2006), p. 368.

119. Parekh, *Colonialism, Tradition and Reform*, p. 228.

120. Terchek, *Gandhi*, p. 112; emphasis added.

121. Terchek quoted in Nicholas F. Gier, 1996, 'Gandhi's Philosophy: Premodern, Modern, or Postmodern?', *Gandhi Marg*, 17(3): 261–81.

122. Mani, *Debrahmanising History*, p. 372.
123. Nagaraj, 'Self-purification versus Self-respect', p. 368.
124. D.N., 1991, 'Gandhi, Ambedkar and Separate Electorates Issue', *Economic and Political Weekly*, 26(21): 1328–30.
125. See Suhas Palshikar, 1997, 'Gandhi and Ambedkar', *Economic and Political Weekly*, 32(30): 1918–19.
126. Palshikar, 'Gandhi–Ambedkar Interface', p. 2070.
127. See Palshikar, 'Gandhi and Ambedkar'.

Critical analysis

Ambedkar, Gandhi, and the Arya Samaj

5

The danger that Gandhi posed to the
greater Sanskritic tradition was exactly this.
He introduced a different system of weightages
and threatened to alter the basic characteristics
of Indian Society by making its cultural
periphery its centre.

—Ashis Nandy[1]

The preceding four chapters of this book
attempted to present a faithful account of
how Gandhi's strategy for abolition of the
caste system evolved as he proceeded with
the struggle. The effort was directed more
towards describing how Gandhi conceived,
organized, and implemented his struggle
against the caste system than towards
critically evaluating his overall strategy. This
approach was adopted for the purpose of:

1. Understanding Gandhi's uncompromising commitment to fight the caste
   system. That his commitment was
   uncompromising is often questioned
   by scholars.

2. Acknowledging Gandhi's remarkable quality of being an extraordinary strategist. This is often acknowledged in the context of his struggle against British colonial rule, but largely ignored and unexplored in the context of his struggle against the caste system.

3. Bringing to centre stage, based on historical facts, Gandhi's strategy against the caste system, which he tactically changed and refined according to the political circumstances of his time.

However, in order to understand the continuing relevance of Gandhi's strategy for the upliftment of the untouchables, it is not enough to acknowledge his commitment to fight the caste system, and/or point out that he was a remarkable and extraordinary strategist in this fight, and/or simply bring to centre stage Gandhi's strategy against the caste system and how he crafted it. It is equally important to understand the efficacy of Gandhi's evolving strategy to abolish the caste system. Therefore, it is necessary to critically estimate Gandhi's life and his strategies in order to understand the effectiveness of Gandhi's ways of fighting the caste system. This will also afford us an understanding of the continuing relevance of Gandhi's strategy for the upliftment of the untouchables. However, to critically analyse Gandhi's life and strategies, one has to consider them in the context of other contemporary movements that emerged during the colonial period to tackle the issues of caste. The apparent divergence between Gandhi's methods—which evolved, undergoing modifications and refinements—and other movements will highlight the limitations as well as merits of Gandhi's strategies.

Though it may have been Gandhi who made untouchability and caste crucial issues in Indian politics, it must also be admitted, in all historical fairness, that he was not the only one fighting caste discrimination and exploitation during the colonial period. Many of his contemporaries, like Ambedkar, E.V. Ramasami Naicker, Narayana Guru, and Gopal Krishna Gokhale, were also involved in this struggle. It was a general concern that emerged among many in a society that was being introduced to liberal education and democratic political systems.

The movements that took on the caste system during the colonial period fall into two categories (ignoring some variations) on the basis of their aims, methods, and the social status of the individuals or organizations concerned. One group consisted of the anti-caste movements of the untouchables, and the second consisted of the social reform movements of the upper castes. The available literature generally categorizes Gandhi's movement under the upper-caste social reform category; it is viewed as a rival to the Dalit anti-caste movements for the purpose of analysis. Though it is true that Gandhi's evolving strategy to fight the caste system was, in more than one way, similar to the social reform movements initiated by upper-caste people, this chapter argues that the differences between Gandhi's movement and the upper-caste social reform movements are too fundamental for the former to be considered as being in the same category as the latter.

As such, this chapter divides the anti-caste movements into three categories for the purpose of analysis. The first category consists of the anti-caste movements of the untouchables, the second consists of the social reform movements of the upper castes, and the third is Gandhi's struggle to abolish the caste system. Since it is not possible to take into consideration all the anti-caste movements for this study, this chapter takes Ambedkar's movement to represent the Dalit campaigns and the Ayra Samaj's *shuddhi* movement to represent the upper-caste campaigns. Besides, these two movements were also very active while Gandhi was at work and had considerable influence in shaping the themes and patterns of Gandhi's strategy as it evolved.

There are several remarkable and scholarly studies available on Gandhi's and Ambedkar's approaches to the issue of caste and its abolition.[2] While some of these works attempt to prove that one was more flawed in its design and outlook than the other, other studies attempt to show how one's reformist commitment towards the downtrodden was greater than his counterpart's. Moreover, several books and research articles have also tried to present the two leaders as arch rivals working in opposite directions and creating problems in each other's paths.[3] In the recent past, there have also been some efforts to present a synthesis of Gandhi's and Ambedkar's methods as the need of the hour by depicting similarities in their concerns, if not in their approaches. Valerian Rodrigues writes: 'They [Gandhi and Ambedkar] differed in their understanding of modernity, in assessing traditions and in proposing options for India and the world. However, across their disagreements there was much that united them, not merely on issues and concerns, but on substantive positions as well.'[4] However, the purpose of this chapter is neither to compare Gandhi's and Ambedkar's highly complicated and multidimensional personalities nor to project them as either archrivals or allies. In fact, such comparisons have no significant bearing on this study. Given the purpose of this chapter, which is to understand the limitations as well as the merits of Gandhi's strategies to abolish the caste system, its next section attempts to highlight the disparities between Gandhi's and Ambedkar's strategies based on their views on:

1. the fundamental issue of the caste system;
2. the primary agent responsible for changing the status of the untouchables;
3. their agenda, relating to whether it unites or creates a division between the classes; and
4. the ultimate objective of abolishing the caste system.

While there is a vast amount of literature on Gandhi and Ambedkar, there are only a few works that seriously study the differences and similarities between Gandhi's approach in tackling the caste system and the Arya Samaj's shuddhi movement for the upliftment of untouchables. Most of the important studies on Arya Samaj's shuddhi movement reflect its communal character; some other works discuss the movement from the gender perspective. However, the caste aspect of this movement is often neglected.[5] Even when some of the major studies on Arya Samaj's shuddhi movement discuss its caste aspect, they hardly take proper account of Gandhi's struggle against the caste system. To address this lack, the chapter attempts to study, in contrast, Gandhi's strategy to abolish the caste system and the Arya Samaj's shuddhi movement.

The focus of this chapter is not so much to explain Arya Samaj's shuddhi movement in depth or to present a historical account of it, as it is to highlight the disparities between Arya Samaj's shuddhi movement and Gandhi's movement, in order to understand the limitations and strengths of the latter.

Gandhi's Strategy against the Caste System versus Ambedkar's Anti-Caste Movement

Bhimrao Ramji Ambedkar (1891–1956), popularly known as 'Babasaheb', was born on 14 April 1891 at Mhow, a small cantonment town in Indore district of Madhya Pradesh. He belonged to the Mahar community, an untouchable caste of Maharashtra. His ancestral village was Ambavade in the district of Ratnagiri in Maharashtra. Ambedkar was an intellectual colossus with extraordinary erudition and talents. He was the first graduate untouchable. He had an MA degree in economics from the famous Columbia University, New York; he also obtained a PhD from the same university. Apart from this, he was awarded an MSc and a DSc from the London School of Economics and Political Science. He also held the degree of barrister-at-law from Gray's Inn in London.

Ambedkar made his entry into the social and political life of India around 1919. In order to institutionalize the sociopolitical struggle for the emancipation of the untouchables, he formed the Bahishkrit Hitakarini Sabha on 20 July 1924 in Bombay. He continued his struggle for the emancipation of the untouchables with the help of the Bombay Legislative Council, to which he was nominated as a member in 1927. He remained a member there for 10 years. During this period, he was not just active in the council but also started a unique satyagraha in 1927 to assert the rights of the untouchables to drink water from the Chawdar tank at Mahad. In 1930, he guided a temple entry satyagraha at Kalaram Temple, Nasik, launched by the untouchables. In order to protect the political interests of the weaker sections, Ambedkar founded the Independent Labour Party in 1936 and the Scheduled Caste Federation in 1942. In July 1941, he was nominated as a member to the Defence Advisory Committee set up by the viceroy; one year later, he entered the Executive Council of the viceroy as a Labour member. He was also appointed as the law minister in the first government of independent India in 1947 and later appointed the president of the Drafting Committee for drawing up the Constitution of India.

Ambedkar is widely appreciated for his contribution to the Indian Constitution. However, his real contribution lies in his effort to challenge the patronage of the upper-caste reformers, including Gandhi. He presented an alternative strategy for the emancipation of the oppressed communities and an alternative vision of society with emphasis on civic equality and economic–political empowerment for the untouchables. Ambedkar's efforts brought him into direct confrontation with Gandhi; this was described by one of Ambedkar's biographers as a 'clash of titans'.[6] In the ensuing paragraphs, an effort is made to understand the differences between the two leaders with respect to their approach to the issue of caste in India.

False Consciousness versus Social, Economic, and Political Difference

Like Gandhi, for Ambedkar too, the individual was of supreme consideration. For both, that social system was best which helped every individual to develop the best that he or she was capable of. Both eventually agreed—for different reasons, however—that the present caste system was not such a social system. For Gandhi, the caste system had created a false consciousness of caste differences and hierarchies and this had not only led to the brutalization of the untouchables but had also dehumanized the upper-caste Hindus. For him, upper-caste Hindus were as much *victims* of the caste system as the untouchables; and in order to abolish the caste system, it was equally necessary for every individual, irrespective of caste, to overcome such caste prejudices.

Since according to Gandhi, everyone needed to overcome the false consciousness of caste differences and hierarchies in order to get rid of the caste system, it was important to understand how this false consciousness was created and justified in Hindu society. According to him, this false consciousness was created and justified with the help of the notion of purity and pollution and by the degradation of manual labour. He firmly believed that the caste differences and hierarchies could be abolished by gradually eliminating the notion of purity and pollution from the minds of the people and by restoring the dignity of manual labour. The previous two chapters offered extensive explanations of Gandhi's evolving strategy to discard such notions and restore the dignity of manual labour.

Ambedkar would agree that in order to become a better human being, it was necessary for the upper-caste Hindus to give up their caste prejudices. However, he had serious difficulty in accepting

Gandhi's views. He could not accept that the upper-caste Hindus were as much *victims* of the caste system as the untouchables. Also, he could not accept that caste differences and hierarchies could be abolished by just removing the notion of purity and pollution from the minds of Hindus and by restoring the dignity of manual labour. According to Ambedkar, Gandhi's analysis of the problem of caste system was shallow in the sense that caste differences and hierarchies are not just one's state of mind or false consciousness that can be abolished by removing caste prejudices from the minds of Hindus. For Ambedkar, the caste differences and hierarchies were real; in Hindu society, wealth, political power, knowledge, and other real as well as symbolic sources of higher status were apportioned according to caste differences and hierarchies. He knew that these differences and hierarchies were not just symbolic; political power, knowledge, and economic wealth were also divided unevenly and according to caste hierarchies. The consequence of this was that a group of people who were at the bottom of this system were deprived of not just the opportunity to attain the best that they were capable of, but their very basic needs for survival. In other words, the caste system, according to Ambedkar, was a hindrance to social justice and equality of opportunity for the untouchables.

Moreover, Ambedkar would argue that even if it were accepted that caste differences and hierarchies were just a state of mind, they could not be abolished by just removing the notion of purity and pollution from the minds of people and restoring the dignity of manual labour. He agreed that the caste differences and hierarchies might seem rational and consistent to those who live in the system due to the notion of purity and pollution. However, his view was that they had sustained for so long because they derived justification from religious authority. He wrote:

> The Hindus observe Caste not because they are inhuman or wrong-headed. They observe Caste because they are deeply religious. People

are not wrong in observing Caste. In my view, what is wrong is their
religion, which has inculcated this notion of Caste. If this is correct,
then obviously the enemy you must grapple with is not the people
who observe Caste, but the Shastras which teach them the religion
of Caste.... The real remedy is to destroy the belief in the sanctity
of the Shastras.[7]

Therefore, for Ambedkar, the false consciousness of caste differences and hierarchies could not be overcome just by removing
the notion of purity and pollution from the minds of the people.
Rather, it was necessary 'to destroy the belief in the sanctity of the
Shastras', an idea which Gandhi would not accept. D.N. wrote that
Ambedkar proposed the reorganization of Hindu society on the
basis of the principles of 'Liberty, Equality and Fraternity'. D.N.
added that for this, the 'sense of religious sanctity behind caste and
varna' must be destroyed, and this sanctity 'can be destroyed only by
discarding the divine authority of *Shastras*'.[8]

Gandhi himself did not believe in the sanctity of the Shastras.
He once said: 'Words have, like man himself, an evolution, and
even a Vedic text must be rejected if it is repugnant to reason and
contrary to experience.'[9] But unlike Ambedkar, he did not believe
that destroying the sanctity of the Shastras would be a good way
to go forward to abolish the caste system. This was for the following two reasons. First, though he accepted that seemingly religious
sanctions make many social evils, including caste—justifiable and
acceptable in Hindu society as they might in any other society—
he similarly believed that the masses in general also observed
moral values because of religious sanctions. As Joseph Prabhu
wrote: 'Gandhi makes ethics, both personal and social, the core of
religion.'[10] Gandhi believed this sanctity of religion and religious
texts served as a foundation for moral practices in society and provided the foundation for man to preserve morality in the critical
moments of life. Therefore, he held the view that while destruction
of belief in the sanctity of the Shastras would help the masses see

the evil or sin involved in practising the caste system, it would also encourage people to question the validity of their perception of morality. Hence, distortion of the sanctity of the Shastras or any other authority might result in the collapse of morality in society. Gandhi wrote that a hollow devotion to truth and non-violence is likely to break down in a difficult situation. He added: 'Hence I have said that Truth is God.'[11] Therefore, Gandhi concluded that relinquishing the Shastras may not be the best way to tackle the caste issue. The second reason for which Gandhi did not directly attack the religious sanctity of the caste system was a pragmatic one. He believed that if he did so, his movement could easily be interpreted as an attack on the Hindu religion itself and render it (the movement) unpopular. This, in turn, would make difficult the removal of false consciousness of caste from the minds of Hindus.

Community Responsibility versus State Protection

The last two chapters showed that instead of destroying the authority of the Shastras, Gandhi decided to educate the masses by stating that caste differences, hierarchies, and practices based on the notion of purity and pollution are not an integral part of their religion and should be abolished if they contradicted reason and morality. The methods he used were argument, persuasion, and personal example. He tried to create an army of devoted coworkers who would go from village to village to set example through action, and persuade people to realize that caste restrictions based on the notion of purity and pollution were not an integral part of their religion. He created several organizations and travelled across the country with this purpose in mind. For Gandhi, it was the individual or the community concerned that was the real force behind his movement, and he always remained uneasy about the importance of the state not only in abolishing caste differences and hierarchies but also in other social reform movements. While explaining Gandhi's arguments against state-initiated reforms, Parekh wrote: They [state-initiated reforms] treated men as 'donkeys compelled to carry a load' against their will and dehumanized them. They encouraged moral inertia and a culture of dependency. Rather than explore ways of mobilizing their own and others' moral energies, citizens got into the 'lazy' habit of rushing to the state every time they felt uneasy about a social practice.[12]

Therefore, in Gandhi's scheme of thought, social reform must remain the responsibility of the community concerned and the state must not gain ascendancy in this respect.

On the other hand, Ambedkar knew that the people for whom he was fighting were socially and educationally backward, economically subservient, and culturally oppressed; they would need the necessary constitutional protection to be assured equal access to all the real sources of higher status in society to facilitate their upward mobility. In his scheme of thought, the state had to play a major role in abolishing caste differences and hierarchies by safeguarding the interests of the untouchables. It is evident from the life and struggles of Ambedkar that he never lost any opportunity to work with the government, whether British or Congress, for the social, economic, and political upliftment of the untouchables. According to him, this was the real approach by which caste differences and hierarchies could be abolished. Christophe Jafferlot wrote: 'He [Ambedkar] also tried hard to influence the governments in his personal capacity, whether they were of the British or Congress, for better serving the cause of the Untouchables.'[13]

Gandhi held the state to be as dangerous as the caste system in destroying the autonomy of the individual. He believed that the 'state does the greatest harm to mankind by destroying individuality, which lies at the root of all progress'.[14] He was of the opinion that the best method was one which tried to appeal to the conscience of the individual as well as that of the community, rather than one which was dependent on some external agency like the state. To him, the state was nothing more than concentrated and organized violence. It was with a lot of hesitation that he was ready to accept it as an instrument for maintaining law and order. But he could not accept it as an agency to bring about revolutionary changes in the lives of human beings and society.

Unity versus Separate Identity

Since for Gandhi, the individual or the community concerned was the real agency to bring about social reform in any society, he believed that the most appropriate method of reform was the one that laid stress on the unity of human beings, minimized differences, and sought consensus among the different parties concerned. This was also why he held that any method which tried to create a separate cultural, religious, or political identity for the untouchables would ultimately fail to abolish caste differences and hierarchies. Since Gandhi did believe that the stigmas attached to Dalit identity were one of the main sources of caste differences and hierarchies, it would be necessary to remove them. However, he did not believe that to do so it was necessary to create a new and separate identity for them. On the other hand, he believed that caste differences and hierarchies could be abolished by removing the stigmas associated with the untouchables and by creating a sense of fellowship among the different caste groups.

In the previous two chapters, it was revealed that Gandhi was trying to create a sense of fellow feeling among the different caste groups and, at the same time, working towards restoring the dignity of certain manual occupations which were looked down upon and considered polluting in Hindu society.

For Ambedkar, the stigmas attached to the untouchables could not be removed by simply educating the Hindus through propaganda or by restoring the dignity of manual occupations that were considered inferior in Hindu society. He felt these stigmas were not simply attached to the untouchable identity; rather, the untouch-able identity itself was/is considered a stigma in Hindu society. He knew from his own personal experience that an untouchable remained an untouchable in Hindu society irrespective of his or her educational qualification or economic status. He also observed that this 'impure' Hindu identity of the untouchable was responsible for their (Dalits') demoralized social status and the indignity of their position in society. Therefore, according to Ambedkar, there was no other way out of this for the untouchables than to completely give up their traditional caste identity, which was one of the main sources of discrimination and humiliation faced by them. However, before coming to such a drastic conclusion, Ambedkar, in his initial years, gave a lot of thought to it and tried to obtain social respect and equality for the untouchables within Hindu society. Thomas Pantham writes that there were two distinct phases in the strategy which Ambedkar actually followed for the emancipation of the untouchables from their oppressive and humiliating situation. In the first phase, which lasted until the end of 1934, Ambedkar sought to gain, for the depressed classes, equality within Hinduism by trying to reform the religion through non-violent direct actions by the untouchables themselves. In the second phase (from 1935 onwards), Ambedkar, while continuing to demand emancipation action and welfare measures by the government for the untouchables, redefined the primary objective of the movement of the depressed classes to ensure social equality. This objective was 'liberation from Hinduism and not reform of Hinduism'.[15]

Ambedkar had another reason to believe that creating a new social, cultural, and political identity for the untouchables would be more effective in removing their hardships than Gandhi's ways to bring unity among the different caste groups in Hindu society. Ambedkar believed that Gandhi's method would help the upper-caste Hindus to justify their claim to majority; this would lead to their enjoying a larger share in political power after the withdrawal of the British from the country. Ambedkar feared that this political power in the hands of the upper castes would only increase the hardships of the untouchables. Ambedkar, therefore, believed that in the prevailing political scenario, the untouchables would benefit better if they projected themselves as a separate minority community to claim more advantages from the state. Ramashray Roy writes that, for Ambedkar, the commonality between upper-caste Hindus and the untouchables was non-existent. For Ambedkar, Roy adds, 'Their [untouchable] upliftment must be detached from the upliftment of the entire community of which the untouchables are claimed to be an integral part'.[16] Roy recalls Ambedkar's discussions with Gandhi on 22 September 1932, when the former made it quite clear to Gandhi that the interests of the upper-caste Hindus and the untouchables were not only different but also irreconcilable. Since the untouchables had lost so much for so long, they must be given adequate compensation.[17] This could only be possible if the untouchables were projected as a separate marginalized community detached from Hindu society.

Ambedkar believed that the process of new identity creation for the untouchables must work in two directions: first, in the direction of creating a separate socio-religious identity by conversion of religion; and second, in the direction of creating a separate political identity by projecting the untouchables as an exploited, marginalized minority community. He believed religious conversion would help them overcome the social stigma attached with their caste identity, hence ensuring social equality. On the other hand, a separate political identity would help them safeguard their political and economic interests, which was essential for their overall development.

Gandhi was against both religious conversion of the untouchables as a means to assuring them social equality and creation of a separate political identity for them for safeguarding their political and economic interests. About conversion, Gandhi wrote: 'I am against conversion whether it is known as *shuddhi* by Hindus, *tabligh* by

Mussalmans or proselytizing by Christians. Conversion is a heart-process known only to and by God. It must be left to itself.'[18] On another occasion, he said: '[I]f a change of religion could be justified for worldly betterment, I would advise it without hesitation. But religion is a matter of the heart. No physical inconvenience can warrant abandonment of one's own religion.'[19]

Though Gandhi agreed that safeguarding the individual's economic benefits and political rights is a prerequisite for realizing self-autonomy, he did not believe that achievement of political power and economic benefits could be considered as an end in itself. He condemned the relentless pursuit of material wealth and believed this could be harmful in more ways than one in the individual's effort to realize self-autonomy. He appreciated the traditional ways of living; through them, according to him, people find beauty and meaning of life in voluntary simplicity, poverty, and slowness. Gandhi rejected the state as the pivotal agency for bringing about revolutionary changes in the life of human beings and society. He, therefore, believed that securing economic benefits and political power for the untouchables with the help of the state by creating a separate identity for them would not be the appropriate way to tackle the caste system. Gandhi also tried to persuade upper-caste Hindus to discover the meaning of life through voluntary simplicity, poverty, and slowness. He wanted that people should learn to regulate their own affairs with minimum help, or without any help, from the state. He believed that the problem was not that the untouchables should be inspired to strive for political power and economic benefits; his concern was how to educate upper-caste Hindus so that they step down from the high pedestal they had occupied all these years. He wrote: 'Whatever appears to be low in them [untouchables] is a reflection of our own [upper-caste Hindus] terrible lowness.' He added, 'We [upper-caste Hindus] must come down from the high pedestal we have occupied all these years and take our natural place with them.'[20] Therefore, for Gandhi, a method which inspires the untouchables, or for that matter anyone, to strive for political and economic advantages by creating a new social, cultural, and political identity and/or religious conversion for assuring social equality was not a suitable solution. He was afraid that such actions would turn the existing caste differences and hierarchies into antagonism between the upper-caste Hindus and the untouchables by creating unnecessary competition and a compulsive rush to accumulate wealth and political power.

Self-Purification versus Self-Respect

Since Gandhi regarded accumulation of wealth and political power as detrimental to the moral development of the individual, he preferred methods which would educate the masses about the beauty that lay in a life of voluntary simplicity, poverty, and slowness rather than methods that encouraged them to strive for material wealth and political power. It was with this purpose in mind that he focused on educating the upper-caste Hindus to give up their caste prejudices rather than on organizing the untouchables to fight for material wealth and accumulation of political power. Basically, Gandhi worked in two directions. The first was to teach the upper-caste Hindus that manual work was of as much value as intellectual work. He insisted that everyone, irrespective of their religion, caste, and economic condition, must do daily manual work. He interpreted the traditional idea of yajna (sacrifice) as manual work, and in his ashrams, spinning the wheel was raised to the rank of a daily *mahayajna* (primary sacrifice). The second was to mobilize the feelings of shame and guilt among the upper-caste Hindus about their failure to treat untouchables as equals. Gandhi also preached that the practice of untouchability is a moral failure or sin on the part of upper-caste Hindus, and that they should purify themselves by giving it up in every form. He wrote: 'Untouchability will not be removed by the force even of law. It can only be removed when the majority of Hindus realize that it is a crime against God and man and are ashamed of it. In other words, it is a process of conversion, i.e., purification of the Hindu heart.'[21] In this way, Gandhi defined his struggle against untouchability and the caste system as a movement of self-purification,[22] in which the upper-caste Hindus were asked to recognize the dignity of manual labour; abandon the practice of untouchability; and help uplift the social, economic, and political condition of the untouchables as a penance for their sins.

Ambedkar found these prescriptions humiliating, maintaining that they consider the untouchables as a mere object in the self-purification exercise of the upper-caste Hindus. Explaining Ambedkar's disagreement with Gandhi's manner of tackling the caste issue, D. Nagaraj wrote:

> Babasaheb had no other option but to reject the Gandhian model. He had realized that this model had successfully transformed Harijans as objects in a ritual of self-purification, the ritual being performed by those who had larger heroic notions of their individual selves. In the theatre of history, in a play of such a script, the untouchables would never become heroes in their own right, they are just mirrors for a hero to look at his own existentialist angst and despair, maybe even glory.[23]

Ambedkar believed that self-help is the best help. He knew from history that injustice is not removed until the sufferer himself does away with it by his own exertions and actions. He diagnosed, perhaps correctly, that as long as the untouchables did not organize themselves to fight to end their own sufferings, there would not be any change in their lives. In a speech, Ambedkar said: 'No borrowed or hired person who does not belong to your class can further your welfare by the least degree. You may rid yourself of internal divisions and organize yourself strongly....'[24] For Ambedkar, the problem of caste was not just moral failure of the upper-caste Hindus in not treating the untouchables as equals. The caste system also created the mental status of self-doubt, self-denial, and self-hatred among the untouchables. Hence, for Ambedkar, the best method was one which created a sense of confidence and self-respect among the untouchables. He concentrated, therefore, on organizing the untouchables to fight for their rights, for that would not only help in abolishing caste differences and hierarchies but also fill the untouchables with feelings of self-respect and dignity and enable them to overcome their socio-economic hardships. Ambedkar thus rejected Gandhi's patronizing idea of self-purification for the upper-caste Hindus as appropriate for eliminating caste differences and hierarchies.

Tradition versus Westernization/Modernization

Westernization/modernization involves, among other things, replacement of the traditional lifestyle—the organization of human society on the basis of beliefs and superstitions—with the modern lifestyle, in which society is organized on the basis of modern institutions, modern knowledge, and rationality. M.N. Srinivas defined it as the changes which appear in a non-Western country by direct or indirect contact with a Western country.[25] Ambedkar, like many other great leaders such as Karl Marx and Jawaharlal Nehru, strongly believed that such changes would lead to the collapse of the caste system in India. At the time of introduction of the railway in India, Karl Marx observed that it would lead to the establishment of a capitalist industry and would eventually trigger the collapse of decadent social systems such as caste. He wrote: 'Modern industry, resulting from the railway system, will dissolve the hereditary divisions of labour, upon which rests the Indian caste system.'[26] Following Marx, many great Indian leaders like Nehru and Ambedkar, who were Western in outlook, also expressed similar faith in the process of westernization/modernization. They believed that the introduction of science and technology in any society would necessarily bring changes in the attitude/world view of its people. Debjani Ganguly writes: 'Ambedkar, in his struggle against caste discrimination, took on board all the values that he imbibed from his English liberal education and declared that the path of Western democracy (with its secular values) was the only way to eradicate the ills of caste.'[27]

A fact which no one can deny is that the process of western-ization/modernization did make difficult, to a large extent, the practice of caste in its ritual form. Most people would be ready to accept that the attitude of educated people in the metropolitan cities is not largely governed by the caste system. However, there are some scholars who feel that though westernization/moderniza-tion played a great role in minimizing the effects of caste system, it generated some other problems in this respect. One such problem, as described by Nagaraj, is the 'phenomenon of willful amnesia towards one's own past'. He explains:

> The working of the caste system has always tried to create mental states of self-doubt, self-denial, and self-hatred among the lower caste individuals in the modern context, and generally these attitudes are collectivized. The birth of the modern individual in the humiliated communities is not only accompanied by a painful severing of ties with the community, but also a conscious effort to alter one's past is an integral part of it.[28]

Gandhi may or may not have been able to predict the 'phenom-enon of willful amnesia' among the 'lower' caste and the 'untouch-able' educated youths in a westernized India. Gandhi's reasons for rejecting westernization may have been different. He rejected blind westernization/modernization not only as a remedy for abolishing the caste system but also as a belief that it is the panacea for every problem in the country. He rejected it because, unlike many other educated Indians, he could not agree with the idea that westerniza-tion/modernization ultimately brings hope for human emancipa-tion by transforming traditional or pre-modern social structures.

Gandhi could not make up his mind whether the Western or modern world presented an age of reason, equality, freedom, and justice. He knew that westernization/modernization indeed brings such notions into prominence in any society, but he also knew that westernization/modernization is not always about equality, freedom, and justice but carries with it its own forms of inequality, domination, exploitation, and normalization. For Gandhi, therefore, the choice between tradition and modernity or westernization/modernization was not about the choice between exploitation and emancipation but the choice between different traditions of exploitation. For him, the process of westernization/modernization was not a method of emancipation but a changed form of exploitation. Therefore, unlike Ambedkar and Nehru,[29] Gandhi did not believe that the imposition of science and technology by any authority would necessarily bring about fundamental changes in the conscience of any individual or society, or even notional changes in their lives.

Gandhi believed that any fundamental changes in people's attitude could not be brought about just by introducing Western science and technology in their daily life. He would have been in agreement with Srinivas who wrote about the driver of a government bulldozer from Rampura village in Mysore:

> Thus the manipulation of western technology does not mean that manipulators have accepted a rationalistic and scientific world view. Far from it. The bulldozer driver in Rampura had mastered the mechanical motions necessary to drive it, and could even do minor repairs; but he was not only traditional in his religious beliefs, he had even picked up some black magic, a knowledge usually confined to small groups. He did not perceive any incompatibility between driving a bulldozer and practicing black magic.[30]

Like Srinivas, Gandhi, too, must have been aware of these practical difficulties. And he could, as a consequence, perceive that westernization/modernization in the form of imposed extensive use of science and technology might make the practice of caste system in its ritual form difficult to practise, but may not necessarily undermine the doctrine of caste or lead to the necessary changes in caste consciousness among the masses. This is a fact; not only about the less educated bulldozer driver of a remote village of India but also about highly educated citizens of the metropolitan cities of India. Although it might seem that the people are free from caste prejudices, their behaviour regarding important issues like marriage and reservation is still determined by caste rules. It may not be an exaggeration to say that far from collapsing, the caste system appears to be growing stronger as far as its doctrine is concerned.

Gandhi, as mentioned earlier, could predict the limitations of the imposed process of westernization/modernization and rejected the belief held by Ambedkar and many educated Indians that the process of westernization/modernization could abolish the power of the caste system. In other words, westernization/modernization was rejected by Gandhi because he believed that it, like many other means, fails to eliminate the consciousness of caste differences and hierarchies from the minds of upper-caste Hindus.

Arya Samaj's Shuddhi Movement versus Gandhi's Evolving Strategy

The Arya Samaj was founded by Dayananda Saraswati (1824–83) in 1875 as an exclusive, constitutionally regulated socio-religious organization, with the avowed aim of 'establishing, protecting and propagating the Vedic religion as expounded by its founder'.[31] At the time of its emergence, certain practices such as animal sacrifice, idolatry, untouchability, ritualism, polytheism, caste rigidities, and ban on remarriage of widows among the upper castes were prevalent among Hindus. Many of these practices were considered as 'sins' and were criticized by Christian missionaries. The Arya Samaj was an upper-caste response to such challenges posed to Hinduism by Christian missionaries. It declared that such beliefs and practices constituted an excrescence upon Hinduism and were not an integral part of the religion. The organization sought to rejuvenate Hinduism in such a way that the religion would become more true to its past and could also face the changing social, economic, and political environment. In this respect, it was basically a revivalist movement, and its reformist aim was to rid Hinduism of the practices and beliefs that were criticized by Christian missionaries and educated Hindus during its time. It projected the Vedic age as the authentic and ideal era of Hindu society. It legitimized rejection of the aforementioned beliefs and practices by arguing that they were not part of Vedic society. It propagated the slogan 'go back to Vedas'. In its attempt to reform Hinduism, the Arya Samaj incorporated many ideas that were foreign to Hinduism, and also radically interpreted some classical ideals in the light of the new circumstances. However, all these ideas were presented to the masses as being part of ancient Hindu philosophy. Shuddhi was one such classical concept which was radically interpreted and reinterpreted to meet the new challenges that had emerged in the social, economic, and political arena at that time in India.

In classic Sanskrit, the term 'shuddhi' is often used to express 'the state of purity'; it designates a group of rituals meant to cleanse members of high castes from impurities with which they may have been tainted by a polluting contact. Yoginder Sikand and Manjari Katju write: 'Shuddhikaran refers to the rite through which this "pollution" is considered to be removed and ritual "purity" restored, thus enabling one to regain one's caste status.'[32] Gandhi had also gone through a shuddhi process to purify himself in order to seek readmission into his caste, for he and his family were declared as outcaste due to his violation of the caste law which forbid voyages across the seas. When Gandhi returned from England, his brother first took him to Nasik where he had a bath in the sacred river as part of his shuddhi process, before going to Rajkot (his hometown). On reaching Rajkot, he had to throw a caste dinner.

Initially, the Arya Samaj considered shuddhi rites as not only a process for purification of upper-caste Hindus who had been tainted by a polluting contact, but also as a method to purify upper-caste Hindus who had left Hinduism and become either Christian or Muslim, in order to bring them back into the Hindu fourfold system. Christophe Jaffrelot writes that in an earlier period, from roughly 1885 to 1895, the Arya Samaj was only concerned about reconverting upper-caste Hindus who had 'gone over' to Islam or Christianity. However, he says that from 1900, the Arya Samaj's shuddhi campaigns were directed towards purifying untouchables and the low castes in order to bring them into the Hindu fourfold structure. And it was, for Jaffrelot, 'no less a modern reinterpretation, as it was not a matter of the purification of high castes having lost their status, but of elevating those who were situated at the bottom of society to the rank of "twice-born"'.[33] In this way, the classical concept of shuddhi, consisting of certain rituals practised by upper-caste Hindus to rid themselves from impurities with which they may have been tainted by a polluting contact, was interpreted and employed to elevate the social status of the lower castes and the untouchables.

There were various reasons for this. The wider context was partly the recognition of communal representation in the political and constitutional reforms introduced by the British government. In this respect, the upper-caste Hindu leaders were afraid that if lower-caste Hindus and untouchables converted to Christianity or Islam, Christians or Muslims stand to get more benefits from the upcoming constitutional reforms. As Swami Shraddhanand, the Arya Samajist behind the shuddhi movement, said: 'If all untouchables become Muslims, then Muslims will become equal to the Hindus and at the time of independence, they will not depend on Hindus, but will be able to stand on their own legs.'[34] Therefore, the focus of the shuddhi movement was not so much on improving the condition of the untouchables and low castes as much as to dissuade them from converting to Christianity and Islam.[35] However, the focus of this study is neither to find out the true motives behind the shuddhi movement nor to present a historical account of this movement. As mentioned earlier, the primary aim here is to study the limitations and strengths of Gandhi's evolving strategy to abolish the caste system by contrasting it with the Arya Samaj's shuddhi movement which had the objective of abolishing the same.

Removing Excrescences versus Removing False Consciousness

While the Arya Samaj emerged as the upper-caste Hindus' response to the proselytizing religions of Islam and Christianity, it sought to make Hinduism, too, a proselytizing religion. The Arya Samaj asserted the superiority of Hinduism over all religions and adopted an aggressive programme for it. It declared that its aim was the restoration of Vedic religion and society. For the Arya Samaj, the different practices and beliefs in Hindu society that were criticized by Christian missionaries were indeed symptoms of the decline of Hindu civilization; these customs were not part of its Vedic civilization. It argued that such aberrations are to be expected in an old and glorious civilization that was long under foreign rule. Following the same line of reasoning, the Arya Samaj said that the practice of untouchability and the subdivisions of the four castes were such aberrant deviations from the original Vedic concept of *chaturvarna* (fourfold division of Hindu society). It wanted these aberrations to be eradicated to rediscover the original fourfold division of Hindu society. K.N. Panikkar writes that Dayananda, the founder of the Arya Samaj, gave a utopian explanation for chaturvarna and sought to maintain it on the basis of virtue. Panikkar adds that Dayananda declared: 'He deserves to be a *Brahman* who has acquired the best knowledge and character, and an ignorant person is fit to be classed as *Shudra*.'[36] Indeed the Arya Samaj wholeheartedly supported the ancient idea of the four castes. Swapan K. Biswas writes: 'The Arya Samaj never talked about annihilation of caste or even to reduce the rigor of the caste system.'[37] The shuddhi movement initiated by the Arya Samaj also worked on the concept of purity and pollution, the cardinal principle which ultimately validates caste differences and hierarchies. In this respect, the shuddhi movement of the Arya Samaj was not an effort to destroy the four-caste division of Hindu society but to revive or purify it by giving up its excrescences, that is, the practice of untouchability and the numerous subdivisions of the four castes.

Gandhi agreed with the Arya Samaj that the practices of untouchability and the numerous contemporary subdivisions of castes are not an integral part of Hinduism but its excrescences. He also agreed that such excrescences needed to be eradicated in order to save Hinduism. However, to him, the practice of untouchability and the caste differences and hierarchies were also a sign of caste arrogance, and of the moral failure of upper-caste Hindus to treat the untouchables as equals. Therefore, for Gandhi, the problems of the caste system could not be solved just by rediscovering the original Vedic society through abolishing the practice of untouchability and erasing the numerous subdivisions of the four castes. Equally for him, the false consciousness of caste differences and hierarchies needed to be removed from the minds of Hindu masses. The last two chapters argued that Gandhi's evolving strategy primarily aimed to remove such false consciousness from the minds of Hindus. It also described how Gandhi went about this, adopting different strategies at different stages.

Upward Mobility versus Downward Mobility

In the shuddhi movement, the Arya Samaj made individuals or groups of people from the Dalit/untouchable castes undergo a purification ceremony in order to free themselves of the impurities attached to them; they would then be admitted into the Hindu fourfold system. It was also expected of these individuals who had been put through the purification ceremony to imitate the different customs and practices of the upper-caste Hindus. In this way, they would get social recognition and acceptance within the Hindu fourfold structure. This meant they would also adopt the practices of the twice-born (*dwij*), be given the sacred thread, and taught the *Gayatri Mantra* and some religious rites. The Arya Samaj evolved a programme for the socio-economic upliftment of the untouchables which involved the establishment of schools and cooperative societies, demanding the right of all to draw water from the village wells or construction of new wells for the untouchables, and so on. In this way, the Arya Samaj developed a multidimensional process for the 'upward mobility' of the untouchables. This can also be called 'Sanskritization'. However, in most of the cases, this process saw ritual take precedence over socio-economic upliftment. This resulted in a mere symbolic acceptance of the individual into the fourfold division of Hindu society but led to little or no changes in their economic and political life.

Gandhi rejected the process of shuddhi, and not just because it failed to bring any substantial changes in the socio-economic status of the untouchables. His disagreement with the shuddhi method was much more fundamental. He rejected it because he could see that the logic of the shuddhi method—'upward mobility'—failed to challenge or weaken the false consciousness of caste differences and hierarchies in society. The logic of upward mobility did not work towards attacking the ideological and moral foundations of the caste system, but was limited to achieving acknowledgement and acceptance of the untouchables within Hinduism's fourfold division. To Gandhi, the logic of shuddhi or 'upward mobility' seemed to have a reverse effect: it consciously or unconsciously strengthened, legitimized, and validated the false consciousness of caste differences and hierarchies rather than weakening or eradicating it. Srinivas explains it this way: 'However, the mobility associated with Sanskritization results only in positional changes in the system and does not lead to any structural change. That is, a caste moves up above its neighbours and another comes down, but all this takes place in an essentially stable hierarchical order. This system itself does not change.'[38]

Gandhi rejected the logic of the shuddhi movement as it only promised a change in the hierarchical position for particular castes or sections of castes within the caste system and failed to actually bring about any definite structural changes within the caste system. Gandhi, on the other hand, adopted a method that can be described as 'downward mobility'. The preceding two chapters explained that Gandhi, through personal example, persuasion, argument, and propaganda, tried to educate the upper-caste Hindus to give up their caste prejudices of purity and pollution in order to purify themselves. According to him, that constituted real shuddhi. He wrote: 'I must tell the Hindus [upper-caste Hindus] to wash off the stain of untouchability. This will be true *shuddhi*.'[39] At another time, when asked whether the untouchables should go through the *upanayan* (sacred thread) ceremony, he rejected it, adding that 'it involves the assumption that they are low and that they have got to be raised to a higher status'. He further argued that the upper-caste Hindus needed to take their natural place with the so-called untouchables by relinquishing their false sense of superiority.[40] Therefore, for Gandhi, the shuddhi movement that aimed to grant the untouchables social acceptance within the Hindu fourfold system, without removing the false consciousness of caste differences from the minds of the Hindus, was an inadequate way to tackle the caste system and its ills.

Pride versus Penance

Arya Samajists had their own disagreement with Gandhi's ways. They were not just concerned with the removal of untouchability. Rather, the removal of untouchability was an approach designed to establish the spiritual superiority of Hinduism in the midst of challenges posed by Christianity and Islam, and to nurture the self-confidence and pride of the humiliated and nervous Hindus. Gandhi's method—'downward mobility'—which demanded that the upper-caste Hindus give up their pride of caste superiority and accept voluntary simplicity and the poverty of the untouchables, was against the Arya Samaj's objective.

The method adopted by the Arya Samaj was that of mobilizing a sense of pride among the upper-caste Hindus to remove certain practices in order to rediscover their glorious past. Lajpat Rai writes that Dayananda's objection was not to give the Hindu matter and occasion for boasting, but to lift him from that slough of despondency into which he had fallen, and to give him leverage for the removal of the great burden that lay on his mind. Rai adds that Dayananda 'wanted to inspire the Hindu with just pride and with confidence in the great value of his heritage'.[41] Another militant nationalist ideologue, Bankim Chandra Pal, praised Dayananda and the Arya Samaj for taking inspiration from evangelical Christianity and Islam in order to create and foster a similar militancy in Hinduism.[42]

Gandhi, however, wanted to remove the false consciousness of caste hierarchies and differences from Hindu society. He, therefore, rejected the Arya Samaj method which created and fostered militancy among Hindus about their religion and caste superiority. According to him, this fake consciousness about caste superiority was the main source of the practice of untouchability and caste differences and hierarchies present in Hinduism. Hence, Gandhi believed that the best method would be one which did not evoke any false sense of caste superiority in Hindus. The method he adopted was to mobilize the feelings of shame and guilt among the upper-caste Hindus. He projected the practice of untouchability as a sin of the upper-caste Hindus, and his movement against the practice as a penance for them. He demanded that the upper-caste Hindus not just abandon their false consciousness regarding caste but also participate in the social, economic, and political upliftment of the untouchables as part of their penance. Gandhi imbued his movement with the character of penance.

Limitations, Strengths, and Continuing Relevance of Gandhi's Strategy

The detailed discussion of the differences between Gandhi's evolving strategy and Ambedkar's anti-caste movement, and Gandhi's evolving strategy and the Arya Samaj's shuddhi movement enables us to understand the strengths and weaknesses of Gandhi's strategy in fighting the caste system, and to understand its continuing relevance for the upliftment of the untouchables. The discussion reveals that Gandhi's evolving strategy suffered from three limitations that are discussed ahead.

First, Gandhi's strategy failed to question, and eventually address, the highly unequal economic structure and the power equation between the upper-caste Hindus and the untouchables created by the caste system. He failed to understand that the caste system is not just a state of mind but also a turbulent political and economic arrangement. Gandhi understood that the caste system was a state of mind based on the false consciousness of caste differences and hierarchies. His diagnosis was that this false consciousness was created and justified by the notion of purity and pollution, and this notion had to be undermined to eradicate the false consciousness. However, Gandhi failed to understand that the removal of the caste system would also involve restructuring of the highly unequal economic structure and power relationship. Though Gandhi had a clear long-term plan to eradicate the false consciousness of caste differences and hierarchies, he could not develop a similar, sophisticated plan to restructure the highly unequal economic structure and power relationship between the upper-caste Hindus and the untouchables. And without restructuring this, the mission of abolishing the caste system could not be accomplished.

Second, Gandhi's evolving strategy for fighting the caste system failed to understand the kind of roles the state and the process of westernization/modernization could play. Though history did prove that Gandhi was right in seeing the state as a soulless machine that crushes individual autonomy and also right in that westernization/modernization had its own forms of exploitation and hierarchy, he failed, however, to see that the state and westernization/modernization were historically inevitable for India. Consequently, he did not develop any plan for using the state and westernization/modernization to restructure the highly unequal economic structure and power relationship between the upper-caste Hindus and the untouchables created by the caste system. He also failed to develop any long-term method to garner state support or to speed up the process of westernization/modernization in order to eradicate the false consciousness of caste differences and hierarchies from the minds of Hindus.

Gandhi remained dependent on the exemplary individual and also organized upper-caste Hindus to carry forward his fight against the caste system. The methods he used were personal example, argument, persuasion, and propaganda. Such methods had their own obvious limitations in reaching out to the masses; these limitations could have been effectively overcome by seeking the help of the state. This Gandhi failed to do. Throughout his struggle against the caste system, Gandhi remained sceptical about the importance of advocating the Western/modern, rational world view, or industrialization and urbanization, for not only eradicating the caste system but also for removing other social evils. In Gandhi's method, there was no scope for expediting the process of westernization/modernization that played an important role in chipping away the false consciousness of caste differences and hierarchies in Hindu society and in restructuring the highly unequal economic structure and power relation between the upper-caste Hindus and the untouchables.

A third significant limitation of Gandhi's evolving strategy was that it demoralized the untouchables. Without doubt,
Gandhi's strategy was paternalistic. In his scheme of things, the
untouchables were to remain as passive objects without their own
individuality/agency, while the upper-caste Hindus practised
penance and virtues. This is ironic, considering Gandhi's emphasis
on the autonomy of individuals. In his strategy, there was no plan
to organize the untouchables to fight for their basic rights. In
the process of evolution of his strategy against the caste system,
Gandhi always thought of assuring self-respect to the untouchables and restoring dignity to the manual occupations that were
traditionally assigned to them. But he never worked out any plan
to enhance their self-confidence. Gandhi, in his long struggle
against the caste system, which lasted almost three decades, did
not succeed in creating even a single Dalit leader of the stature of
Ambedkar, Nehru, or Patel.

Apart from these three limitations, Gandhi's evolving strategy
had the following two weaknesses. First, he did not leave 'a clear
pathway' to continue the fight against the caste system. It was
demonstrated in the book that every time, while extending his
demand regarding what he meant by removal of untouchability,
Gandhi created an institute to set an example as well as actualize
that demand. For instance, in 1920, before articulating that removal
of untouchability meant untouchable children should be admitted into school, he established Gujarat Vidyapith as an example and
effective institute to actualize his demand. In a similar way, after
articulating that the removal of untouchability meant temple entry
for the untouchables, he requested the Congress to set up a committee for removal of untouchability with an objective to open the
gate of the temples for untouchables. And in 1933, after articulating
that the removal of untouchability meant education and social and
economic upliftment of untouchables, he established the Harijan
Sevak Sangh to actualize this demand.

However, the history of his struggle reveals that he alone knew the nitty-gritty of his strategy, such as how long his movement would concentrate on an issue like school entry for the Dalit children, or temple entry for the untouchables, or when the movement would take up other matters. What the real issues of his movement were, which ones were not part of the movement, and what the accepted methods of working were and what were not—all this was decided by Gandhi alone. When caste issues would get priority and when they would be put on the backburner was also entirely dependent on Gandhi's decision. Though Gandhi had created an army of volunteers who were ready to lay down their lives fighting the caste system, most of them were not autonomous individuals governed by their own beliefs, convictions, and principles and, therefore, could not take independent decisions during crises. Most of them depended on Gandhi for guidance. Therefore, as long as Gandhi was around, it appeared that his methods, style, and strategies were viable. However, in his absence, nobody exactly knew in which direction the movement would or should go and hence it would lose all force.

Another weakness of Gandhi's evolving strategy was its slowness, given the size of India's population and the country's large geographical area. India is a huge country and the existing caste differences and hierarchies are based on centuries-old socio-religious prejudices. It seems an almost impossible task to eradicate such age-old religious prejudices from the minds of Hindus who live across such a huge geographical expanse using a step-by-step method of personal example, argument, persuasion, and propaganda. The task became more difficult due to Gandhi's insistence that the caste prejudices must be eradicated without disturbing traditional village life, as he did not encourage industrialization and urbanization that could have speeded up the process of changing the mindset of Hindus towards the caste system.

If Gandhi's strategy had some obvious and serious limitations and weaknesses, it had significant merits too. One of the important merits of Gandhi's evolving strategy was that though it was very slow, it did not bring upper-caste Hindus and the untouchables into direct confrontation with each other. On the other hand, it was designed in such a way that it minimized the differences between them. While Ambedkar's anti-caste movement may seem to be quicker in securing real sources of higher status in Hindu society for the untouchables, it highlighted deep and largely unresolved differences within Indian society that expressed themselves as serious antagonisms during a period when a greater degree of national unity was especially important. In this respect, Gandhi's strategy was very relevant for his time because it tried to maintain the unity of Indian society, which was necessary for the nation's fight against the British Empire. Gandhi's strategy is still relevant, and not just for the simple reason that unity among different sections of society is always important for the maintenance of law and order and for peace and harmony. It is of equal relevance in contemporary India given the prevailing enmity among different caste groups in the country about the policies of reservation and compensatory discrimination. Bhikhu Parekh writes that reservation and compensatory discrimination have aroused considerable hostility between the upper-caste Hindus and the untouchables.[43] In such circumstances, an approach which minimizes this hostility and creates a sense of duty and responsibility in the warring sides would be very appropriate, because an absence of harmony and trust between the upper-caste Hindus and the untouchables would obstruct not only the achievement of peace and harmony in society but also the process of eradicating caste differences and hierarchies.

Another important merit of Gandhi's evolving strategy was that it helped undermine the prejudices of caste differences and hierarchies present in Hindu society, something that other contemporary methods failed to do. The Arya Samaj's shuddhi movement—which strove for upward mobility of the untouchables within the caste hierarchy through purification ceremonies—also aimed to strengthen the unity of Hindu society, but failed miserably to undermine caste prejudices. In fact, the logic of shuddhi movement worked on the principle of purity and pollution which ultimately justified caste hierarchies and differences in Hindu society. Similarly, though Ambedkar's anti-caste movement had many merits, it also failed to undermine the caste prejudices present in Hindu society. Ambedkar's methods that focused on creating a separate identity for the untouchables as a suppressed minority widened the differences between the upper-caste Hindus and the untouchables. Gandhi's strategies, on the other hand, gradually educated the upper-caste Hindus to abandon their beliefs and practices that were based on the notion of purity and pollution, by insisting that they recognize the importance and dignity of manual work that was traditionally done by the untouchables. Since the prejudices of caste differences and hierarchies continue to exist in Hindu society and create hurdles for effective implementation of different policies for the upliftment of the untouchables, Gandhi's strategies, which attack the prejudices at their very root, remain relevant in the present scenario as well.

* * *

This book aims to understand Gandhi's long-term strategy to abolish the caste system and its continuing relevance for the upliftment of the untouchables today. The first chapter argued that despite the enormous difficulties that various scholars had faced in assessing Gandhi's views on the caste system and untouchability due to the inconsistencies in his writings, the subject can be thoroughly examined and understood by studying his life. By citing many examples from Gandhi's life and ashrams, the chapter argued that right from his early childhood, Gandhi dared to disobey caste restrictions and refused to practice any of them at any point in his life. The chapter concluded by revealing the possibility for a new research enquiry; it suggested that since Gandhi did not practise any caste restrictions in his personal life and remained consistent about this until the end of his life, the inconsistencies in his writings on untouchability, caste, and other related issues must be understood as part of his long-term strategy to abolish the caste system.

The second chapter examined the basis of Gandhi's ideal society and ideal form of organizing human society. The examination revealed two things: first, while Gandhi's opinions on many issues underwent changes, his basic ideas about ideal society, ideal governance, and so on, that he developed during his twenty-one-year stay in South Africa and described in *Hind Swaraj*, remained constant. Second, Gandhi learnt during his struggles in South Africa that true swaraj or freedom for India can only be achieved by individuals who had learnt to self-regulate and self-organize their lives. The chapter concluded that it was not parliamentary swaraj based on the modern state, or a Hindu raj based on the caste system, or varnashrama dharma, but the autonomy of the individual that Gandhi advocated and aspired to achieve. The chapter also argued that Gandhi fought against everything—whether it was the modern state, or the traditional caste system, or varnashrama dharma—that crushes the autonomy of the individual. And his fight against the caste system must be understood as part of his larger struggle to safeguard the autonomy of the individual from both external and internal assaults.

The third and fourth chapters discussed the course of Gandhi's evolving strategy against the caste system within its historical context. Both chapters presented a chronological account of Gandhi's writings and life starting from 1915 until his death in 1948. This chronological presentation of Gandhi's writings and life revealed that the writings and works of Gandhi in different periods of time contained different themes on the issues of untouchability, caste, varna, inter-dining, and inter-caste marriage. For instance, Gandhi's writings for the period 1916–20 show that during this span of time, Gandhi emphasized that removal of untouchability meant destruction of the notion that one gets polluted by the mere physical touch of someone. However, his writings between 1920 and 1927 see him argue that removal of untouchability meant that children of the untouchables should be permitted entry in every national school. These two chapters analysed the themes that emerged in the life and writings of Gandhi during different periods of time, and explained their continuity, changes, and strategic inter-relations. In the process of this analysis, it was discovered that the different themes in Gandhi's writings would make greater sense if they are considered as representing different stages of Gandhi's evolving strategy that he designed for the gradual abolition of the caste system.

The fourth chapter also reflected on Gandhi's evolving strategy in its totality and yielded the following three points: first, it was part of Gandhi's strategy to project his movement against the caste system and untouchability as a revivalist movement—a movement to save the 'original tradition' by giving up its excrescences, rather than as a revolutionary movement that aimed to destroy old traditions by adopting new or modern values. For instance, the most revolutionary act of social reform of his time—inter-caste marriage between upper-caste Hindus and the untouchables (a taboo in Hindu society in the present times as well)—was proposed and encouraged by him not for the abolition of caste inequalities but 'to preserve whatever is good in varnashrama' and 'to save Hinduism'. Second, it was also part of Gandhi's strategy to take up different issues related to untouchability and the caste system one by one, on the basis of the intensity of their social impact. It is explained that it was for strategic reasons that Gandhi started his movement against untouchability and the caste system by taking up the least contentious issue, that is, the notion of physical touch, gradually moving to the more contentious issues, that is, school entry for untouchable children and temple entry for the untouchables, and finally, to highly contentious issues, that is, inter-caste marriage between upper-caste Hindus and the untouchables. Third, there was a strategic relation between the changes occurring in Gandhi's views on untouchability, caste, and other related issues over a period of time, and those occurring in the nature and tempo of nationalist politics. As a strategist, Gandhi used both his moral authority over the masses and the favourable conditions in nationalist politics to gradually take his struggle against the caste system to its logical end—its abolition.

The fifth chapter critically evaluated Gandhi's overall strategy to abolish the caste system in order to understand its continued relevance for the upliftment of the untouchables during the present times. For this purpose, it placed Gandhi's strategy in contrast with two other contemporary movements: the Arya Samaj's shuddhi movement and Ambedkar's anti-caste movement. It examined the divergences between Gandhi's strategy and the other two approaches and, in doing so, highlighted the limitations as well as merits of Gandhi's approach. In this process of critical evaluation, some serious limitations of Gandhi's strategy emerged. For instance, while on the one hand Gandhi's strategy failed to undermine the highly unequal economic structure and power relation between upper-caste Hindus and the untouchables created by the caste system, on the other hand, it demoralized the untouchables due to its paternalistic nature. However, the chapter argued that Gandhi's strategy had some important merits too. It did not bring upper-caste Hindus and the untouchables into direct confrontation; it minimized the differences between the upper and lower castes, and finally, it was designed to remove the false consciousness of caste differences and hierarchies from the minds of people, which the other two movements were not. The chapter argued that in the present scenario in which reservation and compensatory policies have generated tension in Hindu society, which in turn poses a danger to the unity of the country as well as to the effective implementation of the different polices for the upliftment of the untouchables, Gandhi's strategy can help foster more cordial relations between the upper-caste Hindus and the untouchables. It is relevant in the present times as it can help overcome fake prejudices of caste that still hold sway over the lives of many educated as well as uneducated Hindus.

Notes

1. Ashis Nandy, 'Final Encounter: The Politics of the Assassination of Gandhi', in *Debating Gandhi*, p. 51.
2. See Roy, *Gandhi and Ambedkar*; Thomas Pantham, 'Against Untouchability: The Discourse of Gandhi and Ambedkar', in Gopal Guru (ed.), *Humiliation: Claims and Context* (New Delhi: Oxford University Press, 2009), pp. 178–208; Nagaraj, 'Self-Purification versus Self-Respect'; Keer, *Dr. Ambedkar*.
3. See Rao, 'Gandhi, Untouchability and the Postcolonial Predicament'; Omvedt, *Dalits and the Democratic Revolution*.
4. V. Rodrigues, 2011, 'Reading Texts and Traditions: The Ambedkar–Gandhi Debate', *Economic and Political Weekly*, 46(2): 56–65.
5. See G. Bhatt, 1968, 'Brahmo Samaj, Arya Samaj and the Church–Sect Typology', *Review of Religious Research*, 10(1): 23–35; V. Dua, 1979, 'Arya Samaj and Punjab Politics', *Economic and Political Weekly*, 5(43 and 44): 1787–91.
6. Keer, *Dr. Ambedkar*.
7. Ambedkar, 'Annihilation of Caste with a Reply to Mahatma Gandhi', pp. 116–17, available at http://drambedkarbooks.word-press.com (accessed on 10 April 2013).
8. D.N., 'Gandhi, Ambedkar and Separate Electorates Issue', pp. 1328–30.
9. M.K. Gandhi, 'Speech at Chamarajendra Sanskrit Pathashala, Bangalore', 30 July 1927, in *CWMG*, Vol. 34, p. 266.
10. Prabhu, 'Gandhi's Religious Ethics', p. 164.
11. M.K. Gandhi, 'Socialism', 13 July 1947, in *CWMG*, Vol. 88, p. 324. Gandhi's position here does not appear to be very convincing; rather, it looks as though he, while opposed to caste hierarchy, is trying somewhat desperately to provide cover for a traditional value system.

12. Parekh, *Colonialism, Tradition and Reform*, p. 230.
13. Jaffrelot, 'Dr. Ambedkar's Strategies against Untouchability and the Caste System', p. 6. According to Gail Omvedt, 'State protection for Dalits had always been seen as essential, even in his [Ambedkar] periods of greater faith in the majority; and now in an atmosphere in which India under Nehru appeared set to adopt planning and a "socialist pattern of society" Ambedkar's main thrust was to look to this state-guided development as a solution.' See Omvedt, *Dalits and the Democratic Revolution*, p. 239.
14. Gandhi, 'Interview to Nirmal Kumar Bose', 9/10 November 1934, p. 319.
15. Pantham, 'Against Untouchability', p. 189. Jaffrelot also reminds that 'by the end of 1920s, he (Ambedkar) had rejected the logic of Sanskritisation which had till then overshadowed the attempts by Untouchables to emancipate themselves'. He adds, 'From the 1930 onwards Ambedkar's career was to delineate two strategies of emancipation. The first, which focused on the organization of political parties, aimed at obtaining a specific representation for Untouchables in India's ruling institutions. The second was none other than the conversion to a religion different from Hinduism.' Jaffrelot, *Analysing and Fighting Caste*, p. 51.
16. Roy, *Gandhi and Ambedkar*, p. 115.
17. Roy, *Gandhi and Ambedkar*, p. 115.
18. M.K. Gandhi, 'Shraddhanand Memorial', 6 January 1927, in *CWMG*, Vol. 32, p. 515.
19. M.K. Gandhi, '"Depressed" Classes', 27 October 1920, in *CWMG*, Vol. 18 (New Delhi: Publications Division, Government of India, 1965), p. 376.
20. M.K. Gandhi, 'Talk with a Harijan Sevak', 15 June 1935, in *CWMG*, Vol. 61, p. 160.
21. Gandhi, 'Temple-Entry', 23 September 1939, p. 184.
22. Gandhi writes, 'The movement for the removal of untouchability is one of self-purification.' See M.K. Gandhi, 'An Impatient Worker', 15 April 1931, in *CWMG*, Vol. 60, p. 381.
23. Nagaraj, 'Self-Purification versus Self-Respect', p. 377.

24. Speech by Ambedkar quoted in Jaffrelot, *Analysing and Fighting Caste*, p. 52.

25. Srinivas, *Social Change in Modern India*, p. 53.

26. Karl Marx, 'The Future Results of British Rule in India', *New York Daily Tribune*, 8 August 1853, available at http://www.marxists.org/archive/marx/works/1853/07/22.htm (accessed on 17 April 2012).

27. D. Ganguly, 2002, 'History's Implosions: A Benjaminian Reading of Ambedkar', *Journal of Narrative Theory*, 32(3): 326–47. Gail Omvedt argues that Ambedkar saw modernity from a perspective quite contrary to that of Gandhi. As Omvedt puts it, 'He looked to the values underlying it as the revolutionary aspirations to liberty, equality and community. Modernisation was something that he sought, not feared.' See Omvedt quoted in C.S. Dharmadhikari, *Trusteeship: A Technique of Social Change*, available at http://www.mkgandhi.org/articles/trusteeship1.htm (accessed on 27 December 2016).

28. Nagaraj, 'Self-Purification versus Self-Respect', p. 366.

29. Sudipta Kaviraj also believes that Nehru and Ambedkar were wrong to disregard traditions entirely, taking the typical Enlightenment view of treating traditional ideas and practices as erroneous. He writes, 'They [Nehru and Ambedkar] also wrongly believed that to rescue people from tradition, their intellectual and practical habits, all that was needed was simply to present a modern option; peoples' inherent rationality would do the rest.' S. Kaviraj, 2000, 'Modernity and Politics in India', *Daedalus*, 129(1): 155.

30. Srinivas, *Social Change in Modern India*, p. 57.

31. Bhatt, 'Brahmo Samaj, Arya Samaj, and the Church–Sect Typology', p. 27.

32. Y. Sikand and M. Katju, 1994, 'Mass Conversions to Hinduism among Indian Muslims', *Economic and Political Weekly*, 29(34): 2215.

33. Christophe Jaffrelot, *Religion, Caste & Politics in India* (New Delhi: Primus Books, 2010), p. 147.

34. Shraddhanand quoted in Lelyveld, *Great Soul*, p. 175.

35. Pauline Moller Mahar writes, 'The nationalistic aims of the Arya Samaj included the cessation of the conversion to Christianity and Islam of the one-fifth of the population who were untouchables.'

P.M. Mahar, 1960, 'Changing Religious Practices of an Untouchable Caste', *Economic Development and Cultural Change*, 8(3): 282.

36. K.N. Panikkar, 'Social–Religious Reforms and the National Awakening', in *India's Struggle for Independence*, p. 88.

37. Biswas, *Gods, False Gods and the Untouchables*, p. 216.

38. Srinivas, *Social Change in Modern India*, p. 6.

39. M.K. Gandhi, 'Speech at Public Meeting, Banaras', 9 January 1927, in *CWMG*, Vol. 32, p. 540.

40. Gandhi, 'Talk with a Harijan Sevak', 15 June 1935, p. 160.

41. Lajpat Rai, 'Religious Ideals and Aims', in J.B. Sharma and S.P. Sharma (eds), *Arya Samaj and Regeneration of India* (Jaipur: Sublime, 1999), p. 99.

42. Pal quoted in Mani, *Debrahmanising History*, p. 217.

43. Parekh, *Colonialism, Tradition and Reform*, p. 241.

The politician

A response to Arundhati Roy's 'The Doctor and the Saint'*

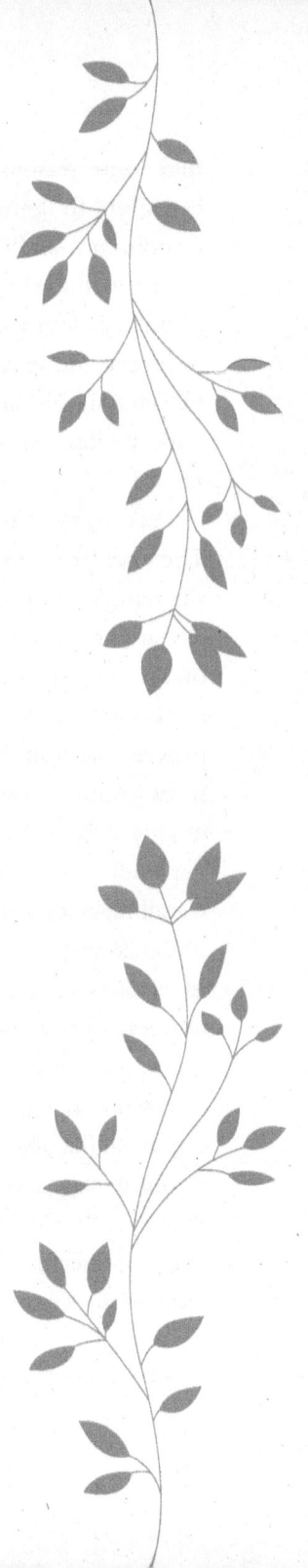

This paper looks closely at Arundhati Roy's introduction entitled 'The Doctor and the Saint' to the annotated edition of Annihilation of Caste *originally authored by Dr. B.R. Ambedkar. The paper argues that the basic problem in Roy's analysis is that from the very outset she assumes (by her own confession she has been raised on a diet of Gandhi hagiographies) Gandhi was a born saint and she expects that his every writing and action should conform to her own perception of Gandhi as a saint. On the other hand, in this paper it is argued that if we accept Gandhi as a politician and examine his writings and deeds within its historical context, keeping in mind that he, as a human being and as a politician, evolved over a period of time, we will be able to better understand his writings, works, and contribution to human society.*

Arundhati Roy's introduction to *Annihilation of Caste: The Annotated Edition*, titled 'The Doctor and the Saint', appears to have been written more to attack Gandhi than to assess the contemporary relevance of this great book and/or the life and works of its author.[1] Therefore, Ambedkarites might find some reasons to ignore the article. However, no Gandhian can afford to ignore her article. The article is a direct challenge to Gandhism. Gandhians are left mainly with two options: accepting the powerful criticism of Roy and reassessing their perception of Gandhi, and/or responding to Roy's criticism of Gandhi. Both are necessary and inevitable elements to have a deeper understanding of Gandhi's life and work, though this response to Roy's article limits itself to the second element only—that, too, only on the issue of race and caste.

Let's begin with a very general note on Roy's method of analysis. The basic problem in Roy's analysis is not that from the very outset she refuses to treat Gandhi as a saint and treats him as a politician alone. The basic problem in Roy's analysis is that from the very outset she assumes (by her own confession she has been raised on a diet of Gandhi hagiographies) Gandhi was a *born* saint and she expects that from his day one in South Africa, Gandhi should have made common cause with the Black Africans to bring down the mighty British rule in British colonies of South Africa. Obviously her reading of Gandhi's life fails to fulfil her expectations regarding Gandhi's sainthood. It appears that while reading Gandhi's writings, she encounters some of Gandhi's odd statements relating to the issues of race, caste, and gender, which appear to her as antithesis to her own perception of Gandhi as a saint. Though she also finds some of Gandhi's statements that might confirm her perception of Gandhi as a saint, she decides not to be deceived this time by Gandhian hagiographies. She not only refuses to perceive this inconsistency in Gandhi's views as a gradual evolution in Gandhi's thought but also decides to unravel consistency in his inconsistency. She seems to argue that inconsistency in Gandhi's views or some of his writings that might conform to his image of sainthood are part of the larger project to create Gandhi hagiographies that Gandhi himself began. She writes, 'In order for Gandhi to be a South African hero, it became necessary to rescue him from his

past, and rewrite it. Gandhi himself began that project.' If we accept
her writing we have to also accept that Gandhi was so confident
about winning the title of Mahatma or saint in India that he started
this project as early as in 1909 (almost six years before his arrival
in India and eleven years before assuming leadership of the Indian
national movement). This realization (some of Gandhi's writings
and acts that conform to his image as a saint are part of a project
to create Gandhi's hagiographies) helps her to reach the conclusion
that in spite of shallow inconsistency in Gandhi's views and deeds,
at a deeper level, 'his [Gandhi's] pronouncements on the inherent
qualities of Black Africans, untouchables and the labouring classes
remained consistently insulting'.[2] Therefore, for her who has been
raised on a diet of Gandhi's hagiographies, it is 'not just disturbing,
it is almost stupefying'.[3]

However, if Roy had thought of Gandhi as a politician and
not a *born* saint, who had two decades of political apprentice-
ship without any mentor in South Africa, she would not have
been disappointed so much. Apart from reading the saint's writings, she should have also looked at the historical circumstances
that had forced a novice politician to accept the role of a public
man. She should have considered the kind of people with whom
the politician was to work, both as associates and as opponents.
She should have also developed a proper understanding of the
social, economic, and political position of the Indian community
in South Africa, as well as the nature and limit of grievances they
could practically think of. In place of blaming the saint for his proposal of an 'imperial Brotherhood' and for citing Queen Victoria's
1857 proclamation for equal treatment to every Indian in Natal,
she should have also contemplated what were the other possible
alternatives available for the politician in South Africa. In place of
blaming the saint for the absence of Black Africans in his Phoenix
Settlement, she should have tried to perceive it as an effort of the
politician to *gradually* do away with the distinction between the

domains of 'home' and 'public'. Along with looking at inconsistency in the saint's *writings* on the issue of caste and varna, she should have also looked at what the politician had been doing, because as Anthony J. Parel writes, 'Nowhere, in his [Gandhi's] entire political career, do we find him attempting to restore the dharma of the discredited varnashrama.'[4]

It should be sincerely accepted that if someone should have studied Gandhi as a politician, it would not have been so disturbing and stupefying for her/him, and she/he should have found some element of saintliness in the politician Gandhi. The problem in Roy's analysis is not that she accidently misses the above-mentioned aspects of Gandhi's life that would have conformed to her own perception of Gandhi as a saint. Instead, her article clearly speaks for her determination to not only refuse to see any aspect of Gandhi's life that would conform her own perception of Gandhi as a saint, but also to tear up her own perception of Gandhi as a saint; even taking the risk of being charged of showing gross disregard for facts, use of 'suitable' quotations out of context, and shallow analysis for deliberate misrepresentation of Gandhi's positions on important issues like race, caste, gender, and so on.

Let us consider the quotation of E.M.S. Namboodiripad that Roy had used in her article to highlight 'the conflict between Ambedkar and the left' as an example. Though the quotation is not used for deliberate misrepresentation of Gandhi's position that is the primary concern of this response, it is important to demonstrate how far she has gone in her article to prove her own point of view. She writes:

> Angered by Ambedkar's display of independence, the communists denounced him as an 'opportunist' and an 'imperial stooge'. In his book *History of the Indian Freedom Struggle*, E.M.S. Namboodiripad ... wrote about the conflict between Ambedkar and the left: 'However, this was great blow to the freedom movement. For this led to the diversion of the peoples' attention from the objective of full

independence to the mundane cause of the uplift of Harijans [untouchables].'[5]

According to Roy, Namboodiripad wrote the above quote to explain 'the conflict between Ambedkar and the left'. However, in fact Namboodiripad wrote the above quote regarding Gandhi's decision to go on fast unto death against the British government's decision to offer separate electorate for untouchables and subsequent events leading to the Poona Pact. In this quotation Namboodiripad blamed Gandhi and not Ambedkar for diversion of the peoples' attention. Namboodiripad wrote that Gandhi:

... subordinated the struggle for Swaraj to the day-to-day activities for the upliftment of the depressed castes. What is more, Gandhi gave a moral (religious) character to this political approach....Thus, the Congress as well as its undisputed leader, Gandhi, which was engaged in a country-wide struggle with the objective of liberating India from the British rule, engrossed itself in the programme of liberating the Depressed Castes and other Hindus from the curse of untouchability from which the entire Hindu religious community had been suffering.... A direct result of this was the weakening of the civil disobedience movement.[6]

This was the context in which Namboodiripad wrote about the shift of focus and Roy uses it for an entirely different purpose— highlighting 'the conflict between Ambedkar and the left'.

* * *

Let us now be more specific and consider Roy's dubious charges against Gandhi that are gross misrepresentation or perhaps deliberate misrepresentation of Gandhi's positions on different issues. Let us also analyse all the explanations and justifications that she puts forward to substantiate her charges against Gandhi. We may begin with her charges against Gandhi on the issue of race that makes an impression on the reader that Gandhi was an outstanding

racist. First, she charges Gandhi for 'always [being] careful to distin-
guish—and distance—passenger Indians from Indentured (bonded)
workers'. She gives two lengthy quotes of Gandhi to support her
argument. In the first quote, Gandhi says:

> Whether they are Hindus or Mahommedans, they are absolutely
> without any moral or religious instruction worthy of the name.
> They have not learned enough to educate themselves without any
> outside help. Placed thus, they are apt to yield to the slightest temp-
> tation to tell a lie. After some time, lying with them becomes a
> habit and a disease. They would lie without any reason, without any
> prospect of bettering themselves materially, indeed, without know-
> ing what they are doing. They reach a stage in life when their moral
> faculties have completely collapsed owing to neglect.[7]

This quote is part of Gandhi's open letter address to the members of the legislative council and legislative assembly,   Natal, dated
December 1984. In this open letter, Gandhi had argued that Indians
are as civilized as British, and being the citizen of British Empire
they are legally entitled to receive equal treatment in Natal. At the
end of his explanation, Gandhi anticipated a possible objection
against his own argument. He writes that one can justifiably argue
that the glorious picture of Indian civilization presented by Gandhi
is imaginary because the practices of most of the Indians in South
Africa—they speak lies and do immoral things—do not conform
to it. He partially accepted the possible objection, but argued 'that
other classes do not fare much better in this respect, especially if and
when they are placed in the position of the unfortunate Indians'.[8]
And he went on explaining the position of the unfortunate Indians
in which they live and develop the practice of speaking lies and
doing immoral things to substantiate his point that in such a position
people from any race will do the same thing. On the other hand,
Roy uses it for a completely different purpose to argue that Gandhi
was always careful to make distance with indentured workers.

The second quote of Gandhi is part of his interview to the *Natal Advertiser*, dated January 1897. This time Roy tries to explain the context in which Gandhi made the remarks regarding his attitude towards indentured Indians in South Africa. She very fairly mentioned that 'in 1897, he [Gandhi] travelled to India where he addressed packed—and indignant—meetings about the racism that Indians were being subjected to in South Africa'. She also informs the reader that 'when Gandhi returned to Durban in January 1897, the news of his campaign had preceded him'. She also tells that 'it took several days of negotiation before Gandhi was allowed to disembark. On his way home, on 12 January, 1897, he was attacked and beaten.' Then she writes the last sentences: 'Two days later, in an interview to *The Natal Advertiser*, Gandhi once again distanced himself from the "coolies"'; this was followed by Gandhi's quote. Gandhi said:

> I have said most emphatically, in the pamphlets and elsewhere, that the treatment of the indentured Indians is no worse or better in Natal than they receive in any other parts of the world. I have never endeavoured to show that the indentured Indians have been receiving cruel treatment.[9]

However, she forgets to explain two important things: first, the context of the question; and second, the meaning of the question in response to which Gandhi had mentioned his attitude towards the indentured Indians. In this interview Gandhi was trying to defend himself from the charge that in India he had indulged in unmerited condemnation of the Natal whites for their cruel treatment of Indians. In the same interview earlier, Gandhi said, 'It has been said that I went to India to blacken the character of the Natal Colonists. This I must emphatically deny.'[10] In this context when the interviewer asked Gandhi the question 'In your Indian campaign what attitude did you adopt towards the indentured Indian question?', the interviewer wanted to know whether Gandhi had said anything in India regarding Natal whites' attitude towards indentured Indian labour that blackened their character. What Roy had quoted is only *part* of Gandhi's response in which he tried to say that while speaking about the indentured labour's condition in Natal Colony, he did not blacken the character of the Natal colonists, and not 'distanced himself from the "coolies"', which is the impression created by Roy. We can understand it better if we read the first full paragraphs of Gandhi's reply keeping in mind the context and the meaning of the question. The first full paragraph of Gandhi's answer goes like this:

> I have said most emphatically, in the pamphlets and elsewhere, that the treatment of the indentured Indians is no worse or better in Natal than they receive in other parts of the world. I have never endeavoured to show that the indentured Indians have been receiving cruel treatment. The question, generally speaking, is not a question of the ill-treatment of Indians, but of the legal disabilities that are placed on them. I have even said in the pamphlet that instances I have quoted show that the treatment that the Indians receive was owing to the prejudice against them, and what I have endeavoured to show is the connection between the prejudice and the laws passed by the Colony to restrict the freedom of the Indians.[11]

When we read this first full paragraph of Gandhi's answer keeping in mind the meaning and context of the question, it gives an entirely different picture of Gandhi than what Roy wants us to believe about him. Apart from this, even if Roy did not go into the details of the work that Gandhi had done in relation with the indentured Indian, and only looked carefully at a single document—*Report of the Natal Indian Congress*—dated August 1895 that she quotes often in her article, she should have got a better picture of Gandhi's work related to indentured Indians. The document says, 'Work has also been done among the indentured Indians. Balasundram, who was badly treated by his master, was transferred to Mr. Askew.' It also informs that two other works were done by the NIC for indentured Indians.

First, '[t]he Congress interfered on behalf of the indentured Indians in the Railway department, in connection with the Mohurrum festivals as well as supply of wood instead of coal. Much sympathy was shown by the Magistrate presiding.' Second, 'the Immigration law, which contemplates imposition of a £3 tax in lieu of indenture, has been strenuously opposed. Petitions were presented to both the Houses.'[12] These are a few examples to argue that Gandhi did work with and for the indentured Indian, and he did not try to distance himself from them as Roy seems to argue.

Let us now take another charge made against Gandhi by Roy. She blames Gandhi for proposing an idea of 'Imperial Brotherhood' and for citing Queen Victoria's 1858 proclamation in order to argue equal treatment for 'passenger Indians'. Roy argues that 'Gandhi was not trying to overwhelm or destroy a ruling structure; he simply wanted to be friends with it'.[13] She also writes that 'when Indian political activists joined the liberation movement under African Leadership in the 1950s and saw their freedom as being linked to the freedom of African people, they were breaking with Gandhi's politics, not carrying on his legacy'.[14] From the following quote of Gandhi, one can infer that why at the initial level he preferred to fight the Indian cause separately. He writes:

> This Association of Coloured People does not include Indians who have always kept aloof from that body. We believe that the Indian community has been wise in doing so. For, though the hardships suffered by those people and the Indians are almost of the same kind, the remedies are not identical. It is therefore proper that the two should fight out their cases, each in their own appropriate way. We can cite the Proclamation of 1857 in our favour, which the Coloured people cannot. They can use the powerful argument that they are the children of the soil....[15]

However, it would be wrong to believe that if he would have stayed longer in South Africa, he would have continued to organize his struggle on the same principle. On the other hand, the history of Gandhi's struggle in South Africa as well as in India clearly shows that as an incisive politician Gandhi developed a new strategy and fixed new aims according to the circumstances. Judith N. Brown writes: 'The techniques he [Gandhi] evolved were those of the pragmatist, in particular he was limited by the people he had to organize, the audience at which he aimed, and the nature of the issue at stake.' She adds: 'As the circumstances and the grievance changed so did Gandhi's political tactics.'[16] It appears that Roy forgets the old proverb that 'the tree does not grow in one day'. She needs to remember that to fight against the policy of racial discrimination of a powerful government is a long-term struggle, and such a struggle advances through stages. As the struggle evolves, its strategy, methods, and aims evolve. Even the Indian National Congress took almost 50 years to officially fix complete political freedom of India as its ultimate objective. Therefore, in spite of vast differences between the methods of early Congress nationalist leaders like Dadabhai Naoroji and Gopal Krishna Gokhale, and the methods of later Congress leaders like Jawaharlal Nehru, Sardar Patel, Maulana Azad, it is believed that the latter were carrying the legacy of the former. Thus, it can be argued that when the Indian political activists joined the liberation movement under African leadership in the 1950s, they were carrying on Gandhi's legacy.

Let us now take the most serious charge of Roy against Gandhi that he had 'shown disdain for Black African' and he 'was not offended by racial segregation'. He was offended that 'passenger Indians—Indian merchants who were predominately Muslim but also privileged caste Hindus—who had come to South Africa to do business, were being treated on a par with native Black Africans'.[17] From the very outset, it has to be accepted that she did not give any evidence to the reader to believe that Gandhi was ever offended because he or some other 'passenger Indians' were forced to travel with native Black Africans or he had started any movement to make different accommodation arrangement for Indian and native Black

Africans in trains. Gandhi, in some of his writings, mentions that British Indians were being treated on a par with raw Kaffirs; however in an altogether different context (the context will be analysed later) than on the issue of common accommodation for Indians and Kaffirs in trains. On the other hand, in the latter part of his life in South Africa when Gandhi started experimenting with simplicity in life, he decided to travel in third-class carriages only. When he was asked about its reasons by one of his friends, he replied: 'I shuddered to read the account of the hardships that the Kaffirs had to suffer in the third-class carriages in the Cape and I wanted to experience the same hardships myself.'[18] In another letter to a different friend, he informs that he along with Kasturba and two friends travelled in the third-class carriage where generally '[n]atives are herded together like cattle!' He also writes that the idea behind travelling in a third-class carriage is 'that only a 3rd-class traveller can bring about reform in 3rd class carriages'.[19] He also strongly advised some of his white friends to travel in third-class carriages only because he believed that 'a few of us doing this will be able to do a great deal for 3rd class passengers'.[20]

In place of giving any evidence to substantiate her argument that Gandhi was offended because 'passenger Indians' were treated on par with native Black Africans, Roy cites the Durban Post Office problem. She writes: 'The Post Office had only two entrances: one for Blacks and one for Whites. Gandhi petitioned the authorities and had a third entrance opened so that Indians did not need to use the same entrance as the "Kaffirs".' It is a fact that the post office had only two entrances; it is also true that the president of the NIC petitioned to the authorities in connection with the separate entrances for the Europeans and natives and Asiatics at the post office. However, Roy's writings create an impression that Gandhi demanded separate entrance for Indians and Kaffirs, and he demanded it because he felt offended to share entrances with Kaffirs. This needs further verification, and since she does not give the source of her information and in the absence of the original petition, we can infer from the writings of Gandhi what might be the issue. In the report of the NIC dated August 1895 Gandhi mentioned that 'a correspondence was carried on by the late President with the Government in connection with the separate entrances for the Europeans and Natives and Asiatics at the Post Office.' He also mentioned that as its result '[s]eparate entrances will now be provided for the three communities'. However, he also writes that 'the result has not been altogether unsatisfactory'.[21] If Asiatics (Indian) were given separate entrances now, they need not share entrances with Kaffirs, then why has this result not been altogether unsatisfactory according to Gandhi? It simply means that the NIC did not demand separate entrances for Indians and Kaffirs because they felt offended to share common entrances with Kaffirs. Gandhi mentioned about the same issue in his appeal to the Indian public; in this appeal he writes, 'In the Durban Post and Telegraph Offices, there were separate entrances for natives and Asiatics and Europeans.' He adds, 'We felt the indignity too much and many respectable Indians were insulted and called all sorts of names *by the clerks at the counter. We petitioned the authorities to do away with the invidious distinction ....*'[22] It is obvious now that Gandhi/Indians neither demanded separate entrances for Indian and Kaffirs nor he/they felt offended to share a common entrance with them, indeed he/they demanded to do away with the invidious distinction because Indians were insulted by the clerks due to this invidious distinction made by the government.

Roy also mentioned that Gandhi was offended because Indians 'were treated on a par with native Black Africans'. It is a fact that on many occasions Gandhi writes about Indians being classified with the South Africans; however a proper investigation is needed to draw a conclusion that he was offended because of it. If we look at those writings of Gandhi in which he mentioned that Indians were being classified with South Africans, it appears he was referring either to the white government policy or biases of white people and not expressing his displeasure for classifying Indians with native Black Africans. Two samples of Gandhi's writings are given below for the ready reference of readers:

> In strict accordance with the policy of degrading the Indian to the level of a raw Kaffir and, in the words of the Attorney-General of Natal, 'that of preventing him from forming part of the future South African nation that is going to be built'.[23]

> A general belief seems to prevail in the Colony that the Indians are little better, if at all, than savages or the Natives of Africa. Even the children are taught to believe in that manner, with the result that the Indian is being dragged down to the position of a raw Kaffir.[24]

Apart from all these, there are also some writings of Gandhi that can help us understand that whenever Gandhi wrote on Indians being classified with Kaffirs, he was simply referring to the white government's policy or whites' prejudices, and not taking offence at it. For instance, in his 'Letter to Maganlal Gandhi', dated August 1910, he writes: 'I regard the Kaffirs, with whom I constantly work these days, as superior to us.'[25] On several occasions, he also writes about Kaffirs and their issues in his newspaper *Indian Opinion*. The *Indian Opinion* issue, dated 2 February 1905, carried an article titled 'Attack on the Kaffirs' in which he expressed his unhappiness because the Johannesburg Town Council passed a regulation that a Kaffir who had a permit to own a bicycle would be asked to wear this permit on his left arm. He writes that they have passed such a regulation because 'the Johannesburg Town Council could not bear to see the Kaffirs riding bicycles like the whites....'[26] In another article titled 'The Kaffirs of Natal', dated 2 September 1905, Gandhi wrote: '[T]his Mr. Dubey is a Negro of whom one should know ... he imparts education to his brethren, teaching them various trades and crafts and preparing them for the battle of life.'[27] In another article titled 'Johannesburg Letter' dated 3 March 1906,

Gandhi wrote: 'Lord Selborne has returned from Masseroo, where nearly 2,000 Basuto Kaffirs had gathered to greet him. These Africans are a very intelligent people. They have their own Parliament, which they call Pitso.'[28] In another article titled 'Terrible Step', dated 1 January 1910, Gandhi wrote about one incident in which the Pretoria Town Council served a notice to the examiners who allowed a Kaffir to sit with the whites in the same hall during examination. He wrote that when the examiners asked for a separate room for the Kaffirs, this too was refused by the council. He added: 'Such instances of injustice are a natural consequence of the whites' refusal to treat the coloured people as their equals. It is in order to put an end to this state of affairs that we have been fighting in the Transvaal....'[29] Let us take a final example from Gandhi's *Satyagraha in South Africa* in which Gandhi describes the life of Negroes in the following words: 'Before British rule men as well as women moved about almost in a state of nudity. Even now many do the same in the country. They cover the private parts with a piece of skin. Some dispense even with this. But let not anyone infer from this that these people cannot control their senses.' He adds, 'It is only vanity which makes us look upon the Negroes as savages. They are not the barbarians we imagine them to be.'[30]

Roy may not accept the last quotation of Gandhi as substantive evidence to accept that Gandhi had not 'shown disdain for Black African' because according to her it was written in 1924, much after the beginning of the project that Gandhi himself along with his followers started to rescue him from his past and to make him a South African hero and the Mahatma. However she might not find it difficult to accept other examples cited from Gandhi writings because they were taken from the writings of Gandhi before the beginning of his project to rescue himself from his past. At the end of this section, it needs to be explained that all the examples from Gandhi's writings cited above and all the explanations given above are not to reconfirm Roy's perception that Gandhi was a born Mahatma.

What is argued here is that if we examine Gandhi's writings and deeds within their historical context, and keep in mind that he, as a human being and as a politician, evolved over a period of time, we can better understand his writings, works, and contributions to human society.

***

Let us now consider Roy's charges against Gandhi related to the issue of caste. Writings of Roy create the impression that Gandhi was an outstanding casteist who was the latest in a long tradition of privileged caste Hindu reformers like Raja Ram Mohan Roy, Swami Dayananda Saraswati, Swami Vivekananda, and so on. She blames Hindu reformers for cleverly narrowing the question of caste to the issue of untouchability, and Gandhi for narrowing it even further to the issue of removing prejudices regarding the works of 'bhangis'. She also blames Gandhi for 'eulogis[ing] a mythical Indian past that was, in his telling, just and beautiful',[31] and ignoring inequality and exploitation present in the Indian past. Another charge that Roy makes against Gandhi is that he was a hypocrite in his practices related to different caste restrictions. To reveal Gandhi's hypocrisy, she quotes from Vijay Prashad's 'The Untouchable Question':

> 'You can offer me goat's milk,' he [Gandhi] said, 'but I will pay for it. If you are keen that I should take food prepared by you, you can come here and cook my food for me'.... Balmiki elders recount tales of Gandhi's hypocrisy, but only with a sense of uneasiness. When a dalit gave Gandhi nuts, he fed them to his goat, saying that he would eat them later, in the goat's milk.[32]

It is important to remember that since Gandhi had a habit of doing experiments with his food, and as part of his experiment he used to observe different rules (not caste restrictions) with respect to food, therefore it is quite possible that he should have asked Dalits or anybody that '[i]f you are keen that I should take food prepared by you, you can come here and cook my food for me'. However, it must be due to his habit of continuous experiment with eating and not due to caste prejudices regarding inter-dining. It is a fact that in the very early years of his life Gandhi overcame the caste restriction of compulsorily dining within one's own caste and throughout his life he ate with people of different faiths as well castes, including untouchables. In his autobiography Gandhi writes: 'I had no scruples about inter-dining.'[33] Just to mention a few examples: first, inter-dining was part of all the four ashrams founded by Gandhi; second, Gandhi adopted an untouchable girl as his own child, and she used to live, play, travel, and share food with Gandhi; and third, in the Sevagram Ashram, one local untouchable boy name Govind used to prepare food for Gandhi along with helping him in other activities as well. Apart from these few examples, Tanika Sarkar's description regarding Gandhi's attitude towards the untouchables is worth quoting. She writes: 'He [Gandhi] worked closely with low-caste coolies and invited Untouchable colleagues to live on his farms. He forced "unclean" work on himself and on his family, and he accepted Untouchables in his social and domestic circles on equal terms.'[34] The examples above and Tanika Sarkar's brief description regarding Gandhi's practice related to the caste restrictions can help us understand that there was no hypocrisy in Gandhi's attitude towards the untouchables. On the other hand, it appears that from a very young age, Gandhi had overcome caste prejudices.

Roy's next charge against Gandhi is that he was the latest in a long tradition of privileged caste Hindu reformers, and he narrowed the issue of caste exploitation to the issue of removal of prejudices against the works of bhangis. Though it is true that Gandhi's methods to deal with the issue of the caste system, in more than one way, were similar to the social reform movements initiated by upper-caste people, the differences between the methods of Gandhi and the upper-caste social reform movements are too fundamental for the former to be considered as being in the same category as the latter. Most of the upper-caste social reform movements work on the principle of upward mobility/logic of Sanskritization. In this method individuals or groups from the untouchable community are encouraged to imitate the customs and practices of the upper-caste Hindus in order to get rid of notions of pollution attached with them. This ensures their admission into the Hindu fourfold system. Some of the upper-caste social reform movements had developed a shuddhi movement in which individuals or groups of people from the untouchable caste needed to undergo a purification ceremony in order to free themselves of the impurities attached to them; they would then be admitted into the Hindu fourfold system. Gandhi, from the beginning of his struggle with caste prejudices, rejected the shuddhi movement/logic of Sanskritization/principle of upward mobility as an effective method to deal with the issue of caste difference and hierarchy present in Hindu society not just because it fails to bring any substantial changes in the socio-economic status of the untouchables. His disagreement with such a method was much more fundamental. He rejected it because he could see that the principle of upward mobility failed to challenge or weaken the false consciousness of caste differences and hierarchies in Hindu society. The logic of upward mobility did not attack the ideological and moral foundations of the caste system but was limited to achieving acceptance of untouchables within Hinduism's fourfold division. To Gandhi, the logic of upward mobility seemed to have a reverse effect by accepting the superiority of Brahminical tradition, culture, and practices. According to him, it consciously or unconsciously strengthened, legitimized, and validated the false consciousness of caste differences and hierarchies rather than weaken or eradicate it.

Gandhi, on the other hand, adopted a method that can be described as 'downward mobility'. In his 30-year-long struggle against caste difference and hierarchies, Gandhi, through personal example, persuasion, argument, and propaganda, tried to educate upper-caste Hindus to give up their caste prejudices of purity and pollution in order to purify themselves. According to him, this constituted real shuddhi or upward mobility. He writes: 'I must tell the Hindus [upper-caste Hindus] to wash off the stain of untouchability. This will be true *shuddhi*.'[35] At another time, when asked whether the untouchables should go through the *Upananyan* (sacred thread) ceremony, he replied 'no' adding that 'it involves the assumption that they are low and that they have got to be raised to a higher status'. He goes on arguing that indeed 'we [upper-caste Hindus] must come down from the high pedestal we have occupied all these years and take our natural place with them'.[36] He idealized the work and position of bhangis (lowest among the lower position in the caste hierarchy) and asked every Hindu to become a bhangi in his thought, words, and action. It is something very different from the logic of upward mobility that accepts the superiority of the Brahminical tradition, culture, and practices, and strengthens the caste differences and hierarchy. Gandhi's method of downward mobility was something very radical, for by doing so, Gandhi was refusing to accept the superiority of the Brahminical tradition, culture, and customs from which the justification for caste differences was derived. By rejecting the superiority of the Brahminical culture Gandhi indeed attacked the very root of the caste system, and perhaps better than any other social reform movement or anti-caste movement did. This is a basic difference between Gandhi's method and the upper-caste social reform movement's method to deal with the issue of caste difference and hierarchy.

There is another significant difference between Gandhi's method and the upper-caste social reform movement's method to deal with the issue of caste system. Many upper-caste movements were not just concerned with the removal of untouchability. Rather, the removal of untouchability was an approach designed to establish the spiritual superiority of Hinduism in the midst of challenges posed by Christianity and Islam, and to nurture the self-confidence and pride of the humiliated and nervous Hindus. The method adopted by these upper-caste social reform movements was that of mobilizing a sense of pride among the upper-caste Hindus to remove certain practices in order to rediscover their glorious past. Lajpat Rai writes that Dayananda's objective was not to give the Hindu matter and occasion for boasting, but to lift the Hindu from that slough of despondency into which he had fallen and to give him leverage for the removal of the great burden that lay on his mind. Rai adds that Dayanand 'wanted to inspire the Hindu with just pride and with confidence in the great value of his heritage'.[37] On the other hand, Gandhi wanted to remove the false consciousness of caste hierarchies and differences from Hindu society. He therefore rejected this method of some of the upper-caste reform movements which created and fostered militancy among Hindus about their religion and caste superiority. According to him, this fake consciousness about caste superiority is the main source of the practice of untouchability and hierarchies present in Hinduism. Hence, Gandhi believed that the best method would be one which did not evoke any false sense of caste superiority in the Hindus. The method he adopted was to mobilize the feelings of shame and guilt among the upper-caste Hindus, and his movement against the practice was a penance for them. He demanded that upper-caste Hindus not just abandon their false consciousness regarding caste but also wanted them to participate in the social, economic, and political upliftment of untouchables as part of their penance. Gandhi imbued his movement with the character of penance. And if the ideology of Hindutva is an offshoot of the upper-caste social reform movement's method to create and foster militancy among Hindus about their religion and caste superiority, it may not be an exaggeration to say that Gandhi's movement to mobilize the feelings of shame and guilt among the upper-caste Hindus has enabled (may be in a limited sense) the government of independent India to enact appropriate legislation to safeguard the interest of untouchables without the fear of popular resistance.

Roy also charges Gandhi of 'eulogis[ing] a mythical Indian past that was, in his telling, just and beautiful',[38] and to ignore inequality present in the Indian past. Though it is a fact that Gandhi appreciated some aspects of the Indian past, it is not the case that Gandhi appreciated everything about the Indian past. Gandhi himself very categorically said that his 'is not an attempt to go back to the so-called ignorant, dark ages'.[39] He was well aware of the totalizing nature of traditions, especially Hindu tradition, and was not any less opposed to the traditional modes of domination. However, for pragmatic reasons alone, he preferred to tackle the traditional modes of domination and hierarchy indirectly. It is important to remember that when Gandhi was talking about his ideal society he was not referring to any geographical area (that is, western, eastern, or Indian society) or time (that is, modern city or ancient village). 'Gandhi though,' Sukumar Muralidharan writes, 'recognised neither past nor present, preferring to focus his attention on the eternal virtues invested in mankind through its intimate contact with divinity.'[40] Indeed Gandhi in his whole life neither idealized India's mythical past as the authentic and ideal era of Hindu society nor did he start any movement to go back to the Vedic golden age as Dayananda Saraswati and some upper-caste social reformers had done. Gandhi, as Muralidharan informs us, was concerned with nurturing the eternal virtues invested in every individual through his intimate contact with divinity.

Roy holds that 'Gandhi never decisively and categorically renounced his belief in chaturvarna, the system of four varnas'.[41] If we look at Gandhi's writings alone, Roy's observation seems to be a fair enough picture of Gandhi's position regarding the issue of the caste system, because Gandhi indeed appreciated some of the positive aspects of the chaturvarna on many occasions. However, Raghavan N. Iyer suggests that political thinkers are properly studied without reference to their personalities and practice, but when we turn to Gandhi we find it peculiarly difficult to ignore his personality and his activities. Gandhi also very categorically says:'To understand what I say one needs to understand my conduct....' [42]

Let us now try to understand Gandhi's conduct related to different caste restrictions in order to better understand his writings. Gandhi, from a very young age, revolted against the practice of untouchability and it may not be an exaggeration to say that in his whole life he did not practice untouchability in any form. It is also mentioned above that throughout his life Gandhi ate with people of different faiths as well as castes, including untouchables. It is worth taking into consideration the fact that Gandhi not only allowed his son Ramdas to marry someone who was from a different sub-caste but also allowed his son Devdas to marry a girl who was from another varna altogether. He also, by design, married off his adopted daughter Lakshmi, who was an untouchable, to a Brahmin boy in 1933. It may not be a coincidence that in the first paragraph of his autobiography, Gandhi writes that over the last three generations, starting with his grandfather, his family had not been pursuing the hereditary or traditional duty assigned to them according to the caste system. He himself never earned his bread and butter by following his ancestors' calling. He also let his children choose their own professions, and never pressed them to follow any pursuit prescribed for their caste. Moreover, he tried to master many activities prohibited for his caste, such as the work of a scavenger, barber, washerman, cobbler, tiller, and tailor. Though it is a fact that Gandhi, on several occasions, said that he believed in the Shastras, it is also true that he did not accept them as the ultimate authority or the word of God. When he was asked 'Where do you find the seat of authority?', Gandhi, pointing to his breast, said:'It lies here.' He also explains:

> I exercise my judgment about every scripture, including the *Gita*.
> I cannot let a scriptural text supersede my reason. Whilst I believe
> that the principal books are inspired, they suffer from a process of

double distillation. Firstly, they come through a human prophet, and then through the commentaries of interpreters. Nothing in them comes from God directly.[43]

Margaret Chatterjee writes that Gandhi was not a temple-goer;[44] Joseph Lelyveld in his recent biography of Gandhi notes that 'Gandhi hardly ever prayed in temples'.[45] Apart from all these let us look at his attitude towards some other caste restrictions; for instance, during his time, it was prohibited for his caste to voyage abroad. Although his fellow caste members were agitated and the caste head—Sheth—declared that if he went to England for studies he would be treated as an outcaste, he still sailed for England to study law. Gandhi also writes: 'On the eve of my going to England, however, I got rid of the *shikha*'.[46] He also gave up his sacred thread—*upavita*. It is also important to remember that none of his ashrams were built on the basic principle of the caste system or varnashrama dharma. And none of the caste restrictions were observed in his ashrams. It seems difficult to accept that a man who violated almost every caste restriction throughout his life and who built ashrams where no caste restriction was observed, held the caste system or varnashrama dharma as an ideal form of organizing human society.

If we look at his sociopolitical activity, we do not find him attempting to restore the dharma of the discredited varnashrama. Nevertheless, like Roy, many scholars believe that it was this ancient original varna system that Gandhi was trying to reinforce and establish in India. However, Gandhi himself rejects such a possibility when he says:

> I have gone no-where to defend varnadharma, though for the removal of untouchability I went to Vaikom. I am the author of a Congress resolution for propagation of Khadi, establishment of Hindu–Muslim unity, and removal of untouchability, the three pillars of swaraj. *But I have never placed establishment of varnashrama dharma as the fourth pillar. You cannot, therefore, accuse me of placing a wrong emphasis on varnashrama dharma.*[47]

Therefore, it seems more difficult to accept that Gandhi held the caste system or varnashrama dharma as an ideal form of organizing human society, as his practices speak otherwise.

On the other hand, Roy who entirely focuses on Gandhi's writings and ignores his practice reaches an erroneous conclusion that Gandhi never decisively renounced his belief in chaturvarna. Even while focusing on Gandhi's writings she treats them as part of the sermon of a saint and takes them literally. She forgets that Gandhi was a politician too and hence fails to notice the possibility of any kind of strategy in Gandhi's defence of some of the positive aspects of the caste system. What she misses can be understood in Rajmohan Gandhi's metaphorical explanation. He writes, 'I see the Varnashrama remarks as sugar-coating for his [Gandhi's] pill for caste Hindus. He wants them to swallow his reforms.' He adds, 'The "caste system" he [Gandhi] was "defending" was nonexistent. Attacks on his "defence" by his foes of the caste system only assured caste Hindus that Gandhi was not their enemy which he was not.'[48]

Notes

* This article has formerly appeared in *Gandhi Marg*, 2014, 36(1): 145–64. *Gandhi Marg* is a quarterly journal published by the Gandhi Peace Foundation, New Delhi.

1. Arundhati Roy, 'The Doctor and the Saint', in B.R. Ambedkar, *Annihilation of Caste: The Annotated Critical Edition* (New Delhi: Navayana Publishing, 2014), p. 134.

2. Roy, 'The Doctor and the Saint', p. 134.

3. Roy, 'The Doctor and the Saint', p. 60.

4. Parel, *Gandhi's Philosophy and the Quest for Harmony*, p. 94.

5. Roy, 'The Doctor and the Saint', p. 115.

6. E.M.S. Namboodiripad and K.M.N. Menon, *A History of Indian Freedom Struggle* (Trivandrum: Social Scientist Press, 1986), p. 496.

7. See Roy, 'The Doctor and the Saint', p. 67.

8. Gandhi, *CWMG*, Vol. 1 (New Delhi: Publications Division, Government of India, 1969), p. 188.

9. See Roy, 'The Doctor and the Saint', p. 68.

10. *CWMG*, Vol. 2 (New Delhi: Publications Division, Government of India, 1976), p. 122.

11. *CWMG*, Vol. 2, p. 123.

12. *CWMG*, Vol. 1, pp. 245–51.

13. Roy, 'The Doctor and the Saint', p. 77.

14. Roy, 'The Doctor and the Saint', p. 87.

15. *CWMG*, Vol. 5 (New Delhi: Publications Division, Government of India, 1961), p. 243.

16. Brown, *Gandhi's Rise to Power*, pp. 3–6.

17. Roy, 'The Doctor and the Saint', p. 66.

18. *CWMG*, Vol. 10, p. 183.

19. *CWMG*, Vol. 11 (New Delhi: Publications Division, Government of India, 1964), p. 443.

20. *CWMG*, Vol. 11, p. 441.

21. *CWMG*, Vol. 1, p. 249.

22. *CWMG*, Vol. 2, pp. 10–11; emphasis added.

23. *CWMG*, Vol. 2, p. 74.

24. *CWMG*, Vol. 1, p. 117.

25. *CWMG*, Vol. 10, p. 308.

26. *CWMG*, Vol. 4 (New Delhi: Publications Division, Government of India, 1960), p. 352.

27. *CWMG*, Vol. 5, p. 55.

28. *CWMG*, Vol. 5, pp. 238–9.

29. *CWMG*, Vol. 10, p. 113.

30. Gandhi, *Satyagraha in South Africa*, p. 9.

31. Roy, 'The Doctor and the Saint', p. 50.

32. Roy, 'The Doctor and the Saint', p. 103.

33. Gandhi, *An Autobiography*, p. 96.

34. Sarkar, 'Gandhi and Social Relations', p. 178.

35. *CWMG*, Vol. 32, p. 540.

36. *CWMG*, Vol. 61, p. 160.

37. Rai, 'Religious Ideals and Aims', p. 99.

38. Roy, 'The Doctor and the Saint', p. 50.

39. *CWMG*, Vol. 70, p. 242.

40. Sukumar Muralidharan, 2006, 'Religion, Nationalism and the State: Gandhi and India's Engagement with Political Modernity', *Social Scientist*, 34(3 and 4): 24.

41. Roy, 'The Doctor and the Saint', p. 41.

42. *CWMG*, Vol. 51, p. 353.

43. *CWMG*, Vol. 64, p. 75.

44. Chatterjee, *Gandhi's Religious Thought*, p. 7.

45. Lelyveld, *Great Soul*, p. 194.

46. Gandhi, *An Autobiography*, p. 355.

47. *CWMG*, Vol. 35, p. 523; emphasis added.

48. Gandhi, *The Good Boatman*, pp. 237–40.

Glossary

ahimsa	Non-violence; conceived by Gandhi as both a personal virtue and a political value as an active agent of change
Arya Samaj	A Hindu reform movement started by Swami Dayananda Saraswati
ashram	A spiritual community; Gandhi established four ashrams (two in South Africa and two in India)
atman	The universal self, according to Hinduism
bania	The sub-caste to which Gandhi belonged, within the Vaishya social order in the system of four varnas
Bapu	Father; a general term of affection and respect often applied to Gandhi
bhangi	Sweepers; lowest among the lowest in caste hierarchy
Bhagavad Gita or Gita	A philosophical dialogue and sacred text of Hinduism that had a profound influence on Gandhi

brahmacharya	A vow of celibacy taken by Gandhi in 1906 to signify devotion to God, self-discipline, and commitment to public service
chamcha	Stooge
charkha	The spinning wheel promoted by Gandhi in his effort to establish the dignity of manual labour
Dandi	A village on the shores of Gujarat on the coast of western India; Gandhi's salt march ended here
dharma	Righteousness; adherence to the Hindu code of morality
dwij	A Sanskrit word, meaning twice-born
Ezhavas	An upwardly mobile caste in Kerala (a state in south India), once considered untouchable
Gayatri Mantra	A highly revered mantra, based on a Vedic Sanskrit verse from a hymn of the *Rig Veda* (3.62.10)
Harijan	The name Gandhi attempted to give the untouchables that stands for 'Children of God'; also, the title of his weekly journal after 1933
haveli	Temple
Hind Swaraj	'Indian Home Rule'; the title of Gandhi's book, published in 1909 in South Africa
karma	The destiny of an individual, shaped by conduct in previous life
khadi or khaddar	Homespun cotton cloth; Gandhi urged its production and use as the dress of nationalist movement to symbolize identification with the masses and practice of swadeshi
Mahatma	'Great Soul'; an honorific title bestowed on Gandhi by the Hindu masses

Modh Banias	The merchant sub-caste into which Gandhi was born
moksha	Spiritual liberation
Panchama	Fifth one; an outcaste or untouchable
Partition	The political division of British India into two independent nations, India and Pakistan, in August 1947
Raj or British Raj	The government; in Gandhi's period it denoted the administrative system of British rule over its colony, India
Ram Raj	'Rule of Rama'; the Hindu ideal of ancient India's golden age, evoked by Gandhi to mean an ideal society
Sarvodaya	'Welfare of all'; Gandhi's term for an ideal system of social and economic equality produced by social reforms
satyagraha	The power or force of truth, love, and non-violence; the word has a broad meaning to include various forms of social and political action
satyagrahi	One who practises the method or employs the power of satyagraha
shikha	A long tuft or lock of hair
Shastras	Old texts that are traditionally considered sacred by Hindus
Shastri	One who is learned in Hindu scriptures
sheth	A rich businessman
shuddhi or shuddhikarana	Rituals of purification in Hinduism; during Gandhi's time, these purification rituals were used for religious conversions by members of the Arya Samaj
Shudra	The lowest order of caste or varna; it traditionally ranks above the untouchables
swadeshi	Self-reliance

swaraj	Freedom; Gandhi offers diverse meanings for the concept of swaraj. Sometimes he uses the term in reference to national independence, and sometimes to mean spiritual freedom of the individual. He also uses it as a synonym for liberty, autonomy, political freedom of the individual, national economic freedom, freedom from poverty for the individual, self-realization, self-rule, freedom from alien rule, and so on
varna	A social order or group, of which there were four divisions in the traditional Hindu social theory
yajna	A spiritual sacrifice
yatra	A pilgrimage

Gandhi's Life
A Chronology

1869	Born on 2 October to Karamchand Gandhi and Putli Bai in the small princely state of Porbandar in the Kathiawad region of the present-day Gujarat, India
1875–86	Develops a dislike for *haveli*, enjoys half-a-dozen meat feasts with a Muslim friend, inclines towards atheism, opposes the practice and doctrine of untouchability
1888	In spite of his fellow caste members' agitation and the declaration by his caste head (sheth) that if he goes to England for studies he would be treated as an outcaste, he sails for England to study law; before going to England he cuts his shikha
1888–91	In England, he experiments with egg-eating; eats food in the company of different persons at different hotels cooked by people belonging to different religions and castes

1891	Comes back to India and gets admitted to the Bombay bar
1893	Again violates the caste rule and sails to South Africa
1893–1910	Drags his wife with the intention of pushing her out of their home because of her prejudices towards one of his Christian clerks, born of untouchable parents; often dines at the homes of friends belonging to different religions and castes and invites them for lunch or dinner at his own home as well; learns washing clothes, cutting his own hair, and a scavenger's work; arranges the marriage of Henry Polak, a Jew, with Millie Graham Downs, a Scottish Christian—after their marriage, this couple lived in Gandhi's Johannesburg house for almost a year; publicly criticizes caste differences, hierarchy, and the practice of untouchability
1904	Founds the Phoenix Settlement to experiment in rural commune living with people belonging to different religions and castes
1908	Opens a school at the Phoenix Settlement for all Indian children irrespective of their religion/caste, including the untouchables
1909	Writes *Hind Swaraj*
1910	Introduces a common kitchen for the settlers of the Phoenix Settlement; establishes Tolstoy Farm to house the families of jailed satyagrahis, who belonged to different religions and castes; learns shoemaking and carpentry
1912	Gives away his entire belongings and makes a trust of the Phoenix Farm
1915	Reaches back India on 4 January; establishes the Satyagraha Ashram on 25 May 1915 at Kochrab, a small village near Ahmedabad; admits an untouchable family (Dudabhai, his wife Danibehn, and their daughter Lakshmi) in the Satyagraha Ashram

1916	First reference of his calling himself a sanatani Hindu, and saying that he believes in the foundation of the caste system; learns weaving on country looms and fly-shuttle looms to produce khaddar cloth in the Satyagraha Ashram
1917	Learns spinning on charkha; starts a national school for all children irrespective of their caste and religion, where every student needs to learn agriculture, hand-weaving, and the use of carpenter and blacksmith tools; does local experiments to tackle the issue of caste obliquely by taking up issues of hygiene, cleanliness, health, and sanitation in the Champaran region of Bihar
1920	Starts his first all-India movement against caste differences and hierarchy by calling Indians to start national schools and admit untouchable children in them; establishes Gujarat Vidyapith as an example for it; refashions the INC by introducing a new constitution for it
1924	Introduces a minimum spinning qualification for the Congress membership; establishes the All India Khaddar Board at Sabarmati
1925	Sets up the All India Spinners' Association; directly involves himself in the Vaikom Satyagraha (temple-entry movement)
1926	Approves the killing of 60 rabid dogs by one mill owner at Ahmedabad; advises people to enter into marriage alliances within the subdivisions of the major castes, Brahmins, Kshatriyas, Vaishyas, and Shudras
1927	Embarks on an extensive tour to spread the message of the spinning wheel; his son Manilal marries Sushilabehn, who belonged to a different sub-caste of his varna

1928	Commits the greatest Hindu sin of cow killing (*gau hatya*) by killing a calf in order to put an end to its pain
1929	Advises the CWC to set up a committee for the removal of untouchability that would work for opening temples for the untouchables
1932	Undertakes a fast unto death against the MacDonald Communal Award that assured separate electorates for the untouchables to give momentum to his movement against the caste system; founds the Harijan Sevak Sangh for social, educational, and economic development of the untouchables; launches *Harijan*, a weekly English journal
1933–4	Gandhi's son Devdas marries Lakshami, a Brahmin girl, belonging to a different varna; Gandhi arranges the marriage of Lakshmi (an untouchable girl he adopted) with Maruti, a Brahmin orphan boy; undertakes a 21-day fast for self-purification as well as the purification of his associates who were working against the caste system; takes a nine-month-long extensive tour of India, known as the Harijan Yatra, to speed up his struggle against the caste system (during this tour, he faced great opposition and attacks on his life from upper-caste Hindu organizations); founds the All India Village Industrial Association at Wardha for the upliftment of village industry; starts the David Scheme (which provided a scholarship of Rs 2,500 for the duration of five years) for helping untouchable students pursue higher education; for the first time, his writings on varna and other related issues get published in a book, *Varnavyavastha*, on his request
1936	Starts the Sevagram Ashram at Segaon, near Wardha; involves the untouchables in almost all activities of the ashram; starts a tanning centre at Nalwadi

1937	Organizes the All India Education Conference in Wardha and proposes free, universal, and compulsory education for all boys and girls between the ages of 7 and 14
1942	Propagates to make the practice of untouchability a criminal offence
1945–8	Arranges the marriage of Indumati Gunaji, an untouchable girl, with G. Tendulkar, a Brahmin; Prabhakar, a follower of Gandhi from an untouchable background, conducts the marriage; this is also the second time his writings on varna and other related issues are published in a book, *Varnavyavastha*, on his request; starts promoting inter-caste marriage between upper-caste Hindus and the untouchables

Further Readings

Allen, Douglas. 2011. *Mahatma Gandhi*. London: Reaktion Books.

Andrews, Charles F. 2006. *Mahatma Gandhi: His Life & Ideas*. Mumbai: Jaico Publishing House.

Appadorai, A. 1969. 'Gandhi's Contribution to Social Theory', *The Review of Politics*, 31(3): 312–28.

Balaram, S. 1989. 'Product Symbolism of Gandhi and its Connection with Indian Mythology', *Design Issues*, 5(2): 68–85.

Brown, M. 1989. 'Swaraj, the Indian Ideal of Freedom: A Political or Religious Concept?', *Religious Studies*, 20(3): 429–41.

Desai, Mahadev. 1953. *The Diary of Mahadev Desai, Vol. I: Yeravda-Pact Eve, 1932*, Valji Govindji Desai (tr.). Ahmedabad: Navajivan Publishing House.

Dumont, Louis. 1972. *Homo Hierarchicus: The Caste System and Its Implications*. London: Paladin.

Erikson, Erik H. 1969. *Gandhi's Truth: On the Origins of Militant Nonviolence*. New York: W.W. Norton & Company.

Fischer, Louis. 1954. *Gandhi: His Life and Message for the World*. New York: Mentor Books.

Gandhi, M.K. 1958 onwards. *CWMG*. New Delhi: Publications Division, Government of India.

Gavaskar, M. 2009. 'Gandhi's Hind Swaraj: Retrieving the Sacred in the Time of Modernity', *Economic and Political Weekly*, 34(36): 14–18.

Guha, Ramachandra. 2007. *India after Gandhi: The History of the World's Largest Democracy*. London: Macmillan.

Gupta, D. 2008. 'The Importance of Being Inconsistent', *IIC Quarterly*, 35(2): 1–17.

Heredia, R.C. 1999. 'Swaraj, Then and Now', *Economic and Political Weekly*, 34(37).

Ilaiah, Kancha. 1996. *Why I am Not a Hindu: A Sudra Critique of Hindutva Philosophy, Culture and Political Economy*. Kolkata: Samya.

Jodhka, Surinder S. 2012. *Caste*, Oxford India Short Introductions. New Delhi: Oxford University Press.

Jones, K. 1968. 'Communalism in the Punjab: The Arya Samaj Contribution', *The Journal of Asian Studies*, 28(1): 39–54.

Jordens, J.T.F. 1998. *Gandhi's Religion: A Homespun Shawl*. New Delhi: Oxford University Press.

Mandal, J.C. 1999. *Poona Pact and Depressed Classes*. Calcutta: Sujan Publications.

———. 2012. *The Flaming Feet and Other Essays: The Dalit Movement in India*. New Delhi: Permanent Black.

Nandy, Ashis. 1983. *The Intimate Enemy: Loss and Recovery of Self under Colonialism*. New Delhi: Oxford University Press.

Nauriya, Anil. 2006. *The African Element in Gandhi* (e-version). New Delhi: National Gandhi Museum, New Delhi, in association with Gyan Publishing House.

Nayyar, Pyarelal. 1956. *Mahatma Gandhi: The Last Phase*, Vol. 1. Ahmedabad: Navajivan Publishing House.

Nigam, Aditya. 2009. 'Gandhi—The "Angel of History": Reading Hind Swaraj Today', *Economic and Political Weekly*, 34(11): 41–7.

Pande, B.N. (ed.). 1985. *Concise History of the Indian National Congress, 1885–1947*. New Delhi: Vikas Publishing House.

Parekh, Bhikhu. 1989. *Gandhi's Political Philosophy: A Critical Examination*. Notre Dame: University of Notre Dame Press.

———. 2001. *Gandhi: A Very Short Introduction*. Oxford: Oxford University Press.

Parel, A.J. 1969. 'Symbolism in Gandhian Politics', *Canadian Journal of Political Science*, 2(4): 513–27.

Prashad, V. 2009. 'Black Gandhi', *Social Scientist*, 37(1 and 2): 3–20.

Ray, Baren (ed.). 1996. *Gandhi's Campaign against Untouchability, 1933–1934: An Account from the Raj's Secret Official Reports*. New Delhi: Gandhi Peace Foundation.

Rothermund, I. 1969. 'The Individual and Society in Gandhi's Political Thought', *The Journal of Asian Studies*, 28(2): 313–20.

Rudolph, S.H. and L.I. Rudolph. 1987. *Gandhi: The Traditional Roots of Charisma*. Hyderabad: Orient Longman.

Sen, A.K. 1992. 'The Gandhian Experiment in Ahmedabad: Towards a Gramscian Reading', *Economic and Political Weekly*, 27(37): 1987–9.

Sharma, Arvind. 2005. *A New Curve in the Ganges: Mahatma Gandhi's Interpretation of Hinduism*. New Delhi: D.K. Print World (P) Ltd.

Srinivas, M.N. 1956. 'A Note on Sanskritization and Westernization', *The Far Eastern Quarterly*, 15(4): 481–96.

———. 1995. 'Gandhi's Religion', *Economic and Political Weekly*, 30(25): 1489–91.

Trivedi, Lisa. 2007. *Clothing Gandhi's Nation: Homespun and Modern India*. Bloomington: Indiana University Press.

Verma, V. 1999. 'Colonialism and Liberation: Ambedkar's Quest for Distributive Justice', *Economic and Political Weekly*, 34(39): 2804–10.

Wankhede, H. 2008. 'The Political and the Social in the Dalit Movement Today', *Economic and Political Weekly*, 43(6): 50–7.

Zachariah, M. and A. Hoffman. 1985. 'Gandhi and Mao on Manual Labour in the School: A Retrospective Analysis', *International Review of Education*, 31(3): 265–82.

Zelliot, Eleanor. 1988. 'Congress and the Untouchables, 1917–1950', in Richard Sisson and Stanley Wolpert (eds), *Congress and Indian Nationalism: The Pre-Independence Phase*. Berkeley: University of California Press, pp. 182–97.

Index

About the Author

Nishikant Kolge is Assistant Professor at the Department of History, Tripura University, India. He obtained his PhD in history from the Department of Humanities and Social Sciences, IIT Madras. He has contributed to various books and his research articles have been published in leading national journals like *Gandhi Marg* and *Economic and Political Weekly*. Some of his recent articles are 'The Politician: A Response to Arundhati Roy's "The Doctor and the Saint"' (2014) and 'Was Gandhi a Racist?: *His Writings in South Africa* (2016).